To Dad —

John Wayne — my favorite
actor of all time —

1985

Love — Jerdy

75

D0088900

JOHN WAYNE

JOHN WAYNE

My Life with the Duke

PILAR WAYNE
with Alex Thorleifson

McGRAW-HILL BOOK COMPANY
New York   St. Louis   San Francisco
Toronto   Hamburg   Mexico

1 2 3 4 5 6 7 8 9 D O C D O C 8 7

ISBN 0-07-068662-9

LIBRARY OF CONGRESS CATALOGING-IN-PUBLICATION DATA

Wayne, Pilar.
  John Wayne, American.

  1. Wayne, John, 1907–1979. 2. Moving-picture actors
and actresses—United States—Biography. I. Thorleifson,
Alex. II. Title.
PN2287.W454W39 1987   791.43′028′0924 [B]   87-3399
ISBN 0-07-068662-9

Book design by Kathryn Parise

TO DUKE,

THE MOST ADMIRABLE HUMAN BEING I HAVE EVER MET.

AUTHOR'S NOTE

Although my beloved husband passed away over eight years ago, until now I had never written a book about our wonderful life together. Since his death, I have been approached by innumerable persons who tried to convince me to end my silence. I have always declined . . .

I finally decided to break my silence because so many books and magazine articles have been written that misrepresent Duke. This book is about the many wonderful, and sometimes stormy, times we spent together as man and wife. I have been frank and truthful in this book and have tried to set the record straight. I hope I have been able to clear up all the confusion and reflect the true value of Duke, who will always remain foremost in my heart.

Over the years my relationship with Duke's four children by his first wife was always polite and harmonious. However, since Duke passed away, his oldest son, Michael, has seemed to grow much colder toward me, and I have felt excluded from all events commemorating my husband's memory. Needless to say, this hasn't changed the fact that I am Duke's legal widow, and that we spent a quarter of a century as man and wife raising three beautiful children.

In closing I want to go on record to say that I am extremely proud to have spent the better part of my life with John Wayne. He was and always will be a legend, and, even now that he has left us, he remains an example of a great American tradition of strength and dignity.

ACKNOWLEDGMENTS

Without the cooperation of so many friends this book would have been impossible. I would like to thank them here for their continued encouragement and support: The staff at McGraw-Hill, Gladys Justin Carr, Editorial Director, Leslie Meredith, Editor, Mary St. John, Mrs. Mark Armistead, Maggie Glynn, Claudia Mirkin, May Wale Brown, Joseph DeFranco, Richard Curtis, Jerry Kobrin, Bruce Rouleau, Dean Mixon, and most especially my family for standing by me.

CONTENTS

"Wayne is underrated. He's an awfully good actor. He holds a thing together, he gives it a solidity and honesty, and he can make a lot of things believable."

—*Howard Hawks*

"Ordinarily he is one of the kindest and most level-headed men. But when he is crossed, and particularly when double crossed, he can make a nuclear explosion seem like a baby's sigh."

—*Melville Shavelson*

"Sometimes kids ask me what a pro is. I just point to Duke."

—*Steve McQueen*

"God loves John Wayne."   —*Bumper sticker*

"A man's got to have a code, a creed to live by, no matter his job."

—*John Wayne*

JOHN WAYNE

PROLOGUE

"**F**ill your hands, you son of a bitch!" John Wayne's graveled baritone echoed across the mountain meadow. Actor Robert Duvall, playing a villain, had just called him a one-eyed, fat, old man. Fighting words.

Duke, as he was known to his friends, was portraying on film a U.S. marshal as no one ever had. His Rooster Cogburn was a scruffy, unshaven, and overweight roughneck who wore a black patch over his left eye and a sweat-stained wardrobe. But Duke invested Rooster with a warmth, a comfortably aging masculinity, a dignity that went far beyond appearances to the heart and soul of the character.

Watching Duke from the safe vantage of his makeup trailer, I saw my husband spin a Winchester rifle in his right hand as easily as smaller men spin a handgun. Spurring his huge sorrel gelding, he put the reins between his teeth, pulled a six-shooter from its holster with his left hand, and charged the enemy. The horse gathered speed, and Duke began to fire his weapons. The first of four adversaries fell as he passed through their line. Neck-reining, using all his skills as a horseman, he wheeled his mount and charged again.

He'd been repeating that ride all day. The cast began rehearsing the scene at first light, in an alpine meadow high in the Colorado Rockies. *True Grit* had been in production for several weeks by then, but the cast and crew had never filmed at so great an altitude.

That morning, as all of us straggled onto the still dark location, I'd been concerned about Duke's spending a day in the saddle, riding, shooting, and saying his lines at that elevation. Duke was the oldest member of the cast, a 61-year-old man who'd lost

1

a lung to cancer and suffered from shortness of breath under the best of circumstances. People half his age, myself included, were having trouble taking in enough oxygen. Even the younger, more fit members of the film company complained that they couldn't catch their breath. But not Duke, He was a "trouper," in the old-fashioned, theatrical sense of the word. The film's director, Henry Hathaway, had chosen that particular place to shoot that particular scene, and Duke wouldn't utter a word of complaint, no matter how tough things got.

The cast was in the saddle from dawn, rehearsing a tricky action scene that required five mounted men to perform an intricate sequence. Horses and riders had to be in the right place at the right time. The difficulty of the scene, the problems with the altitude, and the long hours were hard on everyone.

Making movies is an exhausting business that requires a passionate commitment. Emotions often run high, especially on location. Bob Duvall and Henry Hathaway had a brief confrontation during the morning shooting, but an hour later, when we all ate lunch together, Hathaway, Duvall, Duke's secretary, Mary St. John, Charles Portis, the author of True Grit, my husband, and I all ate side by side at one long table. The cast laughed and joked about their sore muscles, the morning's anger completely forgotten in the camaraderie of shared hardship. Within the hour they were all back at work.

It was a cold, blue-sky day. Aspen ringed the high field with golden autumn leaves which danced and trembled in the chill wind. The horses' breath frosted the cool air as their hooves churned the dun-colored ground. I spent the afternoon retreating to the trailer to warm up and reemerging a few minutes later, drawn into the open by the beauty of the setting and the excitement of the action.

The shooting lasted throughout the day, as Henry attempted to capture the full splendor of Duke's wild ride against an enemy that outnumbered him. Just before sunset, Henry finally called, "Cut."

Holstering his weapons, my husband guided his mount over to his old friend. Sliding from the huge gelding, Duke handed the reins to a nearby hostler. Then he hunkered down next to Henry Hathaway. "How did it look?" he asked.

"How did it feel?" replied Henry, a man of few words as directors go.

Duke grinned. "Damn good—just right."

Henry smiled back. "That's the way it looked from behind the camera too—damn good." He leaned closer, lowering his voice. "There may be an Oscar for you in this one."

Henry knew what he was talking about—he was one of Hollywood's top directors. But Duke was a realist. He knew that even experienced directors, carried away by the creative process of moviemaking, often started talking about Oscars. Reality usually set in a month or two later, when they began cutting the picture. If Henry was still talking about Oscars then, Duke might begin to take him seriously. Meanwhile, there were a lot more scenes to shoot, a lot more work to do.

Duke rose to his full 6 feet $4\frac{1}{2}$ inch height, a skeptical look in his blue eyes. He knew, better than anyone else, that the critics held his work in low esteem. Other directors had talked to him of Oscar nominations, but he'd only gotten one, thirty years earlier, for playing Sergeant Stryker in *The Sands of Iwo Jima*. He didn't count on it happening again. "Hell, Henry," Duke said, stretching his aching muscles. "Let's get back to work."

PART ONE

★

Preproduction

CHAPTER 1

In 1907, the year of John Wayne's birth, Theodore Roosevelt was president of the forty-five United States of America. He governed a nation that had been growing in power and might for over a century. The United States was a sleeping giant at the end of the Victorian era, ready to emerge in the coming technological age.

The nation's urban population enjoyed the luxury of electric lights and indoor plumbing. Automobiles had become a popular convenience in wealthier households. Henry Ford labored over the design of the Model T, a car that would change the transportation habits of the entire country. Guglielmo Marconi worked in his laboratory, developing transmitters and receivers that would make possible the commercial use of radio.

One result of Thomas Alva Edison's inventions was an increasingly popular diversion called the "nickelodeon." Nickelodeons were small, unpretentious movie theaters, showing films that were little more than a minute in length. Americans, who would have more leisure as machines made their lives easier, were developing an insatiable appetite for all forms of entertainment. They flocked to see pictures that actually moved.

John Wayne couldn't have been born at a more timely moment, although no one knew that he'd be a future giant of the motion picture industry when Mary Brown Morrison bore a healthy baby boy on May 26, 1907, in Winterset, Iowa. Mary, who gave birth at home, was probably more concerned about the immediate past than she was about the unforeseeable future.

Mary and Clyde were wed on September 27, 1906. The ceremony was conducted by a justice of the peace rather than in a church with a minister presiding. When Mary's first baby was born eight months later, rumormongers wagged their heads and tongues knowingly. This inauspicious beginning marked John Wayne's appearance in the world.

His parents called him Robert Michael, and the name was duly recorded on his birth certificate. Then Mary Morrison had a sudden change of heart. Her one wealthy relative was called Marion, and, in an attempt to acquire her child a future inheritance, she renamed him Marion Michael Morrison.

Duke was descended from a mix of Scottish, English, and Irish pioneers who'd made their way to America's heartland before the Civil War. His great-great-grandfather, Robert Morrison, fled Ireland in the late 1700s after being accused of plotting against the British crown. Robert became a ruling elder in the Presbyterian church and a brigadier general in the Ohio militia during the war of 1812. Duke's great uncle, James Morrison, was a minister and one of the founders of Monmouth College. Grandfather Marion fought in the Civil War and was wounded in the battle of Pine Bluff. But, whatever their achievements or adventures, the men of the Morrison clan were essentially farmers who subscribed to the American work ethic.

Duke's father, Clyde, had bigger dreams. Hoping to have a profession someday, he enrolled at the University of Iowa. But impatient to get on with his life, Clyde left prior to graduation. He met and courted vivacious, red-haired, blue-eyed Mary Brown. After marrying they moved to Winterset, the Madison County seat, where he worked as a pharmacist's clerk.

Duke's parents, aside from their son's uncomfortably rapid arrival, were well thought of—indistinguishable from the rest of their white Anglo-Saxon Protestant, God-fearing neighbors. Clyde was a handsome man of medium height with an easy charm and a quick mind. His equally attractive wife had a hot temper and a strong will.

Although the Morrisons lived in a farming community, Clyde wanted nothing to do with raising crops or animals. With his wife's help, he saved enough money to make a downpayment on his own pharmacy in the nearby town of Earlham. During the early years of their life together Mary was confident, despite their minor arguments and differing personalities, that she'd made the right choice in a husband. Clyde was a fine provider, just the sort of man a woman could show off to her family and friends. And show off Mary did, determined to live down the rumors about her reasons for marrying him.

Five years after Marion's birth the Morrisons had another son and named him Robert Emmett. Mary, who had felt compelled to excuse and defend her first son's early arrival, soon turned the full force of her love and attention on the new baby. Marion irritated Mary, but her commitment to Robert Emmett would be unshakeable. In the years to come, when her older son achieved all the things she wanted for her younger, Mary would be angry and baffled. She never understood why her favorite child wasn't favored by the world too.

The happiest part of Duke's childhood ended the day his brother was born. From then on all he heard from his mother was "Bobby this" and "Bobby that." Mary knew the baby needed her, whereas Marion grew more independent with every passing day. Always curious, with an alert, investigative mind, he taxed his mother's patience.

When she wasn't doting on Bobby, Mary argued with Clyde. Duke recalled overhearing a series of battles as his parents fought over how to manage the pharmacy. In Mary's opinion, Clyde trusted his customers too quickly. She objected to his policy of easy credit. A cynical woman, she was inclined to believe the worst about people.

It may seem disloyal to write these things about Mary now, but they are Duke's memories as he told them to me. When Mary and I met in the fifties, Duke's mother had mellowed. I knew her as a dignified, grey-haired lady who very much enjoyed her position as "John Wayne's mother."

Duke was uncomfortable talking about his childhood long after he attained success, fame, and wealth beyond his parents' wildest dreams. He revealed the story in bits and pieces during our years together. He told of feeling unloved by his mother and victimized by his parents' many fights and their poverty. In addition, he had to cope with what he considered a ridiculous name. "Being called Marion," he once confessed, "made me a target for every bully in town. They called me little girl—asked why my mother dressed me in pants instead of skirts—did everything they could to make my life miserable."

By the time Duke passed his sixth birthday he knew the only way to stop the torment was to fight back. Smaller than the other children, he took a beating on the streets when he attacked his adversaries. He often came home dirty and bloodstained in torn clothes to face his mother's anger. (In Mary's mind, street brawls and hoodlums were synonymous. She was determined to make Marion into a gentleman and spent hours teaching him manners.) When she finished lecturing Marion, his father would take him aside and praise him for his bravery, saying that a man should always stand up for what he believed and never run away from a fight. "Mind you," Clyde would continue, "don't go looking for fights, but if you find yourself in one, make damn sure you win." He also told his son that a real man never insults another on purpose and never breaks his given word.

Duke loved his father with a quiet, steady affection. He absorbed his teachings and made them part of his own character. In later years he supported his father's second wife, a woman he barely knew, as a gesture of affection after his father's death.

Loving one parent, unable to admit he didn't love the other, Marion spent his youth trying to meet their opposing demands and expectations. Mary could be tough and unforgiving, a perfectionist and a person of great dignity and not a little harshness. Clyde was affectionate and romantic, an impractical dreamer who had the virtue of being able to laugh at himself. Their oldest son grew to be all of these things.

The Morrison's disagreement about child rearing was just one of their differences. Their battles raged at night: Clyde was a poor money manager, Mary pinched pennies. Clyde doted on Marion, Mary gave her attention to Bobby.

Duke hated hearing them fight night after night. He'd pull the pillows over his head and try to blot out the sound of their angry voices. When the situation grew unbearable, he'd run away, hop a freight train and ride it out of town, sometimes traveling for many miles before someone discovered the small boy and returned him to Winterset. Running away was a frightening experience, but to Duke the terrors of the unknown were not as bad as the situation at home.

Duke remembered that life at home grew even worse when Clyde was diagnosed as having tuberculosis. Mary, who when angry sometimes talked of ending the marriage, now found herself trapped by her husband's illness. She knew that her friends and neighbors wouldn't forgive her if she abandoned a sick man, nor would she be able to forgive herself. "No two ways about it," she was given to saying, "right is right!" Propelled by her sense of propriety, a sense she instilled in her older son, Mary made up her mind to stick by Clyde.

When the family physician told Clyde he had to move to a hot, dry climate if he hoped to recover, Mary agreed to accompany her husband. Clyde's father had moved to the West a few years earlier, purchasing 80 acres on the edge of the Mojave desert outside of Palmdale, California. He'd homesteaded the land and built a small house on it before moving on to the more civilized comforts of Los Angeles. It was to this homestead that the family traveled late in 1915. And then a real hell began for all of them.

Iowa had been flat and fertile, a hospitable land dotted with prosperous farming communities. Duke's first memories of California were of heat and dust and grinding poverty. The Morrisons' new home had no running water or electricity, luxuries the family had taken for granted in Iowa. They used a wood stove to warm themselves against the chill of a desert night and kerosene lamps to chase away the shadows. The nearest town consisted of a couple of churches, a hotel, saloons, a post office, a blacksmith's shop, and a school. The Morrisons had taken a step backward in time to the nineteenth century, a period Duke would return to again and again during his film career.

While the family suffered in rural America, nearby Los Angeles was pushing toward its destiny. In 1907, when Duke was born, construction was begun on the $23 million Owens Aqueduct. Its completion would bring water to the thirsty San Fernando Valley. In 1909 the giant Lankershim ranch, which occupied a big portion of Los Angeles County, was sold by its owners, the Van Nuys family. The promise of abundant water and cheap land opened the area to development.

Then, in 1910, the movie industry came to Hollywood. A group of independent producers, intent on escaping from Edison's monopoly of the Kinetoscope, brought their French cameras and their experimental ideas to the West Coast. By 1914, Jesse Lasky, Cecil DeMille, and Sam Goldwyn had teamed to create *The Squaw Man*. Another film pioneer, D. W. Griffith, set a new standard of excellence in 1915 with his production of *Birth of a Nation*. Hollywood was on its way to becoming the entertainment capital of the world.

But for young Marion Morrison, the loneliness and the isolation of the homestead dominated his daily existence. "There were days," he reminisced, "when I was so hungry, I thought my stomach was glued to my backbone. If we wanted meat, Dad had to go hunting. He wasn't much of a farmer, but he was a damn fine shot. He used to say, 'Marion, if you've just got one bullet you better bag two rabbits—one for your Mom and me and Bobby, and the other one for you.'" Clyde had taught his son to hunt and to handle a rifle and a shotgun with practiced ease. He had also taught Duke to ride and to handle the horses that were a part of each day's work on the primitive farm.

In the first year on the homestead, Duke and his father made the painful transition from being city dwellers to being working farmers. But Mary never stopped hating her new home, the empty vistas, the lack of civilized comforts. Coyotes howled at night. Daylight revealed rattlers and scorpions that terrified her. Marion could take care of himself; little Bobby was still a toddler, and she feared for his safety in that vast loneliness. "You look out for Bobby," she admonished Marion every time the two brothers ventured outside together. "I'll hold you responsible if anything happens to your brother."

Duke recalled wanting to ask, "What about me? Don't you care what happens to me?" But he forced himself to remain silent, to choke down questions that might have precipitated his mother's anger. She spent enough time ranting and raving at his father. The last thing he needed was to have her take on after him too.

By choosing not to reveal his feelings, Duke formed a habit that lasted a lifetime. He never admitted his deepest fears or hurts, not to his mother or father in his childhood, not to me when he was middle-aged, and ultimately not even to himself.

The terrible years of fighting that unyielding desert soil had a long-term effect on the Morrison family. Unable to grow a successful crop (the majority of seedlings were eaten by jackrabbits), lashed by his wife's increasing disappointment, Clyde began to see himself as a failure. Mary, feeling guilty because she no longer loved Clyde, gave a ferociously protective love to her son, Bobby. He, in turn, would never escape from her smothering adoration. Marion, a gregarious boy with a strong need for companionship, had to cope with the lack of his mother's affection as well as loneliness.

By 1916 Clyde admitted that the desert had beaten him. Fortunately, his lungs were clearer, his cough diminished; the dry air had done its job, and he seemed cured. The time had come to move the family back to civilization.

CHAPTER 2

Glendale, California, was a tight-knit community when the Morrisons moved there in 1916, the kind of place where everyone knew everyone else's business. Clyde and Mary, with the help of a small inheritance from Clyde's father, were first viewed as prosperous newcomers.

They rented a comfortable house, enrolled the boys in school, and joined a church. Clyde got a job in a pharmacy, and the family tried to put the difficult years on the desert behind them. But Marion, despite his pleasure in having other children close at hand, had grown awkward, shy and unsure with strangers. Bobby stood in his brother's shadow or hid behind his mother's skirts. And Mary, who'd hoped for a better life, soon learned that her husband's salary didn't stretch very far now that they were back in the city.

After the inheritance was used up, Clyde began to look and act like the failure he had come to consider himself. Unable to save enough money to buy his own drugstore, he drifted from job to job while his family moved from one rented house to another and their standard of living deteriorated.

Marion was uncomfortable with the pitying looks he got from his teachers when he showed up for class in patched pants that didn't reach his ankles, threadbare shirts, and shoes that pinched his feet so badly that he limped. If the family's fortunes were to improve, he knew he would have to help.

Two major events marked his eleventh year. He got his first job delivering newspapers, and he finally left his hated first name behind. The local firemen, perhaps as an act of kindness, began to call the lanky boy "big Duke" when he and his Airedale, "little Duke," delivered the paper.

"You can't imagine what that meant to me," Duke later recalled. "I really looked up to those guys. They were heroes in my book. When they began calling me 'Duke,' I made up my mind to use the name from then on."

In time he convinced his father, his brother, and all his friends to call him by the new nickname, but he never convinced his mother. She refused to call him by "the dog's name." The determined Mary finally stopped calling him Marion when he simply refused to respond. From then on she referred to him by the generic term of "son."

Now known as Duke, the tall, good-looking boy set out to make a place for himself in the hierarchy of Glendale youth. His father's failure had given Duke a monumental drive to succeed. He loved Clyde, but he hoped to do better. Determined to avoid his father's mistakes, he made up his mind to do well in high school, go on to college, and graduate with a degree.

Duke's fans sometimes think of him as a simple, uneducated man, much like the characters he played. In fact, he was very well read. He began going to the local library when he was 12 because it provided him with a form of free entertainment, and he remained a voracious reader all his life. Duke enjoyed a good mystery, read all of Churchill, and perused most new novels looking for stories that would make good movies.

His love of reading and his good memory ensured that he would excel in his classes. Duke's high school achievements are remarkable when one considers that he also worked after school, earning all his own spending money and contributing to the family finances. By his junior year he'd been elected class president and appointed to the staff of the school newspaper. In his senior year he became a member of the National Honor Society, president of the Honor Society of Latin Students, chairman of the senior dance committee and chairman of the ring committee. In addition he was a straight-A student and class salutatorian at graduation and was named one of the finest football players in the state that year.

The Morrisons were justifiably proud of Duke's record. However, it seemed to be their only area of agreement. After one of his parents' fights, Mary confided to Duke that she only stayed with Clyde for Bobby's sake. Duke believed a man should never let a woman talk to him in such a way, and I was to feel his displeasure on this count many times in our marriage.

Fortunately Duke found the role models he needed in his coaches. They were athletic men who preached the virtues of fair play. Life was straightforward out on the football field. There were no confusing emotions, no need to figure out what someone meant by what they said, and no girls—who were a real puzzle to Duke. He'd begun to feel as if the only place he would ever be completely at ease was in the all-masculine world of the playing field.

When he had spare time and a little extra money, he escaped the daily pressures of his life by going to the movies. Films had made tremendous advances since the days of the nickelodeon. The swashbuckling Douglas Fairbanks was one of Duke's early cinematic heroes. He also admired such western stars as William S. Hart, Hoot Gibson, and Harry Carey. And, privately, he thought he could ride and shoot with the best of them.

Duke was realistic and, despite his love of movies, had neither time nor money for make-believe. He was convinced he had to go to college and, in view of the family's finances, that meant getting a scholarship. After careful consideration, Duke decided the U.S. Naval Academy at Annapolis would be an ideal place to get an education. He felt he had all the qualifications for admittance and sent off his application with high hopes.

However, in Duke's senior year his high school football team set state records, and this success gave him his first glimpse of the benefits of fame. In reward for his academic and athletic excellence, the University of Southern California offered him a football scholarship.

Mary, who hoped to see her older son become a lawyer, was overjoyed. Clyde basked in reflected glory as the father of Glendale's most outstanding high school student. Even Bobby could see some potential for gain from Duke's success. If nothing else, he could always make a play for the girls who hung around his brother.

Duke was the only member of the family who wasn't thrilled with the university's offer. He raced home to check the mail each day, hoping to find a letter from Annapolis. When it finally arrived, it proved to be a rejection. It was Duke's first personal failure, and he never forgot it.

Whatever his early misgivings, he enjoyed his first year at U.S.C. Thanks to the newspapers that covered his football career, he was a big man on campus from the beginning. He joined the very social Sigma Chi and financed living in the fraternity house by doing dishes in their kitchen.

Fraternity life seemed like an extension of his experiences on the sports fields. Duke felt at home in the all-male world at Sigma Chi. He'd never dated in high school and remembered being very naive about women, very unsure of himself. "I didn't know what to say to them," he told me, "I sure as hell didn't understand them—and I didn't have enough money to take them out."

In college Duke was pleased to find that these limitations didn't keep girls from being attracted to him. He treated them with the old-fashioned, courtly manners Mary had drilled into him, and from his recollections, they responded positively.

At the end of his first year, just as he was preparing to move back home for the summer, he learned that his parents had separated. Duke wasn't surprised—he'd seen it coming for years—but he was startled by the depth of his own reaction to the news. He felt deeply hurt, ashamed, and embarrassed. Divorce was rare in those days, a cause for scandal. The gossip left Duke feeling alienated and alone. Spiritually, emotionally, and physically, Duke distanced himself from his parents. Unable to choose sides in their dispute, something they both wanted him to do, he simply withdrew.

Fortunately, Duke's football coach, Howard Jones, was beginning to take a real interest in Duke. When Duke asked for help getting a summer job, Howard Jones sent him straight over to the Fox lot to talk to a loyal Trojan fan, Tom Mix, the cowboy star.

Mix loved football, and most of all he loved the U.S.C. Trojans. He took Duke to his favorite speakeasy and proceeded to pump him for inside information about the team. In the course of what proved to be a long, drunken night, Mix promised to put Duke on his own payroll, as his personal trainer. It sounded like a dream job.

When Duke reported to the studio the next morning, he learned that Tom Mix's promise had been nothing more than "drunk talk." The dream job turned out to be working on a swing gang, moving props and furniture from one set to another. Duke, whose fragile sense of dignity had been badly bruised, never forgave Mix for disillusioning him.

One day halfway through the summer Duke was told to report to work on the set of *Mother MacCree*. The film's director was John Ford, one of Hollywood's most visionary talents. In those days scripts were written in great detail, with every scene, every camera angle, every bit of stage business down on paper. They left nothing to the director's imagination or discretion.

Ford chose to ignore large portions of the scripts he was given. He insisted that each of his films bear the stamp of his own particular genius; in so doing, he helped change the movie industry. People on the Fox lot, from the lowliest grip to the biggest star, knew of the already legendary director and hoped to see him in action. Duke was no exception.

On Duke's first day on the *MacCree* set, he was put in charge of a gaggle of geese that Ford intended to use as living props for a farm scene. After a few days with his web-footed charges, Duke was short on temper and long on frustration. It was the wrong day for Ford to notice him.

The tall, pugnacious Irish director had played football in his time. Although he was 31 years old and not in his prime, he couldn't resist the challenge Duke's presence on the set presented.

"You're a football player, aren't you?" Ford asked, surveying the robust athlete.

"Yeah," Duke replied, staring down at the older man. He thought Ford looked soft and out of shape.

The two men eyed each other.

"What position do you play?" Ford probed.

"Guard."

"I used to be a fullback. Think you can take me out?"

Duke gave the older man a long, knowing look. Taking him out, he decided, would be like taking candy from a baby. "Yeah, I know I could."

Ford backed off about 20 feet as Duke started to crouch in the classic football set.

"See if you can stop me," Ford shouted, launching himself at the younger man. His sudden move caught Duke off balance, not fully set yet. The older man was surprisingly strong and agile, far more athletic than he looked. Duke was barely able to secure a partial grip on him as the director rushed past. Ford was about to break free when Duke kneed him in the chest, sending him sprawling in the dirt.

For one frozen second the set was deadly silent. Duke was as dismayed as everyone else. He hadn't meant to knock Ford down. It wasn't exactly the sportsmanlike thing to do. But then, as he told me years later, Ford hadn't exactly played it by the book either. Looking at the crumpled man sprawled in the dirt, Duke reached down and pulled Ford to his feet.

Ford took a moment to straighten his clothes and collect himself. "That's enough bullshit," he said with implacable calm. "Let's get back to work."

Duke couldn't have been more surprised. He'd expected a royal chewing out. But Ford went right about his business as if nothing had happened. A new emotion, akin to hero worship, took hold of Duke. He saw in Ford a man who didn't back away from a challenge, a tough, durable fellow who didn't brood over setbacks. More important, as the days on the set went by, Duke saw a genius at work. Ford could say more, working in the medium of silent film, than most directors could in talkies.

In reminiscing about their first contact, Duke said, "I watched the way he handled people, the way he managed to get the best his actors had to give—in every damn scene. I'd never seen a genius at work before, but I knew I was seeing one now. The man was a great artist, a perfectionist, and I wanted to be like him."

Duke learned a lot about the pursuit of excellence that summer. In the fall he returned to college, determined to redouble his efforts in the classroom and on the football field to be—like Ford—the best.

CHAPTER 3

Josephine Saenz was a petite, dark-haired, well-bred society girl who supposedly carried the genes of the Spanish royal family in her impeccably blue blood. Her father was a wealthy American businessman who'd been appointed consul for the Dominican Republic. Her mother was of French descent and very social. Neither Josephine nor her parents had ever met anyone quite like Marion Morrison.

Duke met Josephine on a blind date and reported being instantly smitten with her cool, ladylike manner. She was beautiful, devoutly Catholic, and determined to remain chaste, although Duke said she had a way of making "no" sound like an invitation. He pursued her with all the passion of his newly awakened romantic nature. Between playing on the varsity team and dating Josephine, he felt certain that 1927 would be the best year of his life.

It certainly proved to be a landmark year for the movie industry. Pictures found their voice that year when *The Jazz Singer* opened to critical acclaim and long lines at the box office. Audiences clamored for more talkies, and the studios worked hard to oblige them. As a result, a number of leading men and ladies whose voices squeaked or squealed on the primitive sound tracks found themselves out of jobs. Movie moguls began a hunt for actors and actresses with good voices.

While the film industry grappled with its new opportunities, Duke was grappling with new opponents on the football field. Playing on the varsity team at the season opener was the opportunity of a lifetime for a mere sophomore, and Duke did his best to make the most of the precious minutes he spent in the games.

Then one hot November Saturday, Duke's dreams of glory came

to a shattering conclusion when his leg was broken during the third quarter of a game. In addition to the pain, the injury put his athletic scholarship, which kept him in school, in jeopardy —he couldn't pay for tuition without it. Clyde and Mary, who were in even greater financial difficulties following their separation, could not contribute a penny to his continuing education.

As the team physician worked on Duke's leg, Duke couldn't help wondering what Josephine would think when her football-hero boyfriend turned out to be a penniless bum. And that, he recalled, hurt even more than his shattered leg.

The next few months saw Duke's worst fears realized. His injury was too severe to allow him to return to the football field. Coach Jones kept him on the active duty roster so that he could finish his sophomore year and get his letter, but there was to be no scholarship the following year.

Meanwhile, Josephine's parents no longer approved of her relationship with Duke. They objected to the fact that he wasn't a Catholic and were horrified that his parents were getting a divorce. In their opinion, he had no breeding, no money, and no prospects. Josephine's father, Dr. Saenz, wasted no time in informing Duke that he was no longer welcome in the Saenz household!

Anyone who ever knew Duke would have realized that Dr. Saenz had made a classic mistake. Duke was a fighter who didn't accept the word "no" but regarded it as a challenge. Duke found ways to see Josephine in secret, and these forbidden meetings had a poignancy that added a new element of romance to their love affair. Duke said he felt like an impoverished "knight" courting a "fair princess." It was the stuff fairy tales—or movies—are made of.

At the end of his sophomore year, Duke returned to the Fox lot and applied for a permanent job. All he wanted was a steady paycheck, a roof over his head, food on the table, and enough money to go on seeing the girl he loved.

Duke was lucky. Movies were increasingly popular with the advent of talkies, and jobs were available for the asking. During the next few months Duke worked on a couple of John Ford films, graduating from the swing gang to being a prop man. At this point he and Ford were not yet friends—the difference in their ages and their circumstances seemed to rule out that possibility in those days. But Duke was determined to win the older man's approval. His first opportunity came one day when John Ford was filming his second talky, Men without Women, off the California coast near Catalina.

As prop man, Duke had to produce a steady stream of bubbles on the ocean's surface to simulate an undersea explosion in a submarine engine room. Duke told me he worked his air pump like a madman, day after day, hoping to catch Ford's eye.

Ford planned to film a sequence showing the men escaping the doomed submarine via the torpedo tubes. He'd hired a couple of stuntmen to double the actors. Their job was to dive into the ocean and then pop to the surface, a simple stunt but for the fact that a storm hovered off the coast. The stuntmen refused to work in the turbulent waters created by the storm.

The third day of waiting found Ford desperate. He didn't want to return to the studio and shoot the sequence in a pool on the back lot. That kind of filming lacked the reality that marked Ford's best work. "Are all you bastards afraid of getting a little wet?" he asked, surveying his crew. Duke stepped forward. "I'm not, Mr. Ford." Duke made a lot of money that day, drawing a stuntman's pay.

More important, John Ford had his first look at Duke on film when he was back in the studio screening the day's rushes. "There was something special about Duke even then," Ford told me years later. "Sure—he was callow and untutored, but he had something that jumped right off the screen at me. I guess you could call it star power. I wanted to keep an eye on him so I offered him a bit part in my next picture." From then on Duke was one of "Ford's boys," a gang of regulars at all levels of the movie industry who worked on most of Ford's films.

Fox gave Ford a new assignment in 1928. The studio wanted him to do a football story, something with lots of action, razzle-dazzle, humor, and patriotism. The movie, titled Salute, was to be filmed on location at the U.S. Naval Academy.

Ford asked Duke to round up some experienced football players for the action sequences that would be filmed on the playing fields of Annapolis. Duke couldn't help laughing at the irony of the situation. He was finally going to the Naval Academy—as an actor rather than a cadet!

The day the cast and crew assembled at the Santa Fe railroad station in Los Angeles, ready to depart for the East Coast, an interloper appeared on the scene. His name was Wardell Bond, and the 220-pound former tackle had never been one of Duke's favorite teammates.

"What the hell are you doing here?" Duke asked Bond, adding, "you're too damn ugly to be in movies."

"Screw you!" Bond replied, straight-arming his way past Duke and boarding the train. "Leave him be," Ford laughed. "You're right, Duke, He is ugly. But I like his style."

When the train pulled out of the station, Duke and Wardell were enemies. When they returned to California several months later, they'd become the best of friends, and both were calling John Ford "Pappy" or "Coach."

The following year, John Wayne the movie star was born. By this time he'd become a familiar figure on the Fox lot, and other directors were taking notice of him, seeing a potential in the big, raw-boned bit player and prop man.

One such director was Raoul Walsh. He was getting ready to film *The Big Trail*, a western that would revolutionize the genre. Walsh had big plans for his new movie. He wanted to take the cast and crew on location around the country, something that had never been done in those days of huge back lots. It was customary to shoot westerns as close to home as possible, and the executives at Fox were balking at the added expense of location filming.

The year 1930 was a bad one for Fox. The studio had lost a large sum of money the year before in the stock market crash, so, although movies were more popular than ever, the executives were cutting budgets. The executives told Walsh that he could go on location if he reduced his other costs. Walsh, who'd been hoping Gary Cooper or Tom Mix would play the male lead in *The Big Trail*, decided to economize by casting an unknown. He was looking for someone to play the wagon-train scout when he noticed Duke for the first time.

He thought Duke looked tough enough to be convincing in the physically demanding part. Deciding to test him, Walsh sent his assistant over to ask Duke to let his hair grow for a couple of weeks. Duke, in the midst of moving some furniture, didn't even bother to ask the reason for the request. Preproduction of *The Big Trail* was well under way when Duke donned buckskins and tried out for the lead.

To Walsh's surprise, Duke looked good on screen and sounded even better. The director hadn't realized what a memorable voice the bit player-propman possessed. Morrison's ability to ride and shoot was an added bonus.

Walsh could see only one drawback to casting Duke. That name, Marion Morrison, would look ridiculous on a marquee—and Duke Morrison wouldn't look much better. "Before we can talk contract," Walsh said after Duke's second and even more convincing test, "We've got to do something about your name."

Duke just grinned in reply. Hell, if they were going to give him a starring part they could call him "Rin Tin Tin" for all he cared. He watched quietly as Walsh paced his office.

"How about Wayne?" the director said suddenly. "It has a nice American ring."

And so Marion Morrison became John Wayne. His new contract paid him $75 a week, a princely sum in the aftermath of the stock market crash. He couldn't wait to tell Josephine. Even Dr. Saenz would have to approve of a man who earned a good living and had his name up in lights.

Sadly, the movie was better received in 1986, when it was restored and reissued by the Museum of Modern Art, than it was in 1930. The movie failed to make a profit, and shortly afterward Fox declared bankruptcy.

Duke, his dreams of instant stardom shattered, found himself looking for a job. Although 1930 was a bad year to be out of work, Duke was swiftly signed by Columbia Pictures. His first assignment was a starring role in *Arizona*, and once again, he hoped he was on the way to the success and security he craved.

Fate, in the form of a jealous studio executive, intervened. Harry Cohn ran Columbia like a private hunting preserve: If he became interested in a young female star, every other male on the lot knew he'd better keep his distance. But Duke was a newcomer and didn't know Cohn's rules. Duke was also handsome, unattached, and almost irresistible to women.

The day after *Arizona* "wrapped," Duke showed up at Columbia and was turned away by the guard at the gate. "I thought it was all some kind of mistake," Duke told me, still indignant three decades after the incident. "All I knew was I had to talk to Cohn and clear things up—or my career was finished."

Cohn proved to be intractable. In a brief and hostile meeting he told Duke, "Keep your goddamn fly buttoned at my studio."

Duke left the lot, as baffled as he'd been when he arrived. Later that night he finally remembered having an idle flirtation with a young female star who was seeing Cohn too. Duke was furious with himself. The girl meant nothing to him. Hell, he was in love with Josephine.

The wily, vindictive Cohn decided to make an example of his new leading man to ensure that no other male on the Columbia lot would ever again make a pass at one of Cohn's girls. He picked up Duke's option, raised his salary, and then cast him in a series of increasingly minor roles in B movies. Cohn's final act of vengeance came when he cast Duke in a part that required no dialogue at all—Duke played a corpse in a coffin. Certain that he'd succeeded in ending his young rival's career, Cohn canceled Duke's contract.

Duke was sick with anger and helplessness. At that time, studios ruled the film industry, and men like Cohn ruled the studios. From then on Duke would be wary of such men. As for Cohn, he lived to regret his actions. Two decades later, when John Wayne was the biggest box office draw in Hollywood, he flatly refused to work at Columbia where Cohn still ruled.

In the wake of the disasters at Fox and Columbia, Duke had developed an unenviable reputation in the movie industry. He'd been labeled a boozer, a skirt chaser, a troublemaker, and, worst of all, box office poison. The big studios wouldn't hire him at any price.

In those days there were three kinds of films—big budget A movies, B movies that sometimes functioned as an apprenticeship for up-and-coming directors and actors, and serials that of-

ten served as the end of the line for has-beens or "never-weres."
The only studio to offer Duke a job, Mascot Pictures, made serials.

Duke told me if he'd known how to do anything other than
make movies, he'd have gotten out of the business then and there.
He hated feeling like a failure, knowing Cohn had made a fool of
him so easily. Duke felt that he'd disappointed the two people
he cared for most: Josephine Saenz, the girl he loved, and John
Ford, the man he admired above all others. And all because of
an idle flirtation.

Thus Duke began his stint at Mascot embittered and disillu-
sioned. If he failed, he had nowhere else to work.

CHAPTER 4

Despite his apprehension, Duke was able to look back on working at Mascot as a fine training period. The serial episodes were filmed in a few days, much like weekly television shows now, and the hurried schedule helped transform him into a professional. He learned to commit a script to memory overnight, to get a scene right in a few takes.

He worked harder than ever before, sometimes completing over 100 setups in a day, compared to the usual 5 to 15 on a big-budget movie. Because of the frantic pace, the studio rotated directors on a daily basis, but Duke had to be present all the time, eighteen hours a day and more. He was paid $500 every eighteen days during this period, little more than $1.50 an hour, but decent money in 1930.

Over the next two years he made three complete serials for Mascot, playing an adventurous airplane pilot in two of them. During this period he lived down all the nasty gossip and became known as a hard-working, untemperamental performer.

By 1932 Duke's future looked more promising than it had after the failure of *The Big Trail* and his run-in with Cohn. When his Mascot contract ran out, Warner Brothers, a far more important and successful studio, signed him to a six-picture deal. Under the Warner banner he worked in B westerns. They weren't the big budget movies he dreamed of making, but they were a significant improvement over the Mascot serials.

Warner Brothers also gave Duke some artistic freedom. He was permitted to reinvent the movie cowboy. Before then Hollywood's cowboy heroes rode white horses, wore white hats and gloves, and acted more like Little Lord Fauntleroy than real he-men. Duke's western heroes proved more realistic; he created characters with a rough quality that mirrored true life. Coincidentally, the cowboys he played in those six Warner pictures were all named John. I think that's one of the reasons critics began to perceive Duke as an actor who always played himself.

Hollywood was a small town in the thirties. Duke was somewhat of a loner and already working outside the studio system. He never signed the typical long-term contract and never got the traditional studio buildup, but he did cross paths with a number of up-and-coming talents who would play a part in his future. The talents included Dick Powell who later directed Duke's film *The Conqueror*, Barbara Stanwyck, Mickey Rooney, Douglas Fairbanks, Jr. (the son of his early idol), William Wellman, who would one day direct *The High and the Mighty* for Duke's own production company, and Loretta Young.

Young, a prominent member of movieland's Catholic community, was Josephine Saenz's best friend. Six years had passed since Duke's first date with Josephine, but he still courted her doggedly. Duke later told me that the relationship, which started as a forbidden romantic adventure, had become little more than a habit, one his sense of honor prevented him from breaking. At this stage of his career, however, he had neither the time nor the inclination to begin a new romance. His early infatuation with Josephine had been supplanted by a new passion. Duke had fallen in love with making movies.

By mid-1933 Duke had fulfilled his contractual obligations to Warner Brothers. He was looking for work when Monogram Pictures, another poverty-row studio not unlike Mascot, made him a proposition. They offered him a chance to star in a series of western films which would be made by Lonestar Productions, a subsidiary established for the sole purpose of making these cowboy pictures. Duke knew it wouldn't be a good career move—he was being typecast, and that was death in the business—but he was flattered that Lonestar had been created to make his movies.

Early in his association with Lonestar, the executives there decided to make him into a singing cowboy. Duke, who needed a job, was willing to try anything once. A test quickly revealed that he couldn't sing, but the studio wasn't discouraged; they could always dub his voice. Duke couldn't play a guitar either, but Lonestar was willing to hire a musician if Duke could simulate strumming the instrument on camera.

Duke made one Lonestar movie as "Singin' Sandy—the most notorious gunman since Billy the Kid." At the end of filming, he said he felt like a "goddamn pansy." Duke had pandered his own talent in order to make a living, and it didn't leave him feeling very good about himself. When the "Singin' Sandy" film wrapped, he went to his boss and said, "Look, I can't play the guitar and I can't sing—and I feel like a damn fool. You can keep the damn job!"

Lonestar, still wanting a singing cowboy, tested then-unknown Gene Autry, and the rest, as they say, is history.

While Duke labored in B westerns that were filmed in less than a week at a cost of $10,000 each, John Ford, his friend and mentor, had moved on to RKO, where he was making *The Informer*, a picture with a big budget. This film firmly established Ford as one of the cinema's reigning geniuses. From then on Pappy enjoyed critical and financial success.

Ford had been jealous when Raoul Walsh chose Duke for the leading role in *The Big Trail*. If anyone was going to make Duke into a star, Ford confessed to me, he thought it should have been him. Although he knew it didn't make sense, he felt Duke had been disloyal. After the two men left Fox, they drifted apart.

Ford's place in Duke's personal life was temporarily filled by a man named Enos Yakima Canutt. "Yak," as he was called, had been a rodeo champion before coming to Hollywood and working as a stuntman. The two men met at Monogram-Lonestar.

Duke was instantly impressed by Yak's physical talents, his daring and courage—he was Duke's idea of a real he-man. Yak worked as a stunt coordinator, stuntman, and bit player on most of Duke's films. When they weren't working, Duke would seek Yak's company after hours. They spent many an evening talking and drinking while Yak told of his life on the rodeo circuit. During the day, between takes, Yak taught Duke to perform a number of stunts, including horse falls, transfers, and bulldogging. Yak made more money than Duke, a fact which led Duke to consider giving up acting to follow in Yak's footsteps. But, after some reflection, Duke concluded that Dr. Saenz would never accept a stuntman in the family.

Most of the films Duke and Yak collaborated on featured at least one barroom brawl, and neither man was satisfied with the way these fights looked on film. In those days screen fights were obviously phony. The fact that the punches never connected with their targets provided audiences with many a laugh the moviemakers hadn't planned.

Duke and Yak changed all that. In their spare time they developed a new technique for filming screen fights, using careful choreography and camera angles to give their fights the illusion of reality. Within a year the entire industry had adopted their methods. Although they never received recognition, money, or praise for their innovative work, they were justifiably proud of this contribution to the business.

Yak went on to become one of the most celebrated stuntmen in moviemaking. His greatest achievement was the magnificent chariot race in *Ben Hur*. He planned the entire sequence and doubled Charleton Heston during the dangerous filming.

While he worked at Monogram, Duke's life was neatly segmented. He spent his days at the studio and his nights in rough-and-tumble parties with new friends who worked in the motion picture business. His weekend dates with Josephine seemed to take place in another world where the niceties of manners and decorum were carefully observed.

Duke was 26 years old in 1933, a very different man from the romantic idealist who had first courted Josephine. He'd experienced success, scandal, defeat. His knowledge of the world and the people in it had been broadened by contact with men like Cohn, Walsh, Ford, and Canutt.

During the long years of their courtship, Josephine had remained at home under her father's guidance and protection. She and Duke were actually worlds apart when they finally married on June 24th, 1933, at the home of Loretta Young, Josephine's bridesmaid. At the time, however, the garden wedding seemed like an ideally romantic conclusion to their long courtship.

In fact, Duke later recounted, it was the beginning of a bad dream. He and "Josie" soon realized how unsuited they were. Duke liked to party and reveled in masculine company. Josie thought his friends were uncouth. The only men she welcomed in her home were priests or socialites.

Duke told me of coming home night after night to find the house full of clerics. After a hard day in front of the cameras riding and doing his own stunts, he wanted nothing more than a long hot bath and an early dinner. Josephine usually had other plans. She wanted Duke to dress for dinner and, in her world, that meant black tie.

Although both longed to have a happy marriage, they couldn't seem to find a common ground. Duke had a passionate nature, but, according to him, Josephine believed sex was permissible for procreation only. In view of her religious beliefs—and Duke's six-year wait to consummate their love, the arrival of four children in short order is not surprising. Michael was born in 1934; Toni, in 1936; Patrick, in 1937; and Melinda, in 1939.

During the first years of the marriage Duke stayed under contract with Monogram. In 1935 the studio merged with Mascot, Lonestar, and Consolidated Film Laboratories to form a new entity called Republic Studios. The power behind the consolidation was Herbert Yates, a Wall Street genius. Yates was a moneymaker, not a filmmaker, and he believed in sure things. Duke's B westerns were as close to a sure thing as there was in the movie business, and Yates kept Duke hard at work acting in them.

Desperate for a change of pace, a chance to stretch and grow as an actor, Duke signed with Universal when his stint at Republic ended. The six action films he made for them took up the next two years. Then it was back to Republic and more B westerns. Duke knew he'd become a victim of typecasting. His career was going nowhere.

He told me of trying to talk his problems over with Josephine, but she didn't understand his frustration or unhappiness. By the late thirties their marriage was maintained for appearances and the sake of the children, and Josephine wasn't concerned about her husband's professional problems. She wanted an orderly existence, a man who came home after work every night, a man who didn't drink, smoke, or swear.

Duke later recalled the years of his first marriage as frustrating, unhappy, and guilt-ridden. He wanted to love his wife—after all, she'd given him four children—but he wanted to be loved in return, for what he was. Josephine tried to change him, to make him into a gentleman like her own father. "Hell," Duke said, "she loved me enough to marry me. The minute we said our 'I do's' she started trying to change me into some other kind of fellow."

The marriage languished in the doldrums of incompatibility. The children didn't bring Duke and Josephine closer together. Duke said he was far too busy working twelve hours a day, six days a week to be a real father. Privately, Duke began to consider the painful possibility of a divorce. Unable to confront Josephine with the truth, he talked around it hoping she would pick up on his overtures. But divorce simply wasn't part of her vocabulary. The marriage had been solemnized by a Catholic priest, and, in view of her strict adherence to her faith, the vows could never be broken.

Duke was to find a haven from his home life on board John Ford's yacht. Since he'd signed with Monogram he'd seen very little of the distinguished director. Then one day, after another spat with Josephine, Duke drove out to the harbor at San Pedro. He was sitting in a local bar, trying to get over his anger, when 10-year-old Barbara Ford walked in. The *Araner* was moored close by, and John Ford had spotted his former protégé. Ford invited Duke aboard, and their friendship picked up where it had left off two years ago.

By then the *Araner* had become a favorite hideaway for a number of men who shared a love of sailing, fishing, drinking, and kicking up their heels away from home. The group usually included actors Ward Bond, Frank Morgan, Grant Withers, Lloyd Nolan; writer Dudley Nichols; and Pappy and Duke.

They called themselves the Young Men's Purity, Total Abstinence and Yachting Association. Weekends, they met on the *Araner*; weekdays, they patronized the Hollywood Athletic Club, sweating out the previous night's intake of booze in the steam room. Eventually the management installed a bar upstairs, which soon served as a private club.

In those days movie people weren't welcomed by the local country clubs. Club membership was offered only to those people who were listed in the social register. Duke, through his marriage, was the only actor to qualify, a fact his peers never let him live down. By contrast, the sole requirement for membership in the Young Men's Purity, Total Abstinence and Yachting Association was a fondness for liquor and steam baths.

The group's motto, "Jews, not dues," was an intentional mockery of the standards which prevailed at the country clubs, and they welcomed men of all religions in their loosely organized group. Eventually the steam room's black attendant, a gentleman named Buck Buchanan (forever after described as the "distinguished Afro-American") was duly elected president of the association, and his presence became a fixture of their gatherings.

Duke helped draw up a charter which defined the organization's purpose as "The promulgation of the cause of alcoholism." Prospective members were required to be "career-oriented or gutter-oriented drunks."

Then, because of their fondness for boating, the group changed its name to the Emerald Bay Yacht Club. Their big annual event was a St. Patrick's Day dinner. The first such dinner took place at the ultra elegant Coconut Grove. All the members bought nautical uniforms for the occasion. Duke's consisted of white trousers, a double breasted navy blue jacket trimmed with an enormous gold star, a matching captain's hat, and a pair of very worn sneakers. The inaugural dinner at the Coconut Grove was capped by a boisterous food fight and permanent eviction from the night spot.

Mazatlan, on the Baja coast, was a favorite port of call when the club met on board the *Araner*. Duke recalled one remarkable trip when he caught seven marlins in just three days, monsters that weighed in at over a thousand pounds each. Fishing by day and partying at night made a great vacation in his opinion.

The Belmar Hotel bar was their beach-side hangout. The group would install themselves in chairs overlooking the ocean, hire a mariachi band to serenade them, and then get down to the real purpose for the trip, some serious drinking. The first man to pass out could count on waking up to find the bartender's pet python placed on his lap. Duke, who never passed out, assured me that he became quite adept at handling that snake.

Those long hours of swilling tequila were responsible for health and personal problems that plagued half the group. Pappy and Grant became alcoholics; Ward died young of a heart attack induced by high blood pressure. Duke was more fortunate. He had an enormous capacity for liquor, could drink for days without any obvious effect on his personality or his health, and could then spend weeks without drinking at all. He enjoyed liquor, but he could live without it.

As Duke's marriage deteriorated further, he spent more and more time aboard the *Araner*. He loved the all-male group, and he gave them the best of himself. His wit, humor, and intellect would always be reserved for his male friends.

So much of my husband's character and lifestyle, the good and the bad, seems a product of those days on the *Araner* and his association with Pappy Ford. Pappy had always wanted a hell-raising, hard-working son of a bitch like Duke for a son. If Duke hadn't existed, Ford would have had to invent him. Perhaps, in a way, he did.

Ford could have given Duke a helping hand any time during the late thirties and saved him from the dreary round of B pictures he was making. I once asked Ford why he waited so long to cast Duke in a starring role in one of his films. "Duke wasn't ready," Ford replied. "He had to develop his skills as an actor. He needed to shed a certain callowness. I wanted some pain written on his face to offset the innocence. But I knew he had what it took to make it in the movie business. He was hungry." Pappy concluded, smiling as if his words were a benediction.

Ford had a genius for justifying his behavior. In fact, the director was happiest surrounded by stooges. Although he wished all his boys well, their later successes aroused the nastier side of Ford's nature. He was content to sit back during the thirties and watch Duke struggle.

Meanwhile Duke worked on his voice, consciously deepening its timbre, and on how he delivered dialogue, developing a halting style that became a unique and often mimicked trademark. He did most of his own stunts, becoming known for athleticism and daring. He listened to his directors as though they were oracles and made a practice of arriving on a set before they did so he'd be ready for work when they were. He studied, watched, and waited.

CHAPTER 5

The year 1939 was significant for the motion picture industry. Box office receipts reached their all-time high as new audiences were attracted to theaters by the increasing realism and technical quality of Hollywood films. The addition of full-length musical scores augmented the dialogue, heightening a script's emotional impact. Technicolor, invented early in the decade, was vastly improved by the development of a three-color process that helped make the 1939 Atlanta premiere of *Gone with the Wind* starring Vivian Leigh and Clark Gable, a phenomenal success.

The industry's renaissance was marked by an explosion of talent and an abundance of films destined to become classics. Premiering that year were *Mr. Smith Goes to Washington*, starring Jimmy Stewart; *The Wizard of Oz*, with Judy Garland; *Intermezzo*, featuring Ingrid Bergman; *Dark Victory*, with Betty Davis— to say nothing of *Goodbye Mr. Chips*, *Gunga Din*, *Wuthering Heights*, and *The Hunchback of Notre Dame*.

Despite this incredible list, the year belonged to Pappy Ford and his rowdy crew. Ford films opening in 1939 included *The Grapes of Wrath*, *Young Mister Lincoln*, *Drums along the Mohawk*, and *Stagecoach*. The first and last made two of his boys, Henry Fonda and John Wayne, overnight stars.

The Grapes of Wrath was a studio picture, made at Twentieth Century Fox under the aegis of the volatile Darryl Zanuck, The equally volatile Ford had been forced to alter some of his ideas about the script—and how to film it—to accommodate the more powerful Zanuck. Zanuck fueled Ford's anger by insisting on making the final cut on all the director's films.

Although Pappy won an Oscar for directing *Wrath*, he preferred *Stagecoach*. Pappy had taken the western's script to Zanuck, who refused to read it. "Nobody goes to westerns anymore," Zanuck told him. The head of Fox Studios had an enormous ego and a bad case of tunnel vision when it came to movies; if he didn't like an idea, he was convinced no one else would either.

Pappy eventually peddled the picture to Walter Wanger, an independent producer who got funding for the project from Universal. The executives at Universal told Wanger they were willing to commit $392,000 to making the western, and not a penny more. When all the other expenses were covered, Ford had a mere $65,000 to pay a cast. It was a tribute to his genius that Claire Trevor, Thomas Mitchell, and John Carradine agreed to work in the picture for far less than their standard fees. Even so, after signing the three, Ford had very little left to pay a leading man. Ford was unconcerned. The actor he had in mind would probably work for free just to have a chance to star in a Ford film.

One long, hot summer day Ford called Duke and invited him to sail to Catalina on the coming Saturday. There was nothing unusual about the phone call, except that Ford indicated they'd be alone aboard the *Araner*. "I need some peace and quiet," Ford explained.

Early Saturday Duke made his usual excuses to Josephine, packed a duffel bag, and drove out to San Pedro to board the *Araner*. That night, after they docked in Avalon, Ford handed him a script. "Read this for me," Ford said. "I'm having a hell of a time deciding who to cast in the lead. You know a lot of young actors, Duke. See what you think."

By the time Duke read halfway through the *Stagecoach* script, he knew the part of the Ringo Kid was tailor-made for him. At the age of 32, he had all the qualifications the part required. He could ride, do his own stunts, and handle guns with authority, and he could act—even though no one had given him a chance to show the depth of his talent. Duke wanted the part and knew he could make it memorable, but he was too proud to ask Pappy for it.

Duke was at a low point in his life, personally and professionally. Privately, he'd admitted that he wasn't much of a husband, at least not the kind Josephine wanted. Because of the tensions in his marriage, he'd also become an absentee father, spending most of his free time away from home. It seemed he faced personal failure no matter where he turned. All the drinking and partying couldn't keep him from confronting the truth: Second rate. He'd become a second rater!

No! He couldn't ask Pappy for the part. Pride was just about all Duke had—and a proud man didn't ask favors of his friends. So when Ford asked, "Who do you think is right for the Ringo Kid?" Duke couldn't let on that the cat-and-mouse game was getting to him. "Why don't you get Lloyd Nolan," he finally replied.

Pappy was enjoying himself too much to stop. "I just wish I could find a young guy who can ride a horse—and act. Hell, Duke, you must know somebody. But I guess you don't run across much talent over at Republic." All Duke could do was grit his teeth and go on fishing.

Pappy didn't offer Duke the part until the *Araner* was moored back at her berth in San Pedro. When he told Duke he'd had him in mind from the very beginning, Duke grinned with more confidence than he felt and said, "I know, Coach."

The film opened in March 1939, and Ford was hailed as a genius, the man who single-handedly made the western movie come of age. The critics mentioned Duke's performance in passing, as an afterthought, but the public's response to him was overwhelming. Exit polls taken after the sneak previews showed that Duke was a sensation as Ringo. Women adored him, men admired him, he'd stolen the picture. The public loved him. It didn't matter that the critics ignored him.

Duke had hoped his performance in *Stagecoach* would liberate him from the dreary round of making quickie westerns at Republic. Herbert Yates didn't see things that way. Capitalizing on Duke's new box office appeal, he threw Duke back into a series of westerns. Duke made seven of them in the fourteen months between finishing *Stagecoach* and starting his next important film. Once again, it was Pappy who came to Duke's rescue, casting Duke as a young and innocent Swedish seaman in the movie version of Eugene O'Neill's classic story, *The Long Voyage Home*.

As he had during the filming of *Stagecoach*, Ford attempted to intimidate Duke throughout the shooting of this new venture. Duke turned in a fine performance, even managing a believable Swedish accent. But the movie didn't advance his career, be-

cause Ford told everyone that he was the only director who could
get a good performance out of John Wayne. It seemed that, bar-
ring unforeseen events, Duke would be forever consigned to making B pictures and an occasional John Ford film.

The "unforeseen event" came in the most luscious package
the movie business had to offer. Marlene Dietrich was the sex
symbol of the early forties, an actress noted for her intelligence
and her ability to get what she wanted. When she saw Duke one
afternoon at the Universal commissary, his fate was sealed. She
took one look at Duke, nudged her agent, and said, "Daddy, get
me that."

Universal was casting *Seven Sinners*, Dietrich's first picture
following her huge success in *Destry Rides Again*. Universal
would have given her any leading man she wanted, and, to everyone's surprise, she wanted Duke. Republic's Herbert Yates was
more than happy to have his leading man out on loan, for a large
fee.

A meeting was set up in Dietrich's dressing room at Universal.
Duke recalled that day quite vividly. He said that Dietrich invited him inside and then closed the door and locked it. He'd
never been in a major star's private dressing room before and
stood gawking at the luxurious appointments.

Dietrich broke the awkward silence, "I wonder what time it
is?" she said, giving him a smoldering look. Before Duke could
glance at his watch she lifted her skirt, revealing the world's most
famous legs. Her upper thigh was circled by a black garter with
a timepiece attached. Dietrich looked at it, dropped her skirt,
and swayed to Duke's side, saying in a husky voice, "It's very
early, darling. We have plenty of time."

Duke recalled doing what any other red-blooded American
male would have done under the circumstances. This first encounter proved Dietrich wrong about one thing, though. There
wasn't enough time that afternoon to put out the fire she ignited.
In fact their love affair wouldn't burn itself out for three
years.

Duke described the Hollywood of the late thirties and early
forties as a combination of Peyton Place and Sodom and Gomor-
rah. Many of movieland's most celebrated citizens, men such as
Hank Fonda, Ray Milland, and Gary Cooper, led exemplary pub-

lic lives while behaving in private like stallions let loose in the mare's barn. Sex and booze were the opiates of the era.

Most of the male stars were relatively uneducated, and many came from deprived backgrounds, so it is understandable that after achieving wealth and power, they took advantage of the discovery that they could attract any woman they wanted. Duke had avoided that kind of behavior following his run in with Cohn, in spite of his unhappy marriage. He'd made a practice of "keeping his fly buttoned" when he was working.

However, Dietrich introduced him to a physical romance quite different from the chaste relationship he had with Josephine. He'd been romantically in love with Josephine and discovered a 19 year old's romantic dream could be a cold bedmate for a passionate man in his thirties. In addition, Dietrich was more than an ideal bedmate: She was the first person in the film industry, excepting John Ford, to tell Duke that she believed in him. Before meeting her he'd been mistreated and ill-used in psychologically emasculating experiences by powerful men such as Cohn and Yates. Dietrich made Duke feel like a man again, both in bed and on the sound stage.

They made three pictures over the next two years and were seen together socially at a variety of Hollywood night spots, including Ciros, the Brown Derby, Mocambo, and the Trocadero. Somehow, through it all, Duke maintained the façade of a happily married man. Perhaps the moviegoing public was more gullible in those days.

Dietrich had a strong influence on Duke that extended from the bedroom to the boardroom. He'd been making a lot of money and spending it all. Dietrich introduced him to her business manager, a Swede named Bo Roos. The two men hit it off, and Duke soon hired Roos, consigning his financial future to Roos's supposedly capable hands.

Duke was always reluctant to talk to me about Dietrich, but he did once say that I looked a little like her, adding, "she was the most intriguing woman I've ever known."

Duke's friends were more talkative about Dietrich. Some described the relationship as purely sexual, but others thought Duke would have married her if he'd been free. (An uneasy truce ex-

isted at home, although he and Josephine were completely estranged.)

Dietrich became Duke's best friend and confidante. She was
also a hausfrau who brought home-cooked meals to the set when
they were doing a movie together. They played chess during lulls
in the shooting and often spent weekends hunting and fishing. More
important, she and Duke shared a passion for making movies.

And then, as quickly as it had begun, for reasons I have never
learned, the affair ended. Duke and Dietrich didn't see each other
for many years. I was an unwilling witness to their final meeting. In 1954, a few months before Duke and I married, Howard
Hughes, one of Duke's friends, called to ask us to fly up to Vegas
to catch Dietrich's new nightclub act. I was reluctant to go, having heard all the gossip about Duke and Dietrich, but I was dying
to meet the elusive and legendary Howard Hughes. So I let Duke
convince me that the trip would be fun.

Las Vegas was just becoming known as a no-holds-barred resort town, and the Sahara offered the best accommodations and
the finest nightclub acts. Dietrich had been playing there to stand-
ing-room-only crowds.

The minute she appeared on stage, she saw our party and threw
Duke a suggestive kiss. From then on, she played to him alone.
Although she was over 50 at the time, Dietrich was still stunning
with a gorgeous figure and perfect legs more revealed than concealed by a $30,000 beaded gown. No one could compete. Half-
way through her performance she launched into "Hey, Look Me
Over," and her eyes locked on mine while she stared with re-
lentless curiosity. Duke had been wrong about the excursion being fun. I wanted to crawl under the table.

When the house lights went on at the end of her act, Dietrich
swayed to the edge of the stage and invited Duke and Howard to
her dressing room. As she walked away, Duke took me by the
arm. "Come on," he said, "I want to introduce you two."

Even though he was 47 at the time, Duke was still hopelessly
naïve about women. He had no idea that a former mistress and
a future wife would mix about as well as oil and water. "You go
on," I replied, trying to return to my seat. "I really don't mind
waiting."

But Duke was insistent. "You're my girl," he declared, "and you go where I go."

When we walked into Dietrich's dressing room, she ignored me, threw herself into Duke's arms, and gave him a passionate kiss. He untangled himself from her embrace, pulled me to his side, and said, "Marlene, I'd like you to meet Pilar, my future wife." Dietrich looked at Duke coldly, turned her back on the two of us, and began a lively conversation with Howard Hughes. Duke and I walked out unnoticed a few minutes later.

CHAPTER 6

In 1940 and early 1941, Duke's affair with Dietrich diverted him from thinking about the growing conflicts in Europe and Asia. Then, on December 7, 1941, the Japanese bombed Pearl Harbor. The United States was at war. Duke's friends, associates, and peers, men like John Ford, Hank Fonda, Clark Gable, Jimmy Stewart, and Ronald Reagan, were soon in uniform. Duke, at 34, was in no danger of being drafted, but he loved his country and planned to serve it.

There was one hurdle to clear before he enlisted. Duke had just signed a new and very lucrative contract with Republic, a contract that gave him a percentage of the profits on his future films. To the best of Duke's knowledge, he was the first star to get that kind of a contract, proof of his bargaining power. Unfortunately, bargaining power didn't help him when he told Herbert Yates he planned to enlist.

The head of Republic wasn't at all sympathetic to Duke's desire to serve his country. "You should have thought about all that before you signed a new contract," Yates told him angrily. "If you don't live up to it, I'll sue you for every penny you've got. Hell, I'll sue you for every penny you hope to make in the future. God damn it! Nobody walks out on me."

Legally, Yates was in the right, and Duke knew it. The celluloid John Wayne would have told Yates what he could do with his contract, marched out of the studio, and gone straight to the nearest recruiter. Duke, certain Yates wasn't bluffing, never enlisted, never got to find out if the service would have taken him in spite of his football injury. He would become a "super patriot"—for the rest of his life trying to atone for staying at home.

*   *   *

Duke spent more and more time away from home as the war dragged on, doing everything he could, out of uniform, to serve his country. In films like *Flying Tigers, Reunion in France, The Fighting Seabees, Back to Bataan,* and *They Were Expendable,* he paid tribute to those who fought in his place. Between pictures he toured with the USO, entertaining troops or selling war bonds.

He said he found life on the road preferable to life at home. He hated subjecting the children to the coldness that existed between him and Josephine. Their relationship might have been easier on their children than the constant fights between Duke's own parents had been on him, but he knew the kids sensed that something was wrong. He remembered getting a sick feeling in the pit of his stomach every time he thought about what he was doing to them.

Finally, on May 2, 1943, Josephine admitted what Duke had known for years: They'd never be able to make each other happy. She went into superior court and asked for a legal separation. The marriage had lasted fewer than ten years.

Duke told me he walked away from the marriage with his clothes, his car, and an overwhelming feeling of guilt he never completely put behind him. Josephine was deeply, mortally angry, although she spoke to him on the rare days she let him see the children. He had given Josephine the house, a car, their savings. He agreed to give her 25 percent of the first $100,000 he made each year and 10 percent of the rest, for his lifetime. He established trust funds for her and their children. Whenever extraordinary expenses came up—braces, a special school or summer camp, Duke paid the bills. And still the guilt tormented him. He was too good a man to have failed in marriage and too subject to human frailties to have made it work.

The part of Duke's personality that was like his father rejoiced in his new freedom, the part that was like his mother punished him with remorse. In those first months alone, he worked and played harder than ever, trying to close his heart and mind to everything but the present. Then, on a trip to Mexico in the com-

pany of Bo Roos and Ray Milland, Duke met the woman who
was to be his next wife.

When Milland introduced Duke to Esperanza Bauer, she
claimed to be an actress. In fact, she was a high-class callgirl
who'd had a bit part in a Mexican film. Milland was one of her
clients. That first night of partying, Milland treated her like a
prostitute, but Duke treated her like a lady. Chata, as Esperanza
was nicknamed, became instantly infatuated. To Milland's and
Roos's horror, so did Duke.

Chata was the exact opposite of church-going, ladylike Josephine. Duke, who had admired and idolized Josephine in their
courting days, lusted for Chata. She was vivacious, blatantly sexual and voluptuous, a combination that was guaranteed to make
her a perfect companion for an emotionally repressed man. They
were inseparable during Duke's stay in Mexico.

Chata was born in the slums of Mexico and grew up in poverty, living by her wits and her looks. Duke, a romantic at heart,
fictionalized her past and admired the courage it took to survive
the childhood she described. Duke told me that Chata talked of
her desire to leave her past behind, to settle down and marry
someone she loved.

Milland and Roos, knowing Chata for what she was, attempted
to tell Duke the truth about his new love. He refused to listen.
Perhaps, like the Ringo Kid, who fell in love with a prostitute in
Stagecoach, Duke thought women such as Chata really had hearts
of gold. Perhaps he even deluded himself into thinking he could
save her, reform her, make an "honest woman of her." Perhaps,
overwhelmed by her sensuality, he didn't think at all.

After Duke returned to California he realized that he wanted
more than a series of one-night stands, he wanted a real marriage, the kind you saw in the movies. Despite fathering four children and having an affair with Marlene Dietrich, Duke was still
unsophisticated when he met Chata. He mistook the lust she in-
spired for a deep, abiding love.

One year after their first meeting in Mexico City, Duke talked
Herbert Yates into giving Chata a screen test. She arrived in Hollywood shortly after Duke and Josephine separated. Josephine
responded to the news of Duke's new love's arrival by suing for

divorce on November 25, 1944. She told the court that Duke had caused her to suffer "Grievous mental and physical pain."

He in turn complained of Josephine's coldness, her lack of interest in the physical side of their marriage. The judge, in disbelief, commented on the fact that Duke had fathered four children. Duke, referring to their sex life, said under oath, "four times—in ten years."

An interlocutory decree of divorce was granted at the end of November. Afterward, Duke learned that Josephine had her own view of their legal situation when she released the following statement to the press: "Because of my religion," she was quoted, "I regard divorce as a purely civil action, in no way affecting the moral status of my marriage."

Although Josephine Wayne had given him the divorce he sought and Duke married Chata on January 18, 1946, Josephine would continue to regard herself as Duke's wife, the only legal wife he would ever have, and that is what she taught their four children. The situation was to cause considerable difficulty in the future when Duke and I married and had our own children.

Back in the forties Duke was too preoccupied with Chata to pay much attention to Josephine. He was learning that Chata had a few peculiarities of her own. She drank—something he wasn't used to in a woman, and she was a nasty drunk to boot. She wanted her mother to live with them, and, hoping that might help keep her sober, Duke agreed.

His former friends, dismayed by the obvious misalliance, avoided the new couple. Duke told me of an angry confrontation with John Ford that ended with Ford screaming, "Did you have to marry that whore?"

"You're talking about the woman I love," Duke replied icily before he walked away. The two men didn't see each other again for two years. By then Duke's marriage was in trouble, and all his friends knew it.

Before the marriage, Chata had spoken of having children and keeping house. Afterward she wanted to shop and go to parties. When Duke first met her, she seemed like a woman who had everything in the world to give. One year later he knew she'd married him because of what he could give her. It was the oldest story in the world, and he felt degraded by his part in it.

His private life was chaos again. Because of Chata, Josephine was reluctant to allow the children to visit Duke at home, preferring that they saw him on location. Milland, Roos, Withers, Bond, Ford, all kept their distance. But Duke couldn't bring himself to admit that he'd made a second mistake. If marriage to Josephine had been a bad dream—marriage to Chata was a full-blown, technicolor nightmare.

The one positive thing in Duke's life was his career. Hollywood was short of leading men during the war years, and Duke had never been in greater demand. He said he felt guilty as hell about that too. However, the money came in handy.

He not only supported Josephine and the kids, he'd bought Chata a 5-acre estate in Encino, near Clark Gable's spread, and Chata was spending a fortune on furniture, clothes, cars, servants, booze, and her mother, who Duke also supported.

In addition Duke gave his stepmother—Clyde Morrison had remarried before dying in 1938—a monthly allowance. Mary Morrison had remarried, and Duke was equally generous to his mother. And not a week passed, without her calling and asking, "What are you doing for Bobby? Have you gotten him a job yet?" Duke did his best to help his younger brother. He persuaded a number of friends in the movie business to give Bobby Morrison jobs, which he never managed to keep. Robert Morrison preferred drinking and chasing women, married or single. He even had an affair with the wife of one of Duke's best friends and was caught by the angry husband while attempting to escape out a bedroom window.

As Mary Morrison Preen put it, "Bobby is a caution!" Duke loved his younger brother too much, felt too responsible for him, to stay angry at him for long. He kept on writing checks and hoping for change.

John Wayne had all the trappings of a major motion picture star by the middle of the forties, including an agent who charged 10 percent for services rendered, a business manager who collected another 5 percent for overseeing Duke's affairs, an ex wife, and a long list of dependents. He needed a private secretary to help him keep track of all of them.

Mary St. John was the woman he picked for the job. She'd

worked for Joe Kane, one of Duke's favorite directors, and he'd known her for years. A petite brunette, she had a wonderful smile, a cheerful disposition, an uncommon amount of common sense, a wide knowledge of the movie industry, and a motherly understanding of human nature. Duke couldn't have made a better choice, He needed a friend as well as a secretary, and St. John never failed him. She ran his office with efficiency, providing an island of calm in Duke's stormy life.

Years after she'd gone to work for Duke, St. John told me about one of the first things he asked her to do. She had just started her new job when he walked into the office with a couple of magazines under his arm. He put them down on her desk and she noticed that the corners of several pages were turned down.

"I want you to order the things I've marked," he said. Mary St. John couldn't help but laugh. It was the last thing she expected from her handsome boss. Duke had been on his way out of the office, but he turned around when he heard her soft chuckle. "Let me tell you something about myself," he said. "When I was a kid we got the Montgomery Ward catalogue. I used to thumb through it and there were a hell of a lot of things I wanted. But we were too damn poor to buy any of them. I made up my mind that if I ever got rich, I'd order anything that caught my eye."

St. John felt guilty about her thoughtless giggle, and from then on she ordered everything Duke wanted from those dog-eared magazines. But she did encourage him to buy quality goods. It was a red-letter day for them both when she got him hooked on the catalogues from Bean and Bauer.

Although she was his employee, St. John always had Duke's best interests at heart. Duke could not say as much for Chata Bauer. The marriage continued to flounder and, following the pattern he'd set with Josephine, Duke spent more and more time away from home. He was making three pictures a year, most of them on location, and traveling for business and pleasure when he wasn't working. The longer he stayed away, the angrier Chata became, and she never hesitated to unleash her fury on his return.

St. John described Duke's coming into the office one day when he wasn't filming, mumbling hello but keeping his face averted as he walked past her desk. She sensed that something was wrong, but, knowing Duke, she decided he'd tell her if and when he felt like it. An hour later when she had papers that needed his signature, she knocked on his office door.

"Come in," he muttered in a low voice.

As she entered he looked up, and she saw four deep red welts running the length of his face. She thought he looked as if he'd had a run-in with a mountain lion. "Oh Duke," she said, "what in the world happened to you? Did you have a fight?"

Duke stared at his desk. "I didn't," he replied, "but my wife sure as hell did. She was drunk again last night. We were at a party and I tried to get her to leave. When she wouldn't, I picked her up—"and his voice trailed off, as if he felt he'd already said too much.

"But, Duke," St. John was dumbfounded, "I thought this was a love match."

"I did too, Mary, I did too," Duke murmured. He turned away too late to hide a sheen of moisture in his eyes.

Things did not improve. Chata had a fiery temper and a jealous nature. She saw every one of his leading ladies as a potential threat. It was a serious mistake on her part.

Duke still believed in all the old-fashioned virtues his parents had taught him. Deep in his heart he was a small-town, midwestern boy who wanted nothing more than a peaceful home life. Things might still have worked out with Chata if she'd been able to accept this simple truth.

During the filming of *The Angel and the Badman*, Duke's young costar, Gail Russell, developed a full-blown crush on her leading man. She was a raven-haired beauty whose fragile appearance mirrored an even more fragile psyche. *The Angel and the Badman* was her first major film, and she started every day's shooting weak with terror, throwing up in her dressing room before appearing on the set. Like many other performers overwhelmed by stage fright, Russell began to find courage in a bottle.

Duke tried to help her as he had helped other novices, by being gentle, patient, and kind. He even loaned her the down payment on a car while she waited to collect her first big check. When he realized she'd fallen in love with him, he asked Mary St. John to "set Gail straight. Make sure she understands how I feel, but do it gently," he said. "The poor kid's having a tough time."

Within a few months Russell had recovered from her schoolgirl crush and married someone else. She and Duke remained friends. They costarred in *Reap the Wild Wind* in 1949, and Duke gave Russell a part a decade later when she struggled to make a film comeback after battling a string of mental and physical problems. But Duke never loved Gail Russell, and he swore they'd never been more than friends.

Chata refused to believe him. She convinced herself that Duke and Russell were having an affair. The night the film wrapped there was the usual party for cast and crew, and Duke came home very late. Chata was in a drunken rage by the time he arrived, and she attempted to shoot him as he walked through the front door. Duke was accustomed to ducking lead on screen but not at home. As the bullet whizzed past his head he suddenly saw Chata as she really was, not as he'd hoped she'd be. Instead of marrying the heroine of his romantic fantasies, he realized he'd married the women whom Ray Milland had labeled, "a Mexican whore."

The next day Chata begged him to forgive her. She swore she'd change, stop drinking, and start acting like a real wife. She spent the following week weeping and moping around the house. Duke was helpless in the face of all those tears. He agreed to a reconciliation.

Chata kept her promise as long as she could. Then her old habits reasserted themselves. She began to drink heavily together with her mother. Duke told me of coming home after a long day at the studio to find the two women in bed together, twined in each other's arms, sound asleep.

He banished Chata's mother to Mexico, sobered his wife up, and asked for a divorce. Chata turned on the tears again. Now the marriage had a pattern, one Duke couldn't seem to break. Chata would go on a binge, she and Duke would fight, they'd make up, and Chata would celebrate their reconciliation by having a few drinks and then a few more, and the whole cycle would begin again.

Despite being trapped in a second unhappy marriage, Duke recalled that life in the late forties wasn't all bad. After the war the

Young Men's Purity, Total Abstinence and Yachting Association had a joyful, hilarious reunion. It felt like old times to Duke, running down to Mexico with Fonda, Bond, Withers, and Pappy Ford. Ford, the die-hard Irish Catholic, had looked into his heart and forgiven Duke for divorcing Josephine. He even forgave him for marrying Chata once he saw how badly that had turned out.

The young men of the association had all reached middle age, but they could still "hurrah" a sleepy Mexican fishing port when they arrived in town. Back they all went to Mazatlan and the Belmar Hotel where the owner's pet python was still available when the most sober of them wanted to play pranks on the drunkest.

"We had some good times," Duke said wistfully, discussing the postwar years and his happiness with his all-male group of buddies.

At this time, however, Duke was approaching his fortieth birthday, and he'd started to take a long, hard look at where he'd been and where he was going, personally and professionally. Early in 1946 something happened that literally changed his life. The distinguished director Howard Hawks called Duke one day to offer him a part in his next picture.

Duke was flattered and accepted at once. He'd been making two and three pictures a year during the war, but he assumed he got so many offers because so few leading men were around rather than because he had talent and ability. Duke still had very little confidence in himself as a performer. He would often tell the press, in an unconscious repetition of John Ford's words, that "I don't act, I react."

When Duke read the *Red River* script, he knew that the part of Tom Dunson would require much more than mere reacting—it would take a consummate actor to perform it. Duke would be playing a man well beyond his own years, a stubborn individual who was wrong more often than he was right. And yet, if the film was going to work, Duke would have to make Tom Dunson likeable.

To add to his difficulties, he would be playing opposite Montgomery Clift, who would be making his screen debut in the film. Clift was a man half Duke's size, an actor who was noted for conveying fragility rather than strength. The film climaxed with a huge brawl in which Clift would best Duke. Duke knew it would take a hell of a lot more than "reacting" if he was to keep audiences from laughing during that scene. He would have to believe in Clift's masculinity and make the people who watched that scene believe in it too. Duke reached deep inside himself during the Elgin, Arizona, filming, using skills he hadn't been sure he possessed, to create one of his most memorable screen roles. Tom Dunson foreshadowed the parts Duke would play when he became too old for traditional romantic leads. When the picture wrapped, Howard Hawks told the press, "I couldn't have made Red River without John Wayne."

"That set me thinking," Duke told me. "It was the first time I felt like a real actor, someone who could make a unique contribution to motion pictures." Before doing the Hawk's film, Duke had been drifting, reacting to life on and off screen instead of taking control. Duke said he'd taken a good hard look at himself after making Red River, and he didn't like what he saw. He wasn't very proud of the things he'd done in the past, and he'd been feeling a little sorry for himself because of how both of his marriages had turned out. But he couldn't change the past. The future was what counted. He wanted to leave a legacy he could be proud of. He wanted the world to be a better place after he was gone than it had been when he arrived. He wanted to do movies he could be proud of, movies that would teach a sound set of values to the younger generation. "I'd kind of put all the things my father taught me out of my mind," Duke recalled, "but when I started looking for a creed to live by I knew I couldn't do better than to believe in the things my father believed in."

A rededicated John Wayne emerged from what had been a midlife crisis. He vowed to be a better man, on screen and off. When word of his bravura performance in Red River got around, all kinds of good offers came his way. Next, Duke chose to do John Ford's Fort Apache with Hank Fonda, Ward Bond, Grant Withers, and a grown-up Shirley Temple. He followed it with another Ford picture, The Three Godfathers, costarring Pedro Armandariz, Bond, and Harry Carey, Jr. The series of Ford pictures was interrupted by a romantic sea story, Wake of the Red Witch, which united Duke and Gail Russell. In 1948 Duke and Pappy Ford returned to Monument Valley, where they filmed yet another classic western, She Wore a Yellow Ribbon. A common thread runs through all three pictures, the triumph of right over wrong. Duke would look for this theme in all his films from then on.

By the end of the decade he was feeling better about himself, and he'd never looked better on screen. Hs friends were aging while he simply weathered. Lines of experience and pain were finally overshadowing the look of "callowness" that Ford had found so unappealing fifteen years before.

Duke was in great demand as an actor and a personality. If it was hell at home, why stay? he reasoned. Not a day went by when he didn't receive a script to read, an invitation to a party, or request to make a personal appearance somewhere. The former serial star had made his way onto the list of top-ten box office draws. It was exciting and gratifying but not as gratifying as finding a cause. With the coming of the cold war, Duke found a way to serve his country.

CHAPTER 7

Duke didn't go to church. He'd been uncomfortable with organized religion since childhood, a feeling which had been reinforced by marriage to the devoted Josephine. But Duke was a believer. He had faith in God and faith in his country. When it came to the United States, Duke was a flag waver who got a tear in his eye when he heard the national anthem or saw the Stars and Stripes outlined against a clear sky. He believed in freedom of speech. His father had taught him that honorable men have a duty to speak out for what they hold dear, to stand up and be counted. That was the American way, and, in Duke's estimation, mankind had yet to invent a better political system. You could call him a "born-again American."

When World War II came to a close, most Americans thought the years of national peril had passed. Hitler, Tojo, and a host of war criminals were either dead or being duly punished by the victorious Allies. People hoped to settle down to a long period of peace and prosperity. Duke had a different view of the world. He saw communism as an insidious threat that could weaken us from within while attacking our friends and allies on a broad international front.

Duke hadn't been swayed by his many liberal friends who were in favor of socialism and who saw communism as the hope of the world back in the days before the war when Russia seemed to stand alone against the insanity of the Nazis. Having voted for Roosevelt, Duke thought of himself as a liberal, a staunch supporter of the principles of Jeffersonian democracy. But he saw a big difference between liberal and left! He made up his mind to dedicate part of his life to fighting communism, whenever, wherever, and however he could.

He'd joined an anti-Communist group, the Motion Picture Alliance for the Preservation of American Ideals, in 1944. Although the Russians were our allies back then, Duke made no secret of his distrust of their political system and their leaders. Nor did men such as Walter Wanger, Dudley Nichols, Clark Gable, Ward Bond, Adolphe Menjou, Robert Taylor, Gary Cooper, John Ford, Cecil DeMille, Walt Disney, and a host of others, who also joined the Motion Picture Alliance (MPA).

Most people working in the industry recognized the movies' potential as a tool for spreading propaganda; their greatest fear was that the industry would be taken over by individuals who secretly belonged to the Communist party. The Motion Picture Alliance had been organized to help prevent such an outcome.

At first the members were wrongfully regarded as radicals and labeled fascist or anti-Semitic. But when the cold war began in the late forties, suddenly anti-Communist sentiments were rampant. The notorious House Committee on Un-American Activities launched an investigation of the motion picture industry and ordered a group of actors and writers to testify. A number of movie people, including writers Ring Lardner, Jr., and Albert Maltz, took the Fifth Amendment, refusing to testify on the grounds they might incriminate themselves. The press dubbed this group the Unfriendly Ten. After their refusal to cooperate with the House committee, the Unfriendly Ten all served jail sentences. These unfortunate individuals, as well as others who appeared to sympathize with the Communist party, were blackballed by the movie industry.

Duke felt relieved that Congress had finally become aware of the danger presented by Communist sympathizers in the entertainment industry, but he never testified before Congress, and he never personally blacklisted anyone. However, he did become president of the MPA and the most outspoken anti-Communist in Hollywood. As a consequence the press associated his name with blacklisting. To his surprise, Duke was labeled an archconservative, described as being right of the right—a bum rap in his opinion but one he would never shake.

Ultimately, however, Duke didn't care about public opinion or the growing frenzy in the press. He cared about fighting com-

munism. When Senator Joe McCarthy began hunting for Communists inside the government in 1950, Duke gave McCarthy his
full and very vocal support. Although the Senator was later dis-
credited, Duke's faith in the man never wavered. He believed
McCarthy was a good though much maligned American.

Duke felt happiest when he had a cause, and his experiences in
the industry showed him that movies could be a powerful way
to affect other people's beliefs. Among his personal heroes were
the men who'd fought in World War II, and he continued to show
his admiration for them after the war by making movies about
their exploits.

The first and best of these movies was Ford's *Sands of Iwo
Jima*. In it Duke played Sergeant Stryker, a professional soldier
with a disastrous home life. In many ways the script paralleled
Duke's own life at the time, so he was able to bring the character
he played vividly to life. He was nominated for an Oscar for the
role, the first nomination of his then twenty-year-long career.

"I wouldn't have minded losing so much," he told me, "if anyone else had won." Broderick Crawford had taken home the Oscar for *All the King's Men*, a film Duke had turned down on the
grounds that it was un-American. He refused to make movies
that showed the United States' faults or portrayed debauched
U.S. citizens. He'd already begun to choose parts on the basis of
the message they conveyed, a practice that limited his career and
the quality of his roles but also helped to make him a legend.

Operation Pacific and *Flying Leathernecks*, both shot in 1951,
were Duke's next salutes to U.S. fighting men. Once, he'd been
in danger of typecasting as a cowboy, but that year it looked as
if he'd never play anything but soldiers. Then Pappy Ford called
and asked Duke if he'd like to star in a love story.

Ford had read "The Quiet Man," a short story by Maurice
Walsh, when it was first published in the *Saturday Evening Post*
in 1933. He bought the story three years later and began planning the film but found financial backing difficult to get. Studio
executives didn't think a script about an ex-fighter and an Irish
girl would sell tickets.

In desperation, Duke and Ford approached Herbert Yates at

Republic, and, to their surprise, Yates struck a deal. Ford had insisted on a $1.7 million budget, and, uncharacteristically, Yates agreed. Then, true to form, Yates began to complain about the expense, the script, the proposed casting. Poor Ford had never worked at a second-rate studio before, had never been treated like anything less than a reigning genius. Duke was furious with Yates and blamed himself for getting Ford involved.

Yates disregarded Duke's anger and continued to complain constantly during preproduction. He even said he didn't think The Quiet Man was the sort of picture Duke should make, although he knew the script had been written with Duke in mind. The situation at Republic Studio grew tense as the cast and crew prepared to depart for location in Ireland.

Duke's situation at home wasn't much better. Chata accompanied him on location despite the fact that Ford had no patience with her drinking sprees. When The Quiet Man cast and crew left Hollywood, they included Ward Bond, Victor McLaglen, Francis Ford, old friends who'd worked together before, and Duke's four children by Josephine, who'd been given parts in the film.

Despite the irritation of Yates's daily phone calls and Chata's presence, making The Quiet Man proved to be a happy experience. The scenery was lush and the pubs warm and welcoming. Duke had his children and his friends, and Ford had Maureen O'Hara.

Ford, in his mid-fifties, had been married three decades. He was an intellectual, interested in politics, literature, sports, as well as a little hell-raising with the boys. His wife, Mary Ford, devoted herself to running their household and raising two children and was a traditional Hollywood wife. She was often forced into the background of her husband's life by women Ford met at work, even though Ford vocally asserted that women were best-suited to doing floors and windows and raising kids.

Ford had had an affair with Katharine Hepburn in the thirties in a classic attraction of opposites. He was a self-declared man's man; Hepburn was a feminist, as strong-willed as Ford. They clashed and loved with equal intensity. Duke told me Ford would have married her in a minute, if he had not been Catholic. The heartbreak Ford felt at having to give up Hepburn in the thirties probably contributed to his resentment of Duke when he left Josephine in the forties.

O'Hara was a Ford favorite. Duke described them on location, their heads close, talking a mile a minute in their native Gaelic. O'Hara first worked for Ford when he directed her in *How Green Was My Valley* in 1940, and she'd been his favorite actress and close friend ever since. He'd teamed Duke and Maureen in *Rio Grande* in 1949 and had been looking for another vehicle for them. Their casting in *The Quiet Man* proved to be pure magic.

Filming *The Quiet Man* resulted in one awkward moment for Duke. O'Hara, Ford, and he were working on the picture's most passionate love scene, photographed in the pouring rain. Through a series of takes, Ford exhorted his stars to make their kisses more passionate, their embrace even tighter. Eventually, Duke could feel every line and curve of Maureen's body through her soaked clothes, and he suspected she could feel every line of his. When I asked Duke years later how Ford could have prolonged the shooting of that particular scene with Maureen, Duke replied, "Hell, Honey, Ford just had me do all the things he wanted to do himself."

Duke returned from Ireland in an expansive mood. He knew he'd done some of his best work there. But Herbert Yates took one look at the picture in rough cut, decided it wasn't commercial, insisted on cuts Ford and Duke didn't want to make, and demanded they change the name to *The Fighter and the Colleen*. In the end, Ford regained artistic control of the film.

But Yates's demands were the end as far as Duke was concerned. He could put up with Yates when it came to his own career, but he couldn't stand by while Yates tormented Ford. Duke had been thinking about leaving Republic. He thought that Yates hadn't learned a thing about the movie business in all the years he'd been running the studio. "The man had the soul of an accountant," Duke explained, adding he'd only stayed with Republic because Yates had promised to finance Duke's favorite project, a film about the Alamo. After the experience of *The Quiet Man*, Duke realized that accepting Yates's backing would be "a pain in the ass." To Yates's dismay, Duke announced that he was leaving.

In the early fifties the studios still controlled the industry, but their grip had been weakened by a 1950 court decision that divested them of their vast chains of movie theaters. The court decision allowed independent producers to arrange distribution of their films. Duke made up his mind to become one of those producers. "Sink or swim," he said, "it had to be better than working with men like Yates and Cohn." He was one of the first stars to form his own production company, which he did in partnership with businessman Robert Fellows. Wayne-Fellows was founded in 1952, after Duke left Republic.

The year of 1952 also proved to be a year for endings. Chata filed for divorce, asking for $12,571 per month for maintenance. Duke countered, offering Chata a lump sum of $375,000 and yearly support of $40,000. Considering the heartbreak of the last four years, he thought he'd been more than generous.

Chata burned with anger when her attorney reported the proposed settlement. She wanted the house, the cars, the savings, all their investments, a repeat of the settlement Duke had given Josephine $6\frac{1}{2}$ years earlier.

I once asked Duke why he and Chata never had a family. "She was too evil to conceive," he replied, the nastiest comment he ever made about any woman during our years together.

It soon became apparent that the property agreement wouldn't be settled easily. Duke made up his mind to leave the whole mess in the hands of his lawyers. The prospect of a second divorce sickened him. He couldn't forgive himself for the kind of behavior he might have expected from his brother, Bobby (and would have forgiven Bobby for). He'd loved Chata and been completely deceived by her. He needed to get out of town and forget the whole mess.

Accompanied by a close friend, Ernie Saftig, Duke left for Peru to check locations for his Alamo film. He'd been told to look up a man named Richard Weldy when he arrived in Lima. Weldy was a big brawling Irishman—Duke's kind of guy—who worked for Pan American and took safaris up the Amazon as a sideline. Weldy was, at that time, my estranged husband.

The three men were to spend several days together in Lima, drinking and seeing the sights. One evening they went to the exclusive roof-top restaurant, the 91 Club, owned by my friend, Dino Prati. Dino later said he was pleased when Duke walked into his restaurant with the group. But they were no sooner seated when a man at a nearby table started to harass them.

"Why don't these Hollywood jerks stay home?" he asked his dinner partners in a loud voice, adding, "They look like a bunch of pansies!"

Duke ignored the comments, but Ernie couldn't resist turning around and saying, "If you're going to talk about us, please lower your voice. We have ladies present and they can hear what you're saying."

The heckler jumped up, took off his coat, and approached Duke's table threateningly. Ernie, who weighed 240 pounds and didn't look like any "pansy," jumped up to intercede. On seeing Ernie's response, the man charged. Ernie lashed out with a short jab that floored his opponent. Somehow, though, the man leaped to his feet and came at the group again. Ernie repeated the jolting jab and this time the man hit the floor to stay.

During the fracas, Duke and Richard Weldy jumped up and stopped two other men from joining in, their imposing size discouraging further violence. During the scuffle, however, tables were overturned and other things damaged as in the best of barroom brawls. Duke, who had wanted to avoid trouble, especially since they weren't in North America, approached the man's wife saying that he was very sorry about what had happened.

"Mr. Wayne," she replied, "I want to thank you for doing what you all did. My husband always starts trouble when he has a few drinks and this is the first time someone has really challenged him and put him in his place."

Duke, on leaving the restaurant, slipped Dino Prati some money that more than covered the damage.

After the fight they decided to leave town for awhile. Weldy knew of a movie crew shooting a film in the jungle in a place called Tingo Maria and volunteered to fly his new buddies there. It sounded, Duke remembered, like a wonderful adventure.

CHAPTER 8

Tingo Maria is a small community bordered by a dense jungle. Outside the town vibrantly colored orchids grow in profusion, and flocks of yellow-crowned parrots sail through the air like children's kites. The greenery photographs like paradise, a Peruvian version of the Garden of Eden. Fortunately the heat, humidity, snakes, leeches, and insects that burrow beneath your skin don't show up on film.

I was there filming *Green Hell,* a particularly appropriate title considering our location. One day while the members of our company shared breakfast and four-day-old newspapers from Lima in the restaurant of Tingo Maria's only hotel, someone saw an article that said John Wayne was in Lima scouting locations for a new film.

I couldn't understand the excitement the news caused. The name, John Wayne, seemed familiar, but I couldn't match it with a face. In those days ten years would pass between the U.S. release of a movie and its release in Lima. I'd seen pictures starring Gary Cooper and Randolph Scott, but westerns were not my favorite movie fare. I preferred melodramatic women's pictures, tearjerkers starring actresses such as Joan Crawford or Ava Gardner.

Back in 1952 I was the rarest of species, a Peruvian movie actress. *Green Hell* was my second picture. I was first exposed to acting in my teens through an amateur theater group, the Lima Theatre Workshop, which I helped found. I was the only Peruvian in the group which was made up of people from the U.S. Embassy and other North Americans who formed the business colony in Lima at that time. We put on plays and musicals in the English language including *Light Up the Sky, Born Yesterday,*

61

Front Page, Oklahoma, and *Mr. Roberts.* I enjoyed participating in these productions but never really wanted to become a professional actress. My career in movies was a fluke—I'd been born the daughter of a prominent politician, expected to make a good marriage to a Latin American aristocrat. But my father had died when I was in my teens, and though married young, I'd separated from my husband, Richard Weldy, taken a screen test when a Hollywood producer came to Lima, and found myself in the movie business—a strange destiny for a woman who hadn't been permitted to go to movies as a child.

So I wasn't familiar with John Wayne's name that morning and couldn't share everyone else's excitement. In any case, John Wayne was in Lima, not Tingo Maria, and I had the morning's shooting to worry about. For a novice, an actress with no training, that was a lot of worry.

When we broke for lunch a few hours later, our director took me aside. "Pilar," he said, "I just got word that John Wayne hired a plane in Lima and is flying over to watch us work. He wants to see what the conditions would be if he did his own film in our country."

"Perhaps he'll like my work and offer me a role in one of his pictures," I replied naïvely, indulging in a bit of wishful thinking. Then, thinking about a difficult dance sequence I had to shoot that afternoon, I dismissed the impending visit from my mind.

Duke and his entourage arrived on location late that afternoon, while I was dancing barefoot by firelight, wearing a low-cut gypsy costume. My skirts whirled around my body as I swayed and turned, trying to forget that so many people were watching. It was a relief when I heard the director call, "Cut. That's a print."

I was flushed and out of breath, my long hair tumbled around my shoulders. Before I had a chance to regain my composure, the director came over, took my hand, and led me to a tall, imposing man. "Pilar," he said, "I'd like you to meet John Wayne."

All I could do was stare. He was the handsomest man I'd ever seen. I couldn't believe anyone's eyes could be so turquoise, so piercing. In Peru most people have plain brown eyes. He looked at me with a lively curiosity. Standing barefoot, my head didn't even reach his shoulder.

"That was quite a dance," he said, studying me from the top

of my disheveled hair to the tips of my dusty toes. His expression held a disquieting interest so powerful and intimate that I gasped, "Pleased to meet you," in a quivering voice. Flustered and out of my element, I turned away to meet the rest of his traveling companions.

While John Wayne and I looked at each other, I'd been oblivious to everyone else. To my pleasure, I realized that my former guitar teacher, Chabaca Granda—later one of Peru's most famous composer-musicians—was part of the group around him. We embraced each other warmly. Next I was introduced to Ernie Saftig, a close friend of John Wayne's.

Then I saw my estranged husband, Richard Weldy, standing in the shadows. What in the world was he doing here? I wondered. We hadn't seen each other in months, and I'd been trying to put the sadness of the failed marriage behind me. Tingo Maria was the last place I'd expected to see him.

After making the introductions, our director told the cast and crew to take the rest of the day off, adding that he planned a dinner in Mr. Wayne's honor that evening and we were all invited. Then John Wayne's party, including our director and my husband, went off to do some sightseeing, and I returned to the hotel.

Later, in my room, I tried to sort out my feelings. I'd never been so immediately and powerfully affected by a casual meeting with a man the way I was by my meeting with John Wayne. It was so much more than sex appeal or good looks, both of which he had in abundance, or his success and fame, of which I had been told. Something elemental about the man, a sense of great strength, appealed to me.

While I attempted to deal with the unexpected and unwelcome emotions he aroused, I continued to wonder about Richard's presence. We'd parted when I learned he'd become involved with another woman, and it had taken me months to deal with this knowledge. Now it was hard to contemplate a festive evening with the memory of that pain upsetting me.

I'd put off filing for divorce because marriage, even in name only, offered some protection in the male-dominated world of moviemaking. Misunderstanding my intentions, Richard had made a few attempts to win me back. As I dressed for the evening,

I found myself wishing I'd gotten divorced when I left Richard. As soon as this picture wraps, I promised myself, I'd see a lawyer.

We'd been asked to gather on the patio of the hotel cantina for cocktails. I'd never realized what a romantic setting it was until I arrived that evening. A great, pale jungle moon illuminated the night sky, candles glowed on the tables, and the soft murmur of a stream flowing a few feet away added to the atmosphere.

When I walked in, John Wayne rose and motioned me to his side, and again I had the feeling that we were alone in the room. As he seated me I noticed that he moved with surprising grace for so large a man. I tried not to stare, although I don't think I succeeded.

"Chabaca has been telling us that you play the guitar," he said, smiling into my eyes.

I tried to keep my voice level as I answered, "Oh, I get by."

"Would you play a song for me?" he asked, in the deep drawl that mesmerized his fans and, now, me.

"Of course," I agreed immediately, sending someone to retrieve my guitar from my nearby hotel room. By the time I held the familiar instrument in my hands, I'd willed my fingers to stop trembling.

I began by playing a few popular Latin American songs like "Criollita," and "Granada." As the music filled the cantina, I kept stealing glances at John Wayne. Every time I finished a song, he looked at me and said, "Please, just one more."

I learned later that he'd fallen in love with Latin America, its music, its food, the languorous pace of life, and—of course—its traditional drink, pisco. But his warm, appreciative expression told me his requests were sincere, not merely courteous. I'd never known a man to be so polite and attentive. Latin American men have beautiful manners, but they are part of a carefully polished façade, whereas Duke's graciousness seemed a natural part of him.

I asked Chabaca to join me, and we launched into a more popular repertoire, songs like "Begin the Beguine," and "Frenesi." We knew each other so well and had played together so much that I could toss her the melody while I built the rhythm, and then she would pass the theme back to me, our minds and hands working in perfect harmony.

Finally, Chabaca and I, growing more daring despite our heavily accented English, decided to sing "As Time Goes By." I didn't know it was one of Duke's favorites, but I saw his eyes fill with remembrance as the melody filled the patio. In my naïvete I hoped that, from then on, he'd think of me whenever he heard it. With the last notes reverberating through the cantina, our eyes met again. I could barely force myself to look away.

Then the crowd burst into boisterous applause, and Chabaca and I took our bows. Shortly afterward the head waiter came in to announce dinner. The entire group rose, but I stayed behind to put my guitar away. Richard stayed too.

"Pilar, we've got to talk," he said, waiting for the rest of the party to drift into the dining room.

"What are you doing here?" I demanded.

"I flew Duke here. In fact, I'm the one who convinced him he ought to watch a Peruvian film company at work. We met in Lima a few days ago, and we've become good friends."

"So quickly?" I asked.

"I wanted to see you anyway," he added.

"What for? We have nothing to talk about! Have you started divorce proceedings?"

"No. I've been hoping we'd get back together."

Richard couldn't believe our marriage was really over.

"You're impossible," I replied, pushing past him. Upset by the confrontation, I paused in the entry to the dining room. As I stood there struggling for composure, John Wayne walked toward me for the second time that night.

As I joined Duke at his table, tremors of apprehension had my stomach doing unpleasant somersaults. I could easily dance while he watched or sing while he listened, but I was very nervous about talking with him during the long course of the traditional Peruvian meal. Realistically, I knew that John Wayne and I had nothing in common. I'd never seen his films so I could not talk about them. I couldn't talk about his private life, since earlier that day I'd asked our director if Duke was traveling with his wife and had been told that he was involved in a messy divorce. Nor did I want to talk about myself now that I knew John Wayne

and my estranged husband had spent a few days together. I hated
to think what Richard might have told him about me. Perhaps
he'd implied I was an overly demanding wife. Perhaps he and
Mr. Wayne had even consoled each other about their mutual marital difficulties.

I sat next to John Wayne feeling very out of place, looking into
those marvelous turquoise eyes, desperately casting about for
something to say. Duke came to my rescue, beginning with small
talk about the country, the local customs, the Peruvian movie
business, and his hope of finding just the right location for *The
Alamo*, a film he hoped to do in the near future. He finally seemed
to run out of words, and we sat staring at each other.

Then I said something so stupid that I still cringe, just thinking about it. "You were wonderful in *For Whom the Bells Toll*,"
I gushed. Complete silence enveloped our table. After what
seemed like an eternity, Duke and his friend, Saftig, started laughing. God, I thought, even his laugh is gorgeous.

"You're thinking of my friend, Gary Cooper," he smiled, those
blue eyes forgiving my mistake. Then he asked, "Have you seen
my last film, *The Quiet Man*? It's one of my favorites."

"Not only have I not seen it," I confessed, "I've never even
heard of it."

Duke looked baffled. "Don't you ever go to the movies?"

"Very rarely," I responded.

"Do you like westerns?" he asked.

"Not really," I replied honestly, before realizing I'd blundered
again.

We lived in such different worlds, I never thought we'd find
a common ground, but my blunders seemed to break the ice. Duke
laughed again, and the entire party began to relax. Or perhaps it
was because everyone had consumed so many Pisco Sours while
we waited for the late Peruvian dinner hour. Whatever the reason, John Wayne and I didn't need to search for words after that.
Our conversation flowed as easily as the stream, which was just
a few feet from our table.

The menu was typically Peruvian: *Cebiche*, heart of palm sal-
ad; *Anticuchos*, shish-ka-bob made of beef hearts; and *Picarones*,
our most popular national dessert. Duke seemed delighted with
the food. "Normally I'm a steak and potatoes man," he com-

mented as the waiter whisked away the last plates, "but I've never had a meal I enjoyed more. Ernie and I are leaving first thing in the morning," he paused and stared at me, "but I won't forget my stay here."

"I won't either," I replied, knowing I would relive the evening again and again in memory. "Unfortunately I've got to be up by five." I rose to my feet.

"Then I guess this is goodbye," John Wayne said, standing and taking my hands in his. I lingered for a moment, savoring the warmth of his touch—and then left the room reluctantly, completely smitten with the famous U.S. movie star.

I went to bed that night feeling a loss. I thought I'd never see John Wayne again, but I consoled myself with the expectation of seeing lots of his movies. I never dreamed I'd be with him while he made the next forty-three.

PART TWO

✯

Lights, Camera, Action

CHAPTER 9

Early in the fall of 1952, I was ordered to Hollywood to dub my dialogue in *Green Hell*. The evening I stepped off the plane at Los Angeles International Airport, my knowledge of the movie industry was confined to my limited personal experience and information and gossip I'd read in fan magazines. Those glitzy publications never mentioned that the film industry had fallen on hard times.

In those days, television, the *enfant terrible* of the entertainment world, was stealing viewing audiences just as VCRs are stealing audiences from the established television networks today. Back in the fifties the studios faced financial problems as they adjusted to a new set of ground rules. B movies and low-budget films that had once served as an important training ground for neophyte performers and crews had become the dinosaurs of the industry. These films disappeared in the fifties, and a lot of jobs vanished with them.

Industry executives, searching for gimmicks that would continue to keep viewers in theaters, experimented with enormous special screens and three-dimensional effects, using processes like Cinerama, Todd-AO, and Cinemascope. Cinerama used a wide, curving screen and film composed of three separate segments; Todd-AO achieved a wide-screen look by using 70-mm film base; and Cinemascope used a distorted lens which squeezed an expanded picture onto normal 35-mm film, expanding it again when the film was projected using special equipment. The new screens were ideal for spectacular films such as *The Robe, The Ten Commandments,* and *Around the World in Eighty Days.* While the number of new films made each year shrank by half, their costs climbed at an astronomical rate. Budgets of $6 to $8 million became commonplace.

The prophets of doom trumpeted the death knell of the film industry and, in fact, Hollywood's boom years had ended. Film companies were scurrying abroad, lured by cheap, nonunion labor. The era of the family-owned, family-run neighborhood theater closed with a thud that drove many small chains of movie houses into bankruptcy.

Throughout the fifties, in what amounted to a frantic treasure hunt, movie moguls searched for box office magic, for a sure way to convince reluctant audiences to part with the escalating price of admission. Major stars, bankable performers with international appeal, filled the bill. Ironically, although the need for big stars had never been greater, the studio system that produced them in the past, guiding a young performer on the path from bit player to household name, had become too expensive to sustain.

The demand for big names soon outstripped the supply, putting great power in the hands of well-known actors and actresses. A new era lay ahead, one which offered performers more freedom but less security. Stars who had formerly made two pictures a year under studio contract were soon on their own, scrambling for good roles in a diminishing market. Some of the more adventurous actors tried their hands at producing and directing.

To Duke, the industry's turmoil was an opportunity rather than a threat. In 1952 his newly formed production company, Wayne-Fellows, released its first film, *Big Jim McClain*. With the formation of Wayne-Fellows, Duke put himself on a business level with John Ford, who was then chairman of the board and creative head of his own Argosy Pictures. From then on Duke and Ford had comparable clout within the industry, although their personal relationship would always be that of father and son.

Founding Wayne-Fellows had been a far-sighted and exceptional act in a year of diminished industry confidence and shrinking ticket sales. Most executives' vision did not extend beyond the next film, the next balance sheet.

Most actors' expectations were similarly limited. I was no exception when I stepped off the plane in Los Angeles. I couldn't look beyond the coming month and dubbing *Green Hell* in English.

Arriving in Hollywood was the biggest thrill of my life. There were two people I hoped to see. The first was John Wayne, although I felt certain he'd forgotten the evening we spent together. I wouldn't have had enough nerve to telephone him, even if I'd known his unlisted number, so I was hoping and praying our paths would cross.

The second person was Patricia Pardo De Zela, a bright American writer who'd become my friend while we worked together in Tingo Maria. I admired her immensely. Although married to a traditional Peruvian man, she managed to keep an intercontinental career in full gear and maintained homes in Lima and Los Angeles. I was to be her house guest during my stay. On the drive to the San Fernando Valley where she lived I kept on staring into every passing car until Pat finally asked me what I was doing.

"Looking for movie stars," I replied, unaware of how naïve I sounded.

"Oh my Lord," Pat groaned, "you really are a greenhorn."

Indeed, I was. After I unpacked and settled into her spare bedroom, Pat gave me a tour of Hollywood and Beverly Hills. Walking down store lined Beverly Drive, lunching at the Brown Derby, shopping at the Farmer's Market, made me feel like Alice in Wonderland. We made a final stop at Grauman's Chinese theater where I lingered by John Wayne's footprints for a moment.

Although I'm not a morning person, my eyes popped open before the alarm rang on Monday. I couldn't wait for my first day at Warner Brothers to begin. As I walked through the gates of the studio two hours later, I had such a sense of unreality. A few days before, I'd been at home in Lima wondering when I'd be offered another part in a movie. And now here I was, about to go to work in one of the business's most successful studios.

The days's dialogue went well, thanks to a crew who never lost patience with my halting English. Worn out from having to concentrate every minute, I heaved a sigh of relief when we finished for the afternoon and I could think about going home. Gathering my purse and jacket, I said goodbye to my coworkers and headed for the stage door.

Normally stage doors are quite heavy but this one responded to my push quite easily, and I realized someone must be on the other side, trying to come in. Then the door flew open, and John Wayne stood there, close enough to touch if I'd dared. He looked every inch the successful movie star in a well-cut suit that emphasized his broad shoulders. He stared at me for the longest time, an expression of complete surprise on his face. Then his eyes narrowed, and a grin spread over his face. "I know you!" he said triumphantly. "You're Pilar Pallete from Lima, Peru."

I guess I just stood there and stared, as surprised as he, because he added, "Will you have dinner with me tonight? I'll pick you up at six, if that's all right."

"That sounds lovely," I replied, trying to appear calm despite the fact that my heart beat so loudly, I knew he had to hear it.

I must be dreaming all of this, I thought, giving him Patricia's address and phone number. John Wayne said a quick goodbye and then he was gone, disappearing through the door of the stage I'd just left. I walked to the studio gates in a daze. Alice In Wonderland had been transformed into Cinderella in the blink of an unforgettable pair of eyes.

It would be wonderful if I could report that Duke had been thinking about me as much as I had about him since our meeting in Tingo Maria. When I knew him well enough to ask, he said he'd known who I was the minute he saw me, although he hadn't given me much thought since leaving Peru.

I didn't walk through Patricia's front door that afternoon, I floated. For two months I'd relived my brief evening with John Wayne again and again. Now, miraculously, we had a dinner date. Checking my watch, I saw that I had an hour to dress, which hardly seemed long enough considering the importance of the occasion.

By six o'clock, the hour when he said he'd pick me up, I was dressed and ready, sitting in Patricia's living room trying to act as if I had dates with men like John Wayne every night of the week. When 6:30 p.m. had come and gone without either the doorbell or phone ringing, I was a nervous wreck. By seven I felt sick! I couldn't believe Mr. Wayne, who seemed like such a gentleman, would play such a cruel trick. Yet I had to accept the evidence of my ears and eyes. He was standing me up without even taking time to phone and make an excuse.

By seven thirty I'd worn a path in Patricia's carpet. I was ready to hide in my bedroom and cry my eyes out, when the phone rang. Struggling to control the tremor in my voice I managed a fairly calm, "Hello."

"Is Pilar Pallete there?" a female voice queried.

"This is she."

"Oh, good!" the stranger exclaimed. "I'm so glad you're still home. We were afraid you might have gone out. I'm Mary St. John, Mr. Wayne's secretary."

Oh boy, I thought, here it comes; a big excuse for standing me up, and he didn't even have the courtesy to call me himself.

"Mr. Wayne asked me to call and I'm very sorry it's so late, but this is the first chance I had to get to a phone. Today he was named top box office star for the second year in a row, and the house has been mobbed ever since. There are thirty reporters here right now, and we're trying to serve them something for supper. Mr. Wayne asked me to apologize for not picking you up on time." Although I didn't realize it, Duke had just become the most bankable star in the industry, a position of tremendous power. But my mind was fixed on the fact that I'd never heard a better excuse for being late.

St. John continued, "Mr. Wayne asked if I could pick you up and bring you back to his house for the evening."

Her warmth and friendliness went a long way toward soothing my injured pride. "I'd be delighted," I replied. I was amazed when the doorbell rang just a few minutes later. A sweet-faced woman with a lively sparkle in her eyes stood there, extending her hand. "I'm Mary St. John. Mr. Wayne is very anxious to see you."

She told me Duke lived on Longridge, just a few blocks away. I couldn't believe it! I'd been thinking about him all weekend, never dreaming he was practically a neighbor.

I'd imagined movie stars living in palaces, but the home we drove up to looked modest. I was not aware that Duke had been battling Chata over a property settlement. She had possession of their Encino estate while he lived in a rented house. The only thing that distinguished it from its neighbors was the crowd of cars and television vans that filled the driveway, spilling over to crowd the street as well.

When St. John opened the front door, chaos confronted us. Reporters thronged the living room, a thick pall of cigarette smoke soiled the air, and everyone seemed to be talking at once. I'd never seen such a group in my life. This was my first exposure to the media, and I was instantly intimidated.

St. John excused herself, and I glanced around, hoping to see Duke. While I stood there feeling out of place, a man came up to me, saying, "I'm Hampton J. Scott, Mr. Wayne's butler." He smiled, adding, "Folks around here call me Scotty. Mr. Wayne will be with you in a minute."

It couldn't happen soon enough to suit me. This wasn't exactly the romantic date I'd hoped for. Mary St. John returned briefly and introduced me to a few people, and I proceeded to try and make polite conversation in my halting English. After what seemed an eternity, a door opened and John Wayne stepped into the room.

He towered over the throng of eager reporters. Looking over their heads, he seemed to be scanning the room for someone. Seeing me, he smiled and began pushing through the crowd, coming straight to my side. All my apprehension vanished as he took both my hands in his, saying, "I'm so glad you're here to share this evening with me." And so was I—very, very glad. Then Duke moved on to say "Hello" to his other guests.

The rest of the evening passed far too quickly. We were served a buffet dinner, but I was too nervous to eat. I watched and listened while Duke fielded a barrage of questions with good humor, clearly enjoying every minute of his encounter with the press. Through it all his eyes would seek mine, and he'd smile his reassurance and pleasure in having me there.

I kept hoping we'd have a private moment, but the opportunity never came. At the time I had no way of knowing that Duke's divorce wasn't final and that he didn't dare show any interest in me in front of the press.

My feelings, already bruised by the way the evening began, were hard to control. A voice in my mind kept saying, "This man will break your heart. He belongs to his fans, to the press, to the world. Tell Mary St. John you want to go home, and get

out of here fast." But then I'd catch Duke looking at me, and I
knew running away wouldn't do me any good—I was already
falling in love.

I was thrilled when he phoned the next day and asked to see
me again. A huge bouquet of fall flowers had arrived by the time
I got home from the studio. A different bouquet came to the door
every day from then on, until Patricia's small house looked like
a posh, Beverly Hills florist shop. Duke called daily, taking me
to dinner each night, always in the company of other friends.
When I looked at him, incredibly handsome, successful, the idol
of half the women in the world, I couldn't help feeling wonderful
that I was with him.

Although he'd passed his forty-fifth birthday, he looked and
acted like a man ten years younger. I'd never known a more confident man, so comfortable with his own body. He never took a
false step or made an awkward move. His star quality was as
potent off screen as on. And the nicest thing was that he seemed
completely unaware of it. He was so attractive, I felt certain there
had to be other women in his life.

One evening we were having dinner at the house on Longridge when I heard the phone ring, and seconds later Scotty came
into the room. "Miss Crawford is calling again," he said.

Duke frowned and replied, "Tell her I'm not in."

A minute later I could hear Scott in the other room, his voice
rising. "Miss Crawford," he said, "there are only two things in
this world I have to do—stay black and die! But I don't have to
let you talk to Mr. Wayne."

That night Duke told me that he'd done a movie with Joan
Crawford back in 1942 and that she'd had a "thing" for him ever
since. At one point in their careers he'd won an award that Crawford had won the previous year. Since he'd been on location the
day the award was made, she'd accepted it for him. Crawford
contacted Mary St. John afterward, trying to arrange to give Duke
the award in her own home.

Duke, sure that he didn't want to be alone with Crawford in
her home, refused the invitation. But, according to Duke, Crawford was a stubborn woman. She couldn't take no for an answer.

No matter what he said, I was quite certain that Duke had to be dating Joan Crawford. Nothing could convince me he wouldn't go back to her, sooner or later.

Two weeks later I was certain he had. Duke didn't call, and no flowers were waiting for me when I got home. I sat by Patricia's phone for hours, sick with apprehension and disappointment, certain my little dream world had come to an end. I convinced myself that Duke was out on the town with Joan Crawford, telling her all about the funny little Peruvian starlet he'd been seeing.

I didn't sleep that night at all. By the time the sun had come up I'd made up my mind to return to Peru as soon as my dubbing job ended. No more impossible dreams for me!

When I returned to Patricia's at the end of the working day she met me at the door with a large package. "It's for you, Pilar," she said, smiling broadly. It was a gift from Duke, a magnificent Martin guitar which I still treasure. The note with it read, "Will you play and sing for me tonight at seven? J.W."

Duke arrived on time and alone. We'd never been alone together, and I hoped for a quiet evening. However, the usual crowd, including Mary St. John, Ward Bond and his wife, Grant Withers and his wife, filled the living room when we walked into Duke's house. "Hail, Hail, the gang's all here," I thought with silent desperation.

Apparently the man I loved loved a crowd. Pasting a smile on my face, I managed to act as though my heart wasn't breaking. After we dined, Duke asked me to play for his guests, and I obliged, sensing that he wanted to show me off to his friends. Once again he requested song after song until, fingers sore, I had to put the guitar aside.

The other guests left when food, wine, and the lateness of the hour finally made them sleepy. But I was wide awake as Duke walked to the fireplace, lit a cheery blaze, opened a bottle of Dom Perignon, and poured two glasses, handing one to me. "Pilar, it's time you and I had a talk," he said in a somber voice. "There are a few things I have to tell you."

Oh, no, I thought, expecting the worst. I stared at him, memorizing the face I'd come to love so much, watching the firelight play across his features as I waited for him to continue. We'd seen each other every day for two weeks, and I couldn't get enough of looking at him.

Duke stared into the flames. "I'm not a rich man," he said softly. "In fact I owe half a million dollars right now, and there's no telling how much the courts will award my wife, Chata.

"I'd like to be able to give you everything a woman could want. Instead, I have to ask you to take a chance on me. I'm a lot older than you, and I thought I knew all about love—but I've never felt this way before." Duke reached for my hand. "Don't go back to Peru, don't leave me," he said, pulling me into his arms, "I love you." Then he kissed me.

Duke and I felt a sort of magic together that we'd never experienced with anyone else. Although we'd been together for only two weeks, our attraction was so powerful that we ignored the difference in our ages, we forgot everything that had happened in the past. The only thing that mattered was being together.

Outside, a storm had begun, and thunder rattled the window panes, but we were oblivious to the wind and rain. I don't think any couple has ever been more in love or needed each other more than we did that night.

CHAPTER 10

Love, being in love, was wonderful, confusing, exciting, frightening, every possible emotion rolled into one. Duke was an intensely romantic and passionate but very moral man. At times the traits clashed. He couldn't go from bed to bed as other leading men did. For a man like Duke, love had one acceptable conclusion: Marriage.

Unfortunately, when we fell in love neither of us was in a position to plan a permanent relationship. Duke, after two failed marriages, couldn't bring himself to think of trying again. Commitment didn't scare him, but the idea of proposing for a third time did. He knew he faced a long and nasty legal battle with Chata.

Events had moved swiftly since my arrival in Hollywood. I'd turned my back on the life I'd known, the strict morality of my Catholic upbringing by beginning an affair with Duke. I loved him so much that I had no thoughts of right or wrong but only thoughts of him.

No matter how I tried, I couldn't see beyond the next few weeks. When my dubbing job ended, I would no longer have the right to remain in the United States. Being Duke's lover, even his fiancée, wouldn't give me legal status—it wasn't a position I could put on my green card.

Duke didn't seem to share my concerns. He knew what he wanted. After our first night together, he wasted no time in asking me to live with him. Of course I agreed, but my heart broke because I thought that I would still be leaving after the dubbing of my film was completed.

The fifties were a schizophrenic era when it came to morality. Women's liberation and the sexual revolution were still in the future; people did not live together as casually as they do today. In fact, the film industry was even more puritanical than society at large when it came to love and sex, and a scandal could have ruined Duke's career as well as his prospects for a fair property settlement with Chata.

To hide the fact that we planned to share his home, Duke rented an apartment for me in a building owned by his long-time friend, Fred MacMurray. I moved a few of my things into the apartment and the rest into Duke's house on Longridge.

Duke hated being alone. At his request, Scotty had been keeping the house on Longridge full of flowers so it would look "lived in." Duke needed companionship the way people need food, and he loved having me with him.

I learned that our meeting at the studio had been pure serendipity. The day our paths crossed, Duke had just completed *Trouble along the Way* for Warner Brothers. He was also working on two new projects, both to be filmed in Mexico, produced by Wayne-Fellows, and distributed by Warner Brothers. The first, *Plunder in the Sun*, would star Glenn Ford. The second, *Hondo*, was a big-budget movie with Duke slated for the lead. He would, of course, be deeply involved in both films as their producer.

When Duke had left Republic in '52 his record at the box office resulted in a steady stream of offers, and he needed to make the most of these opportunities. Although he was making a great deal of money, he was struggling to remain solvent from the settlement with Josephine and the subsequent purchase of an estate for Chata. In addition, a number of his investments had gone sour.

In 1952, Duke signed a very lucrative contract with Warner Brothers, a first-rate studio, in which they agreed to finance and distribute ten Wayne-Fellows films. In return Duke would star in pictures for Warner at a salary of $150,000 per film plus 10 percent of the profit.

The multipicture deal would give Duke the professional and artistic freedom he needed, freedom from men like Yates and Cohn. For the first time in his life he would be in control of his career. It was a marvelous feeling.

Duke liked and respected Jack Warner. The films they would make during the early and middle fifties would include the highly successful Wayne-Fellows productions of *The High and the Mighty* and *Hondo* as well as the Warner Brothers film *The Searchers*. The first two of these would mark Duke's transition from actor to successful moviemaker.

The constant demands on Duke's time made our first days difficult. I was jealous of every minute he was away and frustrated with the number of people who surrounded him at home, and I couldn't forget that my job and my stay would soon be over.

I was marking each day on the calendar with increasing dread when one afternoon Duke came home and flourished a telegram under my nose. "Take a look at this," he said, "and tell me what you think." The telegram was addressed to a man I'd been dating before I left Peru. The message read, "It's a woman's prerogative to change her mind and I have changed my mind about you." It was signed "Pilar Pallete."

Duke grinned impudently as I handed the message back to him. "How dare you?" I sputtered. He continued smiling, obviously very pleased with himself. "All's fair in love and war," he said. Then, becoming serious, he added, "It's time we tried to plan for the future. You'll be finished dubbing in a few days, and you won't be able to stay in the country without a job. I've talked to Bob Fellows, and he's agreed to have Wayne-Fellows sign you to a contract."

I didn't know whether I wanted to kick him or kiss him. It wasn't a romantic proposal but, in his own unique way, he was declaring himself. By signing the contract, I would become financially as well as emotionally dependent on him. I was young, a foreigner, and Duke would be my only resource if I stayed in the United States. It was an enormous step and a frightening one. But I didn't hesitate for a minute. Seeing the impatience and determination in his eyes, I agreed quietly.

Christmas was just days away, and Duke and I wanted to make our first shared holiday very special. He took a child's pleasure in all the trappings of the season, the decorations, the shopping, the gift giving. It was a time for families, and he wanted me to meet his.

Duke was quite fond of his stepfather, Sidney Preen. I was very nervous about meeting Mary Morrison Preen, but she made me feel like a member of the family at once, insisting that I call her

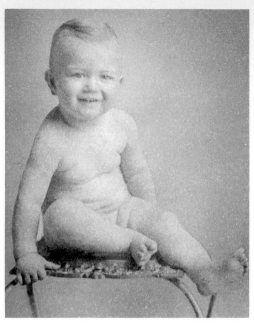

A cherubic Marion Morrison.

A very young Duke in *The Big Trail*. (Andy Shuford)

With his mother;
Robert Mitchum with
his mother. (AP/Wide
World Photos)

John Wayne's birth-
place, 224 S. Sec-
ond St., Winterset,
Iowa. (AP/Wide
World Photos)

TOP: With John Agar, Shirley Temple and Henry Fonda in *Fort Apache*. (RKO Radio Pictures, Inc.)
BOTTOM: On his way to a benefit for servicemen in 1945, with Jesse Lasky, "Duckie" Louie, Ellen Drew, and Anthony Quinn. (AP/Wide World Photos)

With Mary St. John, his super-professional secretary of twenty-eight years.

With Olivia de Havilland.

With Maureen O'Hara.

With longtime friend, Henry Hathaway, in the Sahara.

The famous scene in *Circus World* in which Duke barely escaped uninjured from the out-of-control flames. (AP/Wide World Photos)

Besieged by his fans in France. (Willy Rizzo)

With Greer Garson, in 1952, accepting the golden "Henrietta," symbolic of his selection by the Foreign Press Association of Hollywood as most popular film actor. (AP/Wide World Photos)

With William Holden in 1958, when they were considered two of the twelve actors then ruling Hollywood. (AP/Wide World Photos)

Pilar and John Wayne, taken seconds after he first came up to say hello. (Eduard Ingris)

Two pictures of Pilar Pallette on location of the Peruvian film, *Green Hell*, before she met John Wayne. Third photo is Pilar at age 18. (Eduard Ingris)

Duke, Richard Weldy, Pilar's first husband and friend of Duke's, and Pilar in Tengo Maria (Eduard Ingris).

A romantic shot the night before the wedding.

The wedding in Hawaii, November 1, 1954.

Duke and Pilar leaving Hawaii for the mainland after their wedding.

Learning to hula, during the filming of *Sea Chase*, 1956.

A mid-air wedding celebration, headed for California.

Waterskiing in
Acapulco.

Entertaining
at home.

"Mother." I had a very difficult time reconciling this friendly woman with the cold, unloving mother Duke had described to me. But he quite obviously felt uncomfortable in her presence. The day she and her husband came to dinner, Duke and Sidney retired to the den to watch football, leaving me alone with Mary in the living room. I think Duke was grateful to Sidney for filling Mary's life and keeping her out of his own.

Our next guest was Duke's brother, Bob. I found him to be a pale copy of Duke, a charming man, warm and friendly as a puppy. Duke was obviously very fond of him. At the time, Bobby worked for Wayne-Fellows, but, unlike Duke, he didn't talk shop morning, noon, and night. Duke loved moviemaking, but Bobby was smitten with the glitz, the good living that was part of the Hollywood lifestyle.

The two brothers had a joking, teasing relationship. Duke would pretend to be particularly incensed at Bobby's gorgeous head of thick brown hair. "Damn you, Bobby," Duke would say, pointing to his own thinning hair, "I'm the actor in the family. I'm the one who needs hair. When the hell are you going to lend me some of yours?"

Although my first two encounters with Duke's family had gone well, I was concerned about meeting Duke's children. He told me they meant a great deal to him, but he'd spent very little time with them, a pattern that never changed during all our years together. He explained that they blamed him for divorcing their mother. He added that because of the children's religious training, they believed that their parents were still married in the eyes of the church. With all that in mind, I knew our first meeting would be difficult, but I hoped, in time, to earn their friendship, if not their affection. They had no reason, after all, to resent me.

Duke described the four of them in detail: Michael, the oldest, was the least like him in looks, temperament, and personality. "He's still angry at me," Duke told me, "and I'm afraid he always will be. It breaks my heart. I let those kids down, leaving them and their mom. And it was roughest on Michael because he's the oldest." His voice grew warmer when he spoke of Toni, the next in line. "She's beautiful, like her mother, and a real lady. You'll like her." Duke was very fond of his younger son and daughter: "Patrick's a hell of a nice kid, a lot better looking than his old man." Duke described Melinda, the baby of the family, as a pert, vivacious charmer.

"Don't expect too much from them at first," he warned. "They haven't forgiven me yet."

"But the divorce was ten years ago!" I objected. "Surely they're over that by now."

Duke shook his head sadly. "Hell, I don't blame Josephine for being bitter. I'm not proud of what I did. But they're good kids. They'll come around when they see how happy you make me."

My heart went out to the four of them that day, but Michael touched me most of all. He was in his late teens, not quite a man but trying hard to act like one. The other three were more relaxed and at ease with their father and, consequently, with me too. Once the cheer of the holiday season conquered our initial awkwardness, all four of Duke's children seemed to have a good time. By the end of the day I felt certain that we'd all get along.

Duke was delighted with the way the day went. "You've given me the best Christmas present in the world," he said after they'd left. "For the first time in years, I feel like I have a real home."

Those words meant a great deal to me. I made up my mind to give Duke the best holiday of his life, with a home-cooked turkey and all the trimmings. Duke was enthusiastic when I told him my plans. "Great," he said. "I'll give Scotty the day off."

I neglected to tell him that I'd never cooked a meal by myself. When he walked in the kitchen on Christmas morning, he found me scrubbing the turkey in a sink full of detergent.

"What in the world are you doing?" Duke asked.

"The instructions said 'Wash Bird,'" I replied. Duke laughed until he cried.

We cooked that dinner together, and it was as memorable a Christmas as I could have wished. In fact, Duke never let me forget it. He told that story for years.

During our first weeks together, Duke screened his best films for me. "I've lived a lot of years without you," he said. "This is one way you can catch up."

I think he enjoyed seeing his own movies as much as I did. It gave him a chance to introduce me to his past. Hearing anecdotes about things that happened during their filming gave me insights into his life and his relationships with other people.

The first picture he showed me was *The Quiet Man,* one of his favorites. I remembered him asking if I'd seen it when we first met in Tingo Maria. At the time I'd never imagined watching it while holding hands with the star. Although many of Duke's films included a love interest, *The Quiet Man* was the only contemporary love story he ever made.

Many of Duke's films were westerns, and he teased me about not liking westerns. "You're going to be watching a lot of them from now on," he said. "I like making them, and people like seeing them."

As it turned out, I loved almost all of his. One or two nights a week we continued to escape into the fantasy world of his films. His concentration as he studied himself on screen surprised me. I'd suffered agonies the first time I saw myself in *Lost Emeralds.* My acting ability, or lack of it, embarrassed me. Duke had no such qualms. He could deftly dissect his own performance, knowing exactly when he'd been at his best and why. Seeing those movies with Duke gave me my first exposure to his dedicated professionalism.

I'd enjoyed being an actress, but acting had never been more than a job, which was fortunate since there wasn't room for two careers in our relationship. My contract with Wayne-Fellows enabled me to stay in the United States, but Duke didn't want me to work—he wanted me free to spend all my time with him. Although I wasn't reluctant to give up acting, I hated being completely dependent on Duke, especially since neither of us could predict when and if we would marry.

Duke was an honest and open man, and thus keeping our relationship secret was hard on both of us. Our free time was spent with his friends, and, although I liked them very much, I resented seeing so much of them.

Shortly before the new year, Duke had to make a public appearance at an awards ceremony, and, of course, I couldn't go with him. He asked me to wait at the house until he got back. I remember admiring the way he looked in a tuxedo as he walked out the door.

True to his word, he was home early—roaring drunk. I'd never seen him that way before and had just realized the condition he was in when I saw a large blotch of lipstick on his face.

"Who have you been kissing?" I gasped.

He wiped his cheek, staring at the splotch of bright red which now stained his fingertips. "Oh hell, Pilar. It must have been Hedda Hopper or Louella Parsons," he replied, pulling an immaculate white handkerchief from his pocket to scrub away the offending stain.

All the doubts and insecurities which had tortured me for weeks rushed to the surface. "I don't believe you!" I cried, bursting into tears. Before Duke could react, I pushed past him and out the door.

Duke had been completely honest with me about his first marriage. He told me he'd been unfaithful to Josephine, with Marlene Dietrich and then Chata. When he talked of regret and remorse, I believed him. But he had a past I couldn't ignore.

Who does he think he's kidding, talking about Hedda or Louella, I thought, driving back to my apartment. My imagination kept conjuring up pictures of Duke locked in a passionate embrace with Joan Crawford.

Duke knew that I couldn't deal with infidelity, that I'd left my first husband because of it. He knew the kind of relationship I wanted. I thought he felt the same way until I saw that scarlet slash of lipstick on his face.

As I walked through the door of my apartment, the phone rang insistently. I picked it up to hear Duke's deep drawl saying, "Honey, I swear it was Louella or Hedda, congratulating me." I hung up.

He called constantly the next day and the day after, filling my apartment with flowers. More unsure of myself than ever, I clung to my misery. In my more rational moments, I knew my behavior was unreasonable. I wanted to believe Duke, but I was so afraid of being hurt. I simply couldn't share him.

Finally Scotty arrived at my doorstep one day and deposited a box in my hands. It was a gift from Duke, twelve beautiful and obviously valuable gold coins—part of Duke's treasured collection, but I completely misinterpreted the meaning of the gift. I thrust the box back at Scotty, sputtering "Does he think he can buy me?" It seemed proof that Duke put a dollar value on my companionship. And I knew what that made me!

An hour later Duke knocked at my door. When I opened it he pushed past me. "Pilar," he began soberly, "you're riled up over nothing. I told you what happened, and you're going to have to trust me. We've got enough problems without you making up ones that don't exist. The last couple of days have been hell. I want you back." Then he took me in his arms and the world felt instantly right again.

But things didn't stay that way, not with Chata still legally married to Duke and making every effort to hurt or embarrass him. She had an evil genius for public relations and used the tabloids to create sympathy for her position. Things were so bad that reporters had started camping outside the Longridge house. It seemed miraculous that my name had been left out of all the gossip.

In talking one day about the problems we faced, Duke made a suggestion: "I've got to leave for Mexico soon," he said, "to spend some time on location with the *Plunder in the Sun* company. There's a part for a Eurasian girl in the film. Why don't you come down with me and test for the role?"

So I followed him down to Mexico, did a dreadful screen test but had a wonderful time. The film's star, Glenn Ford, soon realized why I was in Mexico, and he was very sympathetic and supportive. Then Gary "Coop" Cooper, one of Duke's oldest friends, stopped by on his way to another location, and Duke told him we were in love.

Cooper was sympathetic. Hollywood rumor had it that he'd been in love with Patricia Neal in 1951 when she starred with Duke in *Operation Pacific*, and that Coop used his friendship with Duke to explain his constant visits to the set. Cooper was married to Rocky, a patrician blonde socialite with an iron will, at the time. Rocky Cooper was one of the smartest women I ever met, while Coop was shy, sweet, sensitive. We knew we could depend on him to keep our secret. But, in view of the circumstances, it seemed that half of Hollywood, including Chata, would soon know the truth.

Duke's career had survived his break with Josephine. We had no way of knowing if he could get through a second scandal unscathed. When *Plunder in the Sun* wrapped, the time had come to part, temporarily. Duke had been invited to President Eisenhower's inauguration in Washington, D.C., an event I couldn't possibly attend as his date, so I boarded a plane to return to Los Angeles.

Months before, when I was preparing to come to the United States, I'd applied for a green card which entitled me to work in California. When I passed through Immigration on arrival I gave the officials all my documents, including my birth certificate, an affidavit from the police stating I had no record, a chest x-ray, and my passport. I was told I'd receive my green card once the paperwork had been completed. The day I arrived back in L.A., the first thing the immigration official asked for was my passport.

"But I don't have it," I objected, "you do! I handed it over when I applied for my green card."

The uniformed civil servant looked at me as if I'd lost my mind. "Lady," he grunted, "didn't anyone tell you not to leave the country until you got your green card?"

I'd been so excited the evening I arrived in California that I hadn't paid attention. "I don't remember," I explained.

"I'm sorry," he said, "but I'm going to have to send you to Terminal Island for the night."

At first, I was too tired to be upset. Tomorrow, I consoled myself, I'll get the whole mess straightened out.

My case wasn't called until two o'clock the next afternoon. When I explained my situation, the judge said, "You have two choices, Miss Pallete. You can stay at Terminal Island while you wait for your green card, or you can go back to Mexico. But you can't return to Los Angeles."

The choice seemed obvious. I didn't want to spend another minute in a Terminal Island cell. My jailers allowed me to use the phone, and I called Patricia Pardo De Zela. She came to my rescue without a word of complaint, arriving in time to join me on a one-way bus trip to the airport. The ever-ingenious Patricia had smuggled a bottle of scotch in her purse, so my mood had improved considerably by the time we boarded a plane and headed south.

CHAPTER 11

Patricia and I checked into a Tijuana hotel, and then she volunteered to try to track Duke down in Washington. The capital was caught up in the confusion of an inaugural, and finding someone, even someone as noticeable as Duke, proved difficult. Pat finally located him at a White House reception. She took a minute to tell him where we were and then handed the phone to me.

"What the hell are you doing in Tijuana?" Duke's voice boomed in my ear.

"It's better than being stuck in Terminal Island," I replied, choking back a sob.

Duke paused, "I'm sorry, sweetheart. Why don't you tell me exactly what's going on."

I explained the whole thing, from my aborted reentry into the United States to the trip to Tijuana with Patricia. When my recital ended I heard Duke break into a hearty laugh.

"Don't worry," he said, "I'll take care of everything. There ought to be someone in Washington who can cut through a little red tape."

I still smile when I remember that one of President Eisenhower's first official acts had been to expedite my green card. It was waiting for me at Immigration in Los Angeles the next day. Encino seemed like heaven when Pat finally delivered me to the door of my small apartment.

Within days it was to feel more like hell. Duke returned from Washington to find himself in the headlines again. Chata wanted the bulk of Duke's income and property; she orchestrated a flood of negative publicity as the date for the preliminary hearing approached. Duke hated his situation. He was being pilloried by the press, his divorce tried in the newspapers long before it got to court.

I went through each day sick with anxiety. Then one dreadful morning I realized worry wasn't the sole cause of my nausea. I'd been feeling sick and run-down for weeks. Despite the fact that my nausea often kept me from eating, I'd been gaining weight. It had been easy, at first, to attribute my condition to the emotional trauma of the last few months. The passage of time finally forced me to admit the truth. Duke needed to be told that I might be pregnant.

"Why haven't you been to see a doctor?" he asked, looking and sounding dumbfounded when I confessed my fears.

"Because I don't know one here!" I replied honestly.

"Well—hell—neither do I!" Choosing a gynecologist hadn't been his responsibility before. He finally called Bo Roos. Aside from being a financial adviser, Roos was a sophisticated "man about town," with all kinds of connections and information. When Duke returned from the phone a few minutes later, he said, "You've got an appointment with a doctor tomorrow."

Somehow the news only added to my worry. I still didn't want to face the truth. I'd always dreamed of marrying and having a houseful of children. That hadn't happened in my brief marriage to Richard Weldy. But Duke and I loved one another; we wanted to have children after we married. Dear God, I thought, why now? Why did this have to happen now? I sat in stunned silence, reality sinking into my dazed mind, while Duke left the room to make another call.

He came back a few minutes later, saying, "I just talked to my attorney, baby. I told him to give Chata whatever she wants. I'll get a quickie divorce in Mexico and we can get married right away."

I fell into his arms, finally letting the tears come. Things were going to be all right after all.

*   *   *

The next day the doctor confirmed my fears. "I'd say you're about three months pregnant," he said, a look of sympathy warming his eyes.

"Oh, no! Three months!" Had I really been ignoring the possibility that long? The doctor, taking one look at the expression on my face, seemed to read my mind.

"Are you thinking of terminating this pregnancy?" he asked.

"I really want this baby," I answered, "but the timing couldn't be worse." I went on to explain that I was in love with a famous married man whose divorce wouldn't be final before the baby's birth. Then I asked the doctor if he could help me.

"I don't do that kind of thing myself," he replied, walking to his desk and scribbling on a prescription pad, "but if things don't work out for you, call this number. The man who answers can help. And Miss Pallete, please don't wait too long."

My voice trembled as I asked, "What's too long?"

"Yesterday," he answered grimly.

His words burned into my mind. How could Duke settle things with Chata in a matter of days when months and months hadn't sufficed?

The next week was torture. Duke's attorney, Frank Belcher, called daily, filling us in on the negotiations. He seemed hopeful at first, but his calls grew grimmer as the days passed. He told us that Chata couldn't be moved. She wanted more than money, she wanted to humiliate Duke, and the best way to do that was to put him through the three ring circus of a name-calling public divorce trial. Nothing else would satisfy her.

"Why does she hate you so much?" I asked Duke. I couldn't imagine anyone feeling that way about him. He'd always been loving and kind in my presence, to everyone.

"I don't know," he answered, looking miserable. "I'm so sorry, baby. I wish things were different. We've got to face it—I'm not going to be divorced in time to give that kid my name. But I'll do whatever you say. The decision is yours. You can have the baby if that's what you want. I'll take my chances as far as my career is concerned. Whatever happens, I don't want to lose you."

I buried my head against his chest, and we held each other wordlessly. Somehow I'd known this particular story wouldn't have a happy ending.

When I look back at the miserable days that followed, it all seems so sad and unnecessary. Today a pregnancy can be confirmed at home, quickly and easily, shortly after conception. Abortion—although I have reason to hate the word, the deed, the whole concept—is legal.

But that wasn't the case in the fifties. There were no legal abortions then. I'd heard of women dying because of illegal operations, of others who were so badly butchered that they were never able to have children. Those were the risks of that kind of back-alley surgery in those days.

Having an out-of-wedlock child would have been even more disastrous in the early fifties. Society was unwilling to accept illegitimate children or the women who bore them. They were confronted with the cruelest forms of censure and discrimination.

In our case the situation was complicated by the fact that Duke had the standard morals clause in his contract, a clause the studios could use to ruin his career if it became known that he'd fathered an illegitimate child. I knew Duke loved me, but his deepest commitment was to making movies. I could not and would not endanger his happiness.

But then I'd think, what about me? What about the baby? Duke's professional life, his hope of ever being free of Chata, hung in the balance while I struggled to reach a decision. To add to my torment I faced the choice as a Catholic, knowing I'd be damned for ending the pregnancy.

Hollywood, in the fifties, had to be one of the most hypocritical societies on the face of the earth. Stars could do as they pleased in secret as long as their public images remained untarnished. One leading lady, with a talent for keeping her private life "private," had managed to convince the world that she'd adopted a baby girl who was, in fact, the actress's own illegitimate daughter. By contrast, Ingrid Bergman's career came to a stop the day she confessed she was bearing an out-of-wedlock

child by the brilliant director, Roberto Rosselini. Years passed
before American directors dared to hire her.

I feared Duke might face Ingrid's fate if he became involved in
a similar scandal. Like Ingrid, he often portrayed characters with
the highest moral standards. Moviegoers were beginning to con-
fuse Duke, the private man, with his screen image. I was certain
they'd be unforgiving if he disappointed them.

We had to keep my condition secret. That meant I couldn't go
home to Peru either. I was too well known to return to South
America pregnant and unmarried. The scandal would break my
mother's heart and ruin my family's good name. There were so
many lives to consider: my sisters and brothers, Duke's children,
all the people who depended on him.

When I turned to him for advice he said, "Do what you have
to, and I'll back you all the way."

I didn't choose to have an abortion because it was easy, ex-
pedient, or convenient. I loved Duke enough to do what was best
for him. But the decision almost destroyed me.

When I didn't dare wait a day longer I called the number the
doctor had given me. The next day I went to an address on Sunset Boulevard where I was met by a man who turned out to be a
doctor practicing without a license. He took me into a small examining room and explained what he had to do.

The next few hours were hell. I know I called out for Duke,
blamed him. Yet when the operation ended the only thing I
wanted was to feel Duke's arms around me.

When it was over my physical ordeal had ended, but the mental trauma had barely begun. Despite my need for him, I could
hardly face Duke when I went back to his house.

Lying in bed that night I made God a promise. If I was ever
lucky enough to have another child, I'd be the best mother in the
world. I'd put the baby's needs before everything else. Only,
please, God, let me have another baby.

I hadn't fully recovered when Duke told me he thought it would
be best if I went back to Peru. "I've got to go down to Camargo

to film *Hondo*, he said, "and it wouldn't be smart to take you with me."

"Why not?" I protested. "I'm well enough to go any place."

"It's not that," Duke explained gently. "Camargo is a one-horse border town—not much more than a cantina, a store, and a few houses. A beautiful woman like you would stick out like a sore thumb down there. I don't want your name used in my divorce. Chata would have all the evidence she needed if I took you with me. I'll be on location for a few months, and I need to know you're safe with your family while I'm gone."

Although Duke swore that he loved me, that we'd be together soon, I couldn't help feeling he wanted to be rid of me. And why not? I'd been moping around the house for weeks.

The day we said goodbye I wasn't sure we'd ever be together again. Logic told me Duke had been completely honest about his reasons for sending me home. If I continued to share Duke's life, it would be only a matter of time before Chata named me as a correspondent in the divorce. But logic had nothing to do with feelings. I cried and cried, all the way to Lima. And I continued to cry once I got there.

My mother couldn't console me. No one could. I needed to be with Duke, to feel his arms around me, to hear his voice. Life had no meaning without him. I kept praying he'd call, but he had no access to phones on *Hondo's* remote location. Our cables had to be sent under assumed names to keep Chata's detectives, who'd followed Duke to Mexico in hopes of finding me with him, off my trail. I didn't think the nightmare would ever end.

In Peru there is a superstition that unhappiness causes jaundice. In my case the old wives' tale proved prophetic—I became quite ill, eventually turning as yellow as a banana. Duke heard of my illness just as he finished *Hondo*. His next cable read, "If you can't meet me in Mexico City in three days, I'm coming down to get you."

I could just imagine what Chata would do if she heard he'd gone to Peru to see a sick friend, especially if she found out the friend was me. So I booked a night flight and traveled wearing huge, dark sunglasses and a concealing scarf.

Duke and Ernie Saftig met me at the airport. When Duke took a good look at me, thin as a twig and a ghastly shade of yellow, he groaned, "Oh, baby, what happened to you?"

"I missed you," I answered, collapsing in his arms, "I just missed you."

We didn't know whether to laugh or cry, so we did a little of both as we clung together.

CHAPTER 12

When I arrived in Mexico City, we'd been apart for three months. On the trip from the airport to our hotel, Duke held me in his arms and made all the hard-to-keep promises that lovers make. "I'll never leave you again. I'll never hurt you again. You mean more to me than anything in the world." I needed to hear those things, Duke needed to say them, and we both wanted to believe them.

I arrived 10 pounds underweight and suffering from jaundice. Duke was the best medicine in the world. His presence made our suite feel more like home than my mother's house I had so recently left behind. The simple act of hanging my clothes in the closet next to his banished the black misery of our separation. Life seemed full of happy possibilities again.

While I settled in we talked about our months apart. My story was brief. Missing Duke had been the focus of my life in Lima. It was some consolation to hear he'd been equally miserable. His sons, Michael and Patrick, accompanied him on location, and his costars, Ward Bond and Jim Arness, were old friends, but, Duke said, their presence didn't make up for my absence.

He also complained of having a series of problems with his leading lady, Geraldine Page. His former leading ladies had all been "movie stars," a different breed from a New York-nurtured stage actress such as Page. "She may have been great on Broadway," Duke said, "but she didn't know a damn thing about making movies." His face soured with distaste. "I don't know where some of these arty New York theater people get their manners. Would you believe she sat down at dinner one night and ate her mashed potatoes with her fingers."

His list of complaints continued. He was accustomed to glamorous costars who thought preparing for a role meant getting to makeup on time. From what he said, Geraldine didn't care much for makeup—or soap and water for that matter. He told me that one night when her table manners brought him to the boiling point, he'd dumped his dinner plate over her head. "And," he declared, "I'm not sorry!"

Their already poor relationship hit rock bottom when they had to reshoot a love scene. John Ford instigated the incident. He visited the location in the middle of shooting, took one look at Geraldine Page, and declared that audiences wouldn't believe a handsome man like Duke could be in love with such a homely woman.

"Damn him," Duke growled. "Shooting that scene the first time was bad enough."

Duke talked about his friend, John Ford, a great deal. I had yet to meet the famous director and was beginning to feel nervous at the prospect. According to Duke, Ford had a low opinion of most women. Like many producers and directors, he used them—on screen and off—to feed a giant ego. Ford, along with most of those in the male-dominated movie industry, expected actresses to be pretty, docile creatures. Geraldine Page didn't fit the mold.

It never occurred to Ford, Duke, or John Farrow, *Hondo's* director, to consider how she would feel about having to redo the love scene with the additional lines they wanted her to say. They told her to look into Duke's eyes adoringly, and murmur, "I know I'm a homely woman, but I love you." It's no surprise that their relationship was less than cordial after that. Duke was shocked a few months later when Miss Page received the first of many Oscar nominations for her performance in *Hondo*.

By the time *Hondo* wrapped, Duke's patience, a short commodity at the best of times, had worn thin. His role had been physically demanding, the location rough, hot, and uncomfortable. He'd been shadowed by the press and worried about me.

Duke arrived in Mexico City needing a rest, and the tension caused by his pending divorce continued to etch new lines of worry on his face. He hated feeling as if he'd lost control of his life. It brought out the worst in him. The warm, loving man I'd known in California had a new, hard edge that worried me. His anger was always close to the surface. Other people had told me of Duke's legendary rages, but I'd never seen them.

My luck was due to run out. One evening we were having cocktails in one of Duke's favorite restaurants, and our companions, including the Saftigs, laughed and joked while the waiter served our meals. Duke sat back in his chair, looking remote and disinterested, drinking tequila, and smoking cigarettes at a furious rate. He'd ordered his customary steak, and the minute his plate appeared he cut a large portion of meat, jammed it on a fork which he pushed hard into my face, saying in a vicious tone, "Here, try this."

The room grew quiet while everyone looked at the two of us. I stared at Duke in shock. I could taste blood; my bruised lip began to swell. Pain and humiliation brought tears to my eyes. I jumped up, determined to get away from there, away from Duke as quickly as possible. All the doubts that tormented me in our first weeks together returned in a rush as I ran through the restaurant. He didn't love me, couldn't truly love me or he wouldn't treat me that way. I'd been an idiot to think I could make him happy when two other women had failed. I stood on the curb in front of the restaurant, looking for a cab, when the Saftigs reached my side and begged me to stay.

"He's so upset over Chata and the way the newspapers are covering the divorce," Ernie began. "Can't you see he's half crazy over what's been happening. For God's sake, Pilar, if you walk out on him now, when he needs you so much—oh hell—" Ernie's voice trailed off.

Half crazy? I thought. Completely crazy is more like it. I'd never experienced the darker side of Duke's nature. The Saftigs stayed outside with me, talking quietly until I calmed down.

Duke came outside and asked me to return. "God, Pilar, I'm sorry," he said. "Believe me, baby, I'll never do anything like that again. I don't know what the hell got into me." But Duke wasn't able to keep that particular promise. Of course he was always dreadfully sorry after he lost his temper, and he never understood why I couldn't forget the incidents as quickly as he did.

That night, returning to our table, I learned how irresistible he could be when he was contrite. His anger had passed completely, and he held my hand tightly while laughing and joking, entertaining everyone as if the incident had never happened. But I knew there'd be no peace until he was free of Chata. Fortunately his attorney, Frank Belcher, called a few days later, asking Duke to fly back to Los Angeles for his court appearance.

The divorce trial was as bad as we all feared. In her testimony Chata described Duke as a drunken, vicious brute. She listed twenty-two specific acts of physical cruelty, giving dates and places, using the word "clobber," over and over. According to Chata, Duke had clobbered her in California, Hawaii, Mexico, London, Dublin, and New York. She called him a drunk and blamed him for turning her into one too. She complained of his infidelity, naming Gail Russell as one of the other woman in his life. Chata was on the stand for $2\frac{1}{2}$ days, detailing the horrors of her marriage.

When Duke took the stand the third afternoon of the trial, he was at an all-time emotional low, suffering from the flu, looking and feeling terrible. He denied ever abusing Chata, related stories of her reckless spending habits and alcoholism. All the while his heart was breaking because he had loved Chata as he'd never loved Josephine. Then Scotty was called to testify, and he told of the week Nicky Hilton had been a constant visitor while Duke was away on location. Scotty produced notes in Chata's hand filled with doodles where she'd written "Chata Hilton, Chata and Nicky," many times.

The trial ended on October 28. By then Chata had achieved one of her goals. Duke's name had been blackened, his private life held up to public ridicule. Happily, she failed to achieve her second goal. After listening to all the testimony, the judge permitted Duke to keep the bulk of his estate. Chata was awarded the outright sum of $150,000 plus $50,000 more a year for the next six years.

Chata didn't live to collect all that money. She died thirteen months later, alone in a tiny hotel room in Mexico City, surrounded by empty liquor bottles.

*   *   *

Duke received an interlocutory decree of divorce on October 28, 1953, almost a year after we fell in love. Although the divorce wouldn't be final for twelve more months, we were finally free to be together, anytime, anywhere.

"Baby, you and I have something to celebrate!" Duke declared when he returned to Mexico City. "Let's go down to Acapulco for a while. It's time we had some fun."

I agreed at once, thinking of a warm sun, a blue sea, and several weeks alone, just Duke and me. We needed a quiet time to heal the wounds of the last year, to talk things out, to plan our future. It sounded like heaven!

While I basked in romantic images, Duke added that he'd asked his attorney, Frank Belcher, to bring a companion and join us. "After handling the divorce for me," Duke explained, "the poor guy needs to have fun as much as I do."

I was a good enough actress to hide my disappointment. As it turned out, nothing in the world could have ruined that trip. Duke rented a gorgeous house with sunny patios, quiet red-tiled hallways, bougainvillea-decked walls, and a stunning view of the ocean and coast. The roof became our private place, a sun-drenched lovers' hideaway.

We spent our mornings there and our afternoons waterskiing, scuba diving, sailing. Duke was at home in any water sport, and I had a hard time keeping up with him. When the vacation ended, Duke was anxious to get back to moviemaking, and I looked forward to returning to Hollywood in a new role, that of John Wayne's future wife. The time had come to move out of rented quarters and establish a real home.

"I'd like to move back into my house in Encino," Duke told me, "but I'll buy you anything you want if you don't like it after you've seen it."

"I'll be happy any place," I replied, "as long as we're together."

We'd avoided the house completely during the divorce, but Duke wasted no time showing it to me after our vacation. The two-story Early American home sat on a knoll, surrounded by 5 fenced acres. Duke gave me a tour of the grounds first. The property included a large pool and a cabana-guesthouse, as well as stables and a riding ring.

"Are we going to have horses?" I asked, thinking that might be why he wanted to move back into the house.

He laughed, "Where'd you get that idea?"

"From all your westerns. I just assumed you loved to ride."

"The only time I get on a horse," Duke explained, "is when I make a movie. I hate the damn things."

He walked away from the stables, leaving me puzzled, trailing after him. I was dumbfounded by the revelation that John Wayne didn't like horses.

On the outside the Encino house looked warm and inviting. The inside was dark and dismal. Chata's heavy Spanish furniture overwhelmed the rooms, an unhappy reminder of her stormy occupancy. As we wandered through all 8000 square feet, Duke talked about how much he liked the place. I didn't share his enthusiasm, but we made plans to move back in and redecorate.

"There isn't going to be any more hiding," Duke said as we drove away, "no pretending you're just an actress under contract to Wayne-Fellows. We're going to do things up right, and that includes the house. From here on, sweetheart, you go where I go."

A formal dinner honoring John Ford was the first major Hollywood function we attended as a couple. Duke told me we'd be seated at a table with the Fords, their daughter Barbara, her husband, and Frank Capra and his wife.

I knew Ford had been hostile to Chata. Please Lord, I prayed as I dressed for the party, Let him like me, for Duke's sake.

I expected Ford to be well-dressed, but he looked rumpled, as if he'd slept in his tuxedo. He was tall, wore glasses and a black patch over his left eye, reminding me of an aging, debauched pirate. His manner toward his wife and daughter was brusk and cold. To my surprise and pleasure, he was the soul of old-world Irish charm as he asked me to dance, complimenting me on my appearance and my command of English. In the years to come I would hear John Ford treat other women very badly—He'd look at his wife and say, "Shut up. Don't speak unless I tell you." I knew him as a tease and a prankster, a man who loved Duke more than he loved his own children.

That evening marked my entry into Hollywood society, a wonderful way to begin. Ford's obvious approval had given me a terrific boost. I was energized to redecorate the house and thought we'd have several months to work on the project before Duke made his next picture. But our plans were disrupted.

Duke got word that Spencer Tracy, who'd agreed to play the lead in *The High and the Mighty,* had backed out at the last minute because he didn't want to work with director William Wellman. The Wayne-Fellows picture was scheduled to go before the cameras in mid-November, and it was far too late to get anyone else, so Duke took over the role. The picture, Duke's first in Cinemascope, was a big commercial success. It was also the last film he would make under the Wayne-Fellows banner.

Duke had become obsessed with the idea of making a film about the Alamo, but Bob Fellows wanted no part of such a costly production. So Duke bought Bob out and became sole proprietor of a new production company, which he named Batjac after the Batjack Trading Company in *The Wake of the Red Witch.* Duke spent the next few months organizing his new company.

In May Duke and I left for Utah, where *The Conqueror* would be filmed in the Escalante Desert. It proved to be the worst picture of his long career. He was no more qualified to portray Genghis Khan than I would be to play Eleanor Roosevelt. Yet he chose to do the role, was even anxious for the experience, thinking it would stretch him as an actor.

Once shooting began he couldn't wrap his tongue around the script's archaic English dialogue. When the movie was released in 1956 audiences howled as Duke drawled his dreary way through lines like, "You are bewdiful in your wrath."

Some movies are lucky. Not this one. During the filming, Duke's costar, Susan Hayward, developed a wild passion for him. She was headstrong and determined. My presence in St. George fed her jealousy, and her heavy drinking diminished her inhibitions.

One night a group congregated at Duke's house for one of those impromptu gatherings that are so much a part of life on location. We were all talking and drinking when Susan came up to me, a wild gleam in her gorgeous eyes. "Take off your shoes," she challenged, kicking her own high heels into a corner, "and fight me for him!" I knew at once the him was Duke, and I didn't know whether to laugh or put up my fists.

Although nothing came of this particular confrontation Susan continued to be a problem—but not the only one. The weather, scenes that didn't work, minor accidents all delayed production. And the bad luck didn't end at the conclusion of the filming. In the years to come the principal players and the director would all die of cancer, a remarkable and tragic coincidence.

I've heard other people attribute these deaths to the atomic energy tests that took place out in the desert near the shooting. But I was there on location day in and out, as were many other people who never became ill. The real culprit in the deaths of my husband, Susan Hayward, Agnes Moorhead, Pedro Armandariz, and Dick Powell was their constant, incessant smoking. They all had a two-pack-per-day (or more) habit. Duke never smoked fewer than three packs a day.

Now we know that cigarette smoking kills—it damages the lungs, the heart, the circulatory system. I watched Duke battle the cancer it caused, watched him battle his addiction to smoking when he had to quit. I'll never forget the day Dick Powell, who had finally given up smoking after being told he had cancer, wryly requested a cigarette sandwich when I asked if I could get him anything.

In view of what happened, I'm entitled to get on a soapbox—to complain about a government that continues to subsidize tobacco farming. And I know Duke would join me in saying, "Don't smoke—whatever you do, don't smoke."

When Duke was filming *The Conqueror* we were not aware of the dangers of smoking, and the more things went wrong, the more Duke smoked. Then one day the world's greatest stress reliever arrived in St. George. His name was Blackie.

A year earlier, when Duke first asked me to stay with him, I'd asked him if I could bring my dog, a Dachshund, to the United States.

"Of course you can," Duke replied. "I don't mind having animals around. I just don't want them eating off my plate and sleeping on my pillow.

"What about that Airedale you told me about?" I asked. "The one called Duke. Weren't you crazy about him?"

"Yeah," Duke replied. "But he was special."

The day Blackie arrived Duke didn't seem very impressed.

"He's really kind of funny looking," he commented as Blackie emerged from his shipping crate. Within days the tiny dog had become the large man's alter ego.

Duke usually got up before me. I'd come down to breakfast to find him seated at the table with Blackie, a cup of coffee in front of each of them. When Duke drove anywhere, Blackie would be draped around his neck like a canine boa. If the dog didn't go on location in the morning, Duke often sent a driver to pick him up in the afternoon. And at night Blackie would prop himself on Duke's lap, and they'd watch television together. Unfortunately we weren't able to take Blackie to Hawaii, where Duke's next picture would be filmed.

CHAPTER 13

Duke had great respect and admiration for the men who directed his movies. Although his name is closely associated with John Ford and the thirteen films they did together, few fans realize that Duke worked two or more times with directors Raoul Walsh, George Sherman, Burt Kennedy, James Grant, Joseph Kane, Budd Boetticher, Edward Ludwig, Arthur Lubin, and Andrew McLaglen. Five of Duke's most memorable films, including *Red River* and *Hatari*, were directed by Howard Hawks, and Henry Hathaway directed six Wayne pictures, among them the classic *True Grit*.

In 1953 and 1954 Duke's work was guided by John Farrow. As the able director of Batjac's *Plunder in the Sun* and *Hondo*, Farrow had agreed to direct *The Sea Chase*, scheduled to begin shooting in mid-September 1954 in Hawaii. Although Farrow was a famous moviemaker, responsible for many fine films, he's probably better-known today as Mia Farrow's father.

William Clothier, repeating the job he'd held in *The High and the Mighty*, was to be the cinematographer. In addition, Duke's close friends Paul Fix and James Arness were in the cast. Mary St. John would join us in the islands to run an away-from-home office.

Duke was now in a position to ensure that a couple of pals would be in the cast or crew of any film he agreed to do. He enjoyed helping people he cared about, but, more important, having pals around ensured that he'd never lack for companionship on location. Eventually his films would employ so many family members and buddies that I'd be amused when the credits rolled.

Duke and I arrived in the islands a few days before *The Sea Chase* began shooting so that he could show me around. We moved into a beautiful house which Warner Brothers had rented for us. As a rule the studio arranged for our housing on location and, whenever possible, our quarters were quite luxurious.

Luxurious quarters were one of the standard perks for leading men, but Hollywood had a double standard when it came to housing female stars. When Duke's costar, Lana Turner, flew to the islands, she found she'd been booked into a single room at the Kona Inn. To make matters worse, her room adjoined Farrow's— a director noted for dramatic flirtations with his leading ladies. Turner was furious. She interpreted the arrangement as another example of the "casting couch" state of mind so prevalent in Hollywood at the time.

Farrow wanted a charming female companion on location. It probably never dawned on him that Turner might be hostile to sleeping arrangements that had been made without her consent. The idea that she involve herself with Farrow was preposterous in any case. She'd just married actor Lex Barker, and he planned to join her as soon as he could.

Turner was looking forward to a second honeymoon and undoubtedly deserved housing as nice as ours. However, movie and television screens were dominated by male-oriented action stories, and, as a consequence, leading ladies didn't receive the salaries or perks their male counterparts did.

Despite Turner's anger, Warner Brothers refused to rent a house for her. She showed up on the set the first day of shooting angry at Farrow and all of male-dominated Hollywood, and some of her hostility spilled over onto Duke. Despite her beauty and talent he reacted to her coldness with a deep freeze of his own. Rumor of a feud soon found its way into the gossip columns. Yet, looking at *The Sea Chase* today, you see some real chemistry between Duke and Lana. Their on-screen characters were involved in a love-hate relationship that sizzled in every scene they shared.

The Sea Chase may have been a forgettable film, but Duke and I had good reason to remember it fondly. Other Californians marry at home and go to Hawaii for a honeymoon. We reversed the pattern. One morning just before we were due to leave for Encino, Duke got a telephone call from his attorney, Frank Belcher. "Duke, I'm holding your final divorce papers in my hand," Frank announced gleefully. "You're a free man." Duke turned to me with a big grin and said, "How would you like to get married today?"

Two long years had gone by since our chance meeting at Warner Brothers. During that time my marriage to Richard Weldy had been annulled. The day I'd dreamed of had finally arrived. Instead of jumping up and down with excitement, I just gaped at Duke in disbelief. "Can we really do it that fast? Aren't there blood tests and paperwork?"

The man who'd gotten President Eisenhower to expedite a green card was undaunted by these problems. "Just leave everything to me," he said. "Take Mary St. John and go get yourself a wedding dress. By the time you get back I'll have everything arranged."

Mary and I went from store to store that day, looking for just the right gown. By the time I made my purchase, half the island's population knew there'd be a wedding that afternoon. I chose a pale pink chiffon dress with a fitted bodice and a flaring skirt. We arrived back home a couple hours before the ceremony to find that Duke had worked wonders. A crew of people were preparing the house and garden for a gala wedding. All I had to do was dress. Mary helped me, twining orchids and sweetly scented frangipani in my hair in place of a veil.

Duke and I married at sunset on November 1, 1954. The ceremony took place in the garden, accompanied by the sound of the surf. I'd asked Mary St. John to be my matron of honor. Francis Brown, another of Duke's friends, served as his best man, and John Farrow gave me away.

We'd done our best to keep the time and place to ourselves, but it's impossible to keep a secret in Kona. As we prepared to take our vows, a crowd of Hawaiians, the women in muumuus and the men in colorful island shirts, appeared in the garden carrying gifts of flowers. It was the most romantic wedding a bride could have wished for.

The next day we flew to Honolulu, where a crowd of reporters met us at the airport. "How about a honeymoon?" they asked Duke. "Where are you and Mrs. Wayne going?"

"Well, fellas," Duke replied, "Pilar and I have been traveling since the day we met. So we're going to honeymoon in our favorite place in the entire world. My bride and I are going home."

Duke planned to stay in Encino for the next six months. The house still needed much work that required our supervision, the staff I'd hired needed some training, and we wanted time to settle into the routine of married life.

I was understandably nervous about my new role, in part because of Duke's reply when a reporter asked why Duke chose me for his next wife: "It's her dignity," he answered proudly. "And her wonderful sense of humor. And of course, her classic beauty." I wasn't sure I could live up to that glowing appraisal.

In fact, I soon realized how poorly prepared I was for my new role as Mrs. John Wayne. We were talking about redecorating the house when Duke asked, "Do you like antiques?"

I didn't have the vaguest idea what an antique was, having never heard the English word. "No, I don't," I replied.

"That's too bad," Duke said, looking puzzled. "I thought a few antiques would look nice with our Early American architecture."

"If you like them, we'll get some," I responded, not knowing if I was agreeing to buy something to eat, to wear, or to sit on.

Half the time I felt like an impostor. Trying to run our home required skills and knowledge I didn't possess. So many things Duke cared about, his much loved Kachina collection, his western paintings and sculpture, his antique guns, and coins, were things I knew nothing about.

He had his own sense of style in everything he did, from buying clothes to buying art. By comparison, I didn't know the difference between Ting or Ming, Louis XIV or Early American, French or California wines. Obtaining that knowledge suddenly seemed critical. I wanted to learn about things that were important to Duke, and I wanted Duke to be as proud to be my husband as I was to be his wife.

We hadn't seen Duke's children while we were in Hawaii and wasted no time having them over to share the holiday season, our third together. I was still apprehensive about being with them, especially since I was now their stepmother. When they arrived, Michael and Patrick wanted to talk sports with their father, but Toni and Melinda wanted to talk about boys and clothes, two interests I could share.

I'd never seen Duke happier, more relaxed. He told me all his dreams had finally come true. "This is what it's all about," he said, "what I've always wanted—a successful career, a wife I love who loves me back, my family around me."

Duke had put careful planning into Batjac's maiden effort, and, wanting a big star to play the male lead, he'd signed Robert Mitchum. A fortune had been spent on preproduction, including construction of the replica of a small Chinese village. Lauren Bacall, whom Duke admired, had been signed to play the female lead, and William Wellman, who'd directed the box office hit *The High and the Mighty,* was directing. The film also marked Anita Ekberg's screen debut.

The peace and quiet was too good to last. Ten weeks after we got home, Duke got a panic call from San Raphael, California, where the cameras were rolling on *Blood Alley,* Batjac's first production. Wellman reported that Mitchum was raising hell on the set, drinking heavily. Duke understood hell raising, having raised more than his share, but he'd never cost a director one day of shooting because of his behavior on location. Unfortunately, Mitchum didn't share Duke's philosophy of the show must go on.

Wellman felt unable to go on with the picture until Mitchum was replaced, and Duke realized Batjac would lose its investment in the film unless he supplied a new leading man. So he sent Mitchum home and took on the role himself. That put an abrupt end to our six months' stay at home. It was the second time Duke had unexpectedly taken the lead in a Wayne-produced film. In 1953, Duke had stepped into the lead in *The High and the Mighty,* another Wellman-directed film, because Spencer Tracy had refused to work with Wellman. The film was a great hit at the box office, and Duke hoped that *Blood Alley* would repeat that success.

He left for San Raphael at once, asking me to join him in a few weeks. On the date he'd set I took the overnight train up the California coast accompanied by Frances Heneghen, the writer's wife. The two of us had just settled down in the dining car when we spotted Humphrey Bogart having dinner with a friend. I assumed he was on his way to join his wife.

Although married to a major star, I was still awed by someone such as Bogart. Impressed at seeing him in person, I kept glancing toward his table. Frances and I were acting like a pair of starstruck schoolgirls, giggling whenever Bogart glanced our way.

"Let's ask him for his autograph," I suggested, pulling a reluctant Frances to her feet. "It will be all right," I said. "He doesn't know who we are. He'll just think we're fans."

When we stood by his table Bogie rose to his feet immediately, saying, "So nice to meet you, Mrs. Wayne."

I was astonished. "Gee, it's too bad you recognized me. I wanted to ask for your autograph, just like any fan."

Bogie measured Frances and me with the cold, intimidating stare he'd used to terrify a dozen screen villains, saying, "I'd have known you two bitches anywhere."

I fled back to our table, wishing I could disappear. I've never figured out if Bogart was making an instant assessment of my character or if he always addressed women that way. Settling into our motel the next day, I learned the Bogarts would be in an adjoining suite.

Fortunately, his wife, Betty, as everyone called her, proved much friendlier. At the time her career was in a slump; her studio had suspended her because she refused to accept the awful parts they offered. Duke found her to be completely professional, always prepared on the set, never moody or temperamental, and intelligent and articulate. Although she and Duke were at opposite ends of the political spectrum, he liked her spunk, humor, and outspokenness. She wasn't afraid to stand up and be counted, a trait he admired—even though she was standing up and being counted in the ranks of Adlai Stevenson supporters. By the end of the film she and Duke had become friends.

Lauren Bacall was a perfect example of the type of woman Duke liked as a pal—worldly, confident, firm in her beliefs. The list of his leading ladies who fit this mold included Patricia Neal, Katherine Hepburn, and Claire Trevor. In view of their rapport, Duke hoped he and Betty would have some of the same chemistry that was so obvious when she played opposite her husband.

Betty did her best and so did Duke, but their on-screen love affair looked dull, dull, dull.

We were back in Encino by the end of March, scheduled to
stay there for a few weeks before Duke's next film. He'd worked
steadily from the day we met, jumping from one project to another with only a few weeks' rest. His box office record guaranteed a constant demand for his services, and a steady stream of
scripts passed across his desk. A full-time reader struggled to get
through them, giving Duke only the best material. Sometimes
the best of the current lot proved to be dreadful, but that didn't
guarantee Duke wouldn't make the picture.

Although he said he loved being home, he couldn't stand being idle long. Duke was a fanatic about the rigorous schedule
imposed by film making: up at four or five o'clock, at makeup by
six, on a set from first light to the end of the day. He also believed the only way to improve his skills was to practice them,
so he made a number of second-rate films, learning from the experience. Unfortunately, the critics devoted more time and attention to his failures than his successes.

While he made pictures I struggled to transform myself into
the perfect wife. Although he talked about wanting privacy, we
were almost never alone. In public fans besieged us, and I quickly
learned to cling to his arm in a crowd so I wouldn't be swept
aside by eager autograph seekers who didn't know or care who
I was.

In private, our home served as a club for Duke's friends, who
included John Ford, Ward Bond, Grant Withers, Victor McLaglen and his son Andrew, Charlie Feldman (Duke's agent), Web
Overlander (his makeup man as well as our neighbor), Johnny
Weismuller (of Tarzan fame), Yakima Canutt, and Jimmy Grant
(Duke's favorite screenwriter). I made sure all felt welcome in a
way they never had been in Josephine's or Chata's homes.

Shortly after we moved into our house in Encino, Pappy Ford
began to appear at odd hours, unannounced and unexpected. He
continued to treat me cordially, but I began to suspect he was
testing me. Duke's unhappy marriages had never threatened
Ford's dominant position in Duke's life, but Ford, knowing ours
was a genuine love match, suffered the same kind of jealous anxiety that a mother feels when her only son brings home a bride.

To ease his mind I tried to make him feel welcome no matter what time he came calling. I wanted all Duke's friends to know our doors would always be open to them.

Privately, I couldn't wait to have Duke to myself. Late at night, after everyone had gone, we finally had quiet times. Duke enjoyed television, and we had a set built into our bedroom ceiling. A push of a button dropped it to viewing level. We'd watch the late shows, snacking on salami, which Duke loved, smoking—for by now I'd acquired the habit, and reading out loud together. Weekends were spent aboard our boat, the *Nor'wester*, with the Fords, the Bonds, the Coopers, or any number of other famous couples and friends.

Shortly after we returned from Hawaii, Jack Warner gave a glittering, star-studded party in our honor. Elizabeth Taylor was one of the two hundred guests who came to wish us well, and Duke and I liked her instantly. Her astonishing beauty would have been intimidating if she hadn't been so down to earth. Taylor was pregnant with her first child, a condition I envied so much I had to fight back tears. She and her husband, the English actor Michael Wilding, had been married about as long as Duke and I. At the end of the evening, Taylor and I exchanged addresses and phone numbers, planning to see each other again, neither of us knowing that our lives would be intertwined through twenty years of public triumph and personal tragedy.

CHAPTER 14

Duke had a favorite expression engraved on a plaque that he kept on board the *Nor'wester*. It read, "Each of us is a mixture of some good and some not so good qualities. In considering one's fellow man it's important to remember the good things, and to realize his faults only prove he's a human being. We should refrain from making judgments—just because a fella' happens to be a dirty, rotten son-of-a-bitch."

Duke wasn't a "son-of-a-bitch," but he wasn't perfect. His character reflected a lifelong association with John Ford, who had helped mold Duke both as a man and a performer. Their first collaboration in *Stagecoach* in 1939 had been a particularly difficult period for both of them. Ford recognized that Duke would always, to some extent, have to play himself. He knew that a man of Duke's size and physical attributes could not be a chameleon; his body, face, and voice were too recognizable to be hidden with makeup or costuming. "Part of being an actor," Ford told him, "is knowing your strengths, weaknesses, and limitations." And, "For God's sake, Duke," he'd add, "don't try to act. React!"

Duke recalled those first three weeks in Monument Valley back in 1939 as the toughest in his entire career. He and Ford had left California for the location as close friends and drinking companions. The day they began filming *Stagecoach* on the Navajo Reservation, Ford began to bully and demean Duke, calling him "a dumb bastard," or "a big oaf" in front of the cast and crew. In the past Ford had commented favorably on Duke's athleticism and how well he moved. Yet one day while Duke strode across the set, Ford shouted, "Can't you even walk? for chrissake, instead of skipping like a goddamn fairy."

Coming from any other man on the face of the earth, those would have been fighting words. But Ford wasn't any other man, he was Duke's best friend. Duke bowed his head and took the unending stream of invective Ford hurled his way, wondering if he'd ever be able to satisfy him. The pressure continued until Duke felt like quitting.

Ford, knowing Duke wasn't a quitter no matter how rough things got, kept the pressure up. Pushing Duke to the limit, he forced Duke to react in every scene.

Duke's fresh, honest performance in *Stagecoach* was a tribute to Ford's directing genius. Duke played the Ringo Kid with vulnerability and innocence, and a depth of emotion that would have never been there if Ford hadn't pushed so hard.

In the early years of their friendship people who never saw beyond the surface were often shocked by just how far Ford would push Duke on a set and even more shocked by the fact that Duke took it without complaint. Duke told me that when he made a Ford movie he simply surrendered himself completely, placing his trust in a man he admired and loved. He said, "I'll never be able to repay Ford for everything he did for me."

Duke was a constant visitor at the Ford home. They had lived in their house for so long that Ford was almost obsessively attached to the old place, even though the Hollywood neighborhood had become increasingly unfashionable and run down. He'd been horrified when a surveying crew knocked on his door one day to tell him the house stood squarely in the path of the soon-to-be-built Hollywood freeway.

Despite loud protests to the mayor, the governor, and any other influential person who would listen, the Fords were forced to make way for progress. Mary Ford, in keeping with their affluence and celebrity status, chose a new home in Bel Air, a fitting place to park her Rolls.

When Ford and Duke weren't working, their deep affection often found expression in rough humor and outlandish practical jokes. The Ford home, scene of so many gatherings of the clan, was the focus of one of Duke's all-time favorite tricks.

Duke waited a year to pull the prank he had in mind, holding back until it became obvious that Ford was putting down roots again. Then Duke borrowed a replica of a city truck from Warner

Brothers, hired a couple of actors to impersonate a survey crew, and sent them to Ford's new house to announce that Ford would have to move because a freeway was going to run right through his living room. From their reports, Ford was apoplectic.

In their crazy battle of tit-for-tat, Ford struck the next blow. During a magazine interview he told a reporter that Henry Fonda always had been and always would be his favorite actor on the face of the earth. The remark sent a ripple of shocked gossip through the entire movie industry.

Duke refused to rise to the bait. He held back until Ford called to offer him a part in his next film. "Why don't you get your favorite actor?" Duke growled before hanging up. He drove Ford insane for the next few days by refusing all his calls.

Ward Bond often served as a third member of this wild trio, and he was often the focus of the jokes. Ford and Duke never tired of teasing Bond about his undeniably large rear end. On one memorable occasion the two of them had their picture taken standing next to a horse's backside so they could send Bond the photograph along with a note that read "Thinking of you."

Sometimes the horseplay got out of hand. One evening when Duke and Bond planned to spend the night at the Fords, Bond passed out in the bed assigned to Duke. Duke, wanting Bond to wake up so they could continue the party, poured vodka on Bond's chest and set the vodka on fire. Bond was either too tough or too drunk to allow a few singed chest hairs to spoil the rest of the night.

Another evening at the Fords' house, Bond bet that Duke couldn't knock him off of a newspaper. Duke took the bet at once. Bond proceeded to put the newspaper down in the middle of a doorway and then close the door between himself and Duke, shouting, "Hit me now, you dumb son of a bitch." No one laughed harder than Ford when Duke cocked his fist and punched Ward off the paper, shattering the closed door.

After hearing these stories I was glad that the three of them had mellowed before Duke and I met. My first chance to see them in action in a picture came in 1955, when they filmed *The Searchers* in northern Arizona. Ford and Duke had filmed *Stagecoach*, *Fort Apache*, and *She Wore a Yellow Ribbon* on location there and had an almost mystical attachment to Monument Valley.

"You'll love it," Duke said, when he told me we'd be spending the entire summer hundreds of miles from civilization in the middle of the Navajo Reservation.

He was an incredible optimist. I don't think anyone, including the Navajos who live there year round, really enjoys summering in 115 scorching degrees. When we arrived in mid-June, the spectacular scenery sizzled under a white-hot sun that reminded me of a klieg light. Most of the cast and crew, which included Ken Curtis, Olive Carey (widow of Ford's favorite character actor, Harry Carey), veteran photographer Winnie Hoch, and Duke's son Patrick had been there before. We were quartered at Goulding's Trading Post, a series of red rock buildings that looked as if they'd stood in that spot since the days of the Indian wars.

We'd no sooner settled in when Ford took up the routine he'd established during previous films. He began shooting at first light and worked straight through the day until everyone felt ready to drop from the heat. At sunset we'd return to the Trading Post, wash up, and wait outside Goulding's dining room, the only place to eat in a hundred miles or more, until Ford approached. Then our hosts rang an old dinner bell, and we followed Ford inside as if he was a biblical patriarch. After eating, Ford would invite a few people to his room to play a game that consisted of pitching silver dollars on a felt-covered table.

On location Ford was the undisputed leader. He set the style and tone of our entire stay: Work like hell all day, have a little fun at night, and then early to bed. He loved making films on remote locations because the studio executives couldn't interfere with the day-to-day progress of the movie. Ford brooked no nonsense on his sets. He was a perfectionist who knew exactly how he wanted every frame of film to look long before the cameras rolled. I had the impression that he carried every detail of *The Searchers* around in his head.

By 1955 Ford no longer needed to abuse Duke to get a good performance from him. This picture, and the ones they would make in the future, were true collaborative efforts. Despite the hardships of the location, *The Searchers* was a happy film, one of those lucky movies where everything goes well. There was a rightness, a sureness to Duke's interpretation of the obsessed Ethan Edwards. Costars Jeffrey Hunter, Patrick Wayne, Ward Bond, the lovely Vera Miles, and Natalie Wood gave fine performances as well.

In the early weeks of shooting, Natalie developed an obvious crush on Patrick. She'd been accompanied on location by her sister, and the three youngsters spent most of their free time together. Everyone commented on what a gorgeous couple Natalie and Patrick made. But, as the weeks went by, Natalie spent less and less time with Patrick.

I found myself wondering how Duke's children had been affected by their father's fame, his good looks, his charisma. More important, from my perspective, I wondered how it would change the lives of the children I hoped to have? The question took on new importance midway through the filming when I began to suspect I might be pregnant.

When the picture wrapped, Ford was so proud of it that he told Duke he was thinking of retiring from directing, using The Searchers as his swan song. Sadly, the critics found fault with this movie, as they did with almost every picture Duke made. John McCarten, in the June 6, 1956, issue of New Yorker wrote, "The Searchers' John Ford and his celebrated road company, headed by fearless John Wayne, are back—chasing around Texas, fighting Indians, fighting each other and fighting time."

Duke, never the critics' favorite, was usually unconcerned by what they wrote. He often said, without a trace of bitterness, "I laugh my way to the bank." But in the case of The Searchers, however, it hurt to see Ford's beautiful film go unappreciated. Years would pass before The Searchers achieved the acclaim it deserved. Today it is considered a classic.

But The Searchers wasn't the only wonder created that summer. When we arrived back in Encino my doctor confirmed my hopes. I was pregnant at last. I almost called Duke from the doctor's office to tell him the good news, but I was still enough of a dramatic actress to want to set the scene. So I hurried home, put on my prettiest dress, redid my hair, and was standing at the top of the stairs doing my best Scarlett O'Hara imitation when Duke walked through the front door.

"Darling," I said, "I have the most wonderful news. We're going to be parents."

Responding on cue, Duke did his best Rhett Butler routine, taking the stairs two at a time and sweeping me into his arms.

Later that evening there was a hint of tears in his eyes as he talked about the baby to be. "This is my second chance at being a father," he said. "It isn't often a man gets a second chance in life. This time, Pilar, I swear I'll do it right."

CHAPTER 15

Webster's International dictionary defines "compulsion" as an "irresistible impulse." From 1955 on Duke and I were driven by incompatible compulsions. His was to make films which took him away for months at a time; mine was to stay at home and raise a family.

When we learned of my pregnancy, we were so happy that neither of us recognized the challenge a baby would present in our lives. Throughout the three years we'd been together, Duke had been adamant about wanting me to share locations with him. Making two or three films a year kept him away from home six to nine months. To complicate matters, he often filmed in remote, uncivilized places that were hard on his own health and would endanger a baby's.

I recognized that to maintain a good Hollywood marriage I had to travel with him, and I wanted to be his constant companion, but I'd vowed to be a good mother too. What is best for a child does not include leading a gypsy life.

Fortunately we didn't have to deal with the impending problem during the rest of my pregnancy. Although Duke made a cameo appearance in *I Married a Woman*, produced by Universal and directed by Hal Kantor, his next major film, *On Wings of Eagles*, wasn't scheduled to begin shooting until the summer of 1956, after the baby's birth.

Like many middle-aged men, Duke took an almost foolish pride in his coming fatherhood. He could hardly wait to tell his four older children they would soon have a new half brother or sister. We planned a family gathering to give them all the news simultaneously. Duke made the announcement.

"How could you, Dad?" Toni wailed. "You know I'm going to be married next month!"

Duke just stared at Toni with the strangest expression on his face. Then, nodding in my direction, he said, "Don't scream at me. She's the one who's pregnant!"

I felt so indignant and shocked. After all, he did have something to do with it! Now, when I needed him to stand by my side and face his irate daughter, he backed down. This pattern of avoiding family confrontations continued for the rest of our life together.

Duke had always seemed so forceful, so outspoken to me. I'd never seen him back down from a fight before. Learning that he couldn't or wouldn't protect me from his own family came as a great disappointment. Here I was, having a baby at the very time they wanted him to pay attention to their marriages and the children they hoped to have. It must have seemed terribly unfair to all four of them. They couldn't accept the fact that their father was entitled to a new life, a new family. Later, when Toni didn't invite me to her wedding, Duke was properly enraged. He called her and begged her to elope so he wouldn't have to go to the wedding without me. When she refused, he stormed around the house threatening not to attend the ceremony. But he never expressed that anger to his children.

Despite his own quick temper, he refused to be drawn into a battle in the office or at home. He'd lived through enough discord in his childhood and in his first two marriages to last a lifetime. I later learned that he even refused to be drawn into disputes between his employees at Batjac. If any of them asked him to resolve an argument he'd say, "Hell! That's what I'm paying you fellas for." Then he'd disappear, not to return until the problem was resolved.

Duke did his best to ignore the fact that my pregnancy upset his older children. Unfortunately, I couldn't. I told myself they would get over their resentment after the baby's birth. I felt that all I had to do was make their father happy.

Except for his inability to deal with his children's resentment, Duke was marvelous throughout the rest of my pregnancy, putting my needs above his own and everyone else's.

One evening we were invited to Jack Warner's house. The Warners were hosting a gala dinner party in honor of Grace Kelly. She'd just announced her engagement to Prince Rainier, and her stay in Hollywood was drawing to an end. My delivery date was close, and I debated the wisdom of attending the party. But I admired Grace and adored her movies and was dying to meet her, so Duke and I went.

The cocktail hour was exciting but a bit long. My feet were swelling by the time dinner was served in the Warner's large, elegant dining room. Halfway through the meal I began to feel faint. Seeing me grow pale, Duke jumped to his feet and rushed to the French doors that lined one side of the dining room, flinging them all open. Candles sputtered in the cool breeze, and Grace Kelly asked for her wrap.

When one of the guests suggested that Duke close the doors before everyone froze, Duke rose to his full height, saying in a tone that brooked no interference, "My wife is pregnant, and she needs fresh air." Those doors stayed open through dessert and coffee.

My last trimester was acutely uncomfortable. No husband in the world could have been more tender or concerned. He treated me like a china doll, watching over me as if I were the only woman who'd ever had a baby. He was so composed and helpful that I had no doubt he would be equally calm and reassuring during my labor.

On the evening of March 30, we'd gone to bed after having a late supper. I'd fallen asleep while Duke watched an old movie on television, but I woke an hour later, feeling very peculiar. Duke still stared at the television screen, completely absorbed. He watched films with an expert's eye, thinking how he might have handled a scene, picking up ideas for the day when he would direct his own films.

I was looking up at him when I felt a low, deep back pain. "Duke, I think I'm in labor," I said.

He literally leapt from the bed. "What do you want me to do?" he asked, his deep baritone heading toward an agitated squeak.

A wave of pain moved across my abdomen. "Duke, darling, please calm down and call the doctor. Tell him my water just broke!"

Duke seemed to fall apart. He struggled to dial the phone with shaking hands while I pulled my bulky body from the bed. Could he really be as nervous as he seems? I asked myself. After all, he'd been through this four times before.

He finally reached my doctor, who told us to head straight for the hospital. Exhilaration took over as I put on my clothes. In a few hours I'd hold our first baby in my arms, and I couldn't wait. Duke was in such a dither that I retrieved my overnight bag myself and waited for him to finish dressing.

We'd never driven the route to St. Josesph's hospital. Although a few friends had suggested we make the trip just once, Duke had scoffed at the very idea, because St. Joseph's was just down the street from Warner Brothers studio where he was under contract. "I could drive there in my sleep," he'd assured everyone.

The trip shouldn't have taken more than half an hour. Duke wasn't a very good driver, but he certainly was a fast one. We careened up one street and down the next while Duke mumbled, "Do I turn right or left?"

"Honey," I laughed, "you said you could find your way to St. Joseph's in your sleep."

"I know," he groaned, "but I'm wide awake now and lost as hell."

We found the hospital by accident. When my doctor asked what had taken us so long, Duke and I burst out laughing.

Duke rarely left my side during the long hours that followed. He held my hand, paced the floor, blanched when I groaned, and acted as if this was his first child struggling to come into the world rather than his fifth. We'd already chosen names, settling on Aissa if we had a girl. Duke thought it was Peruvian. When my mother, Carmela, heard the name she was convinced it had to be American. Wanting something unique, I'd invented it.

My labor lasted all night and into the next day. I'd been planning the first moment when Duke would see me with our child, and my expectations were based on movies I'd seen. Movie mothers always wore perfect makeup and freshly coifed hair in the labor room. So I'd insisted on applying fresh makeup before going into delivery, not realizing a nurse would mop my face with a damp cloth throughout labor. I was a mess when our daughter, Aissa, was born.

Duke paid no attention to my appearance when the doctor ushered him into the delivery room a few minutes later. He gave me a quick kiss and then turned to the table where Aissa lay swaddled.

"What's wrong with her?" he demanded. "Why isn't she crying?" The pediatrician assured him she was a fine healthy baby, but that didn't satisfy my husband.

"Why isn't she crying?" he demanded again, sounding as if he was about to order a cavalry charge. "Babies are supposed to cry!"

He refused to leave until one of the nurses picked Aissa up and made her wail.

Duke beamed. "Now that's more like it," he said, as if he'd just performed a miracle.

When he joined me an hour later in my hospital room, he took one look at the bed where I was resting and said, "Move over, honey. I'm pooped."

Duke had devoted six months to impending fatherhood, postponing or turning down all offers of new films. Once Aissa made her appearance, his attention quickly returned to making movies. He was especially enthusiastic about his upcoming project, *On Wings of Eagles*, in which he'd play a naval pilot named Spig Wead, a compulsive man, more devoted to country and career than family. Duke, fanatically committed to his own career, understood the part perfectly.

With Aissa to mother, I was beginning to understand compulsion myself. Nothing in the world was going to keep me from being the best mother I could be.

CHAPTER 16

Duke and I had our first serious disagreement in 1957 during the preproduction of *Legend of the Lost*, a Batjac-Robert Haggiag film which would costar Duke, Sophia Loren, and Rossano Brazzi. The picture was to be shot on location in Libya with interiors completed at Cinecitta Studio in Rome.

Duke would be away for three months, and he counted on my going with him. Aissa, who was too small to get all the inoculations she needed for travel to North Africa, would have to stay at home. I felt torn between the two of them. But in the end I couldn't bring myself to leave my baby girl in the care of a nurse, no matter how competent the nurse might be.

"Damn it, Pilar, you're my wife," Duke argued. "The nurse is perfectly capable of taking care of Aissa, and I need you with me."

How could I make him understand that "capable care" wasn't the same as a mother's loving care. In the end, seeing that I couldn't be budged, Duke agreed to a compromise. He would head for the Sahara while I stayed at home, and we'd meet again when the film company moved to Rome.

Sending a husband to a backwater like Godamus, Libya, knowing he'd be doing love scenes with a beautiful woman like Sophia Loren might have given another wife a few sleepless nights. But despite our recent disagreement, I had complete confidence in Duke's love. So I stayed home happily, looking forward to the prospect of a few peaceful, uninterrupted weeks with my daughter.

There'd hardly been an opportunity to start enjoying them when I received a frightening cablegram: "PLEASE HURRY HERE. I NEED YOU. I LOVE YOU. DUKE."

I panicked as soon as I read it. Duke wasn't a man who went back on his word. He'd only ask me to change my plans if something had happened to him. So many things could have gone wrong. He was forever getting scratched, bruised, or otherwise battered during a film. He was a perfectionist who wanted his action scenes to be as real and believable as he could make them. Because of his size and his characteristic walk, few stunt men could successfully double for him. So Duke performed most of his own stunts.

Knowing even simple stunts can be lethal, my imagination ran wild. I pictured Duke in a strange hospital, hurt, perhaps dying. There were no phones on the Saharan location, and I didn't want to waste time while cablegrams traveled back and forth—not if my husband needed me. So I left for North Africa at once, leaving Aissa in the care of her nurse after all.

The two-day trip to Godamus seemed to pass in slow motion. When I finally boarded the single-engine plane that would take me to the northern edge of the Sahara, I felt sick with apprehension. Throughout the journey I kept on praying, Please God, let Duke be all right. Please God, let Duke be all right. But I never expected my prayers to be answered so quickly. When the tiny plane taxied to a stop on Godamus's primitive dirt strip I rushed out straight into Duke's waiting arms!

"Darling," I sobbed, "I thought something terrible had happened to you."

"I'm fine, love," Duke replied, laughter adding extra sparkle to his eyes. "I just wanted you here so you could see the sunsets with me."

Duke had scared me to death, causing me to fly thousands of miles sick with worry, just to share the sunsets in the middle of the Sahara. But I was so grateful to find him unharmed that I didn't say a word.

He was right about one thing, the sunsets were glorious. That is the only positive thing I can say about Godamus. We were quartered in a mud-plastered, thatch-roofed room. Every evening when we returned from the day's shooting, a houseboy would arrive at our door to water the room's dirt floor to keep the dust down. For the next hour Duke and I would slip and slide on fresh mud like a pair of Keystone cops. Our compound boasted a single bathroom which we shared with the rest of the cast and crew. Somehow the stunning sunsets never quite made up for the primitive living conditions or for the fact that I missed Aissa more each day. Duke, knowing I'd left her in expert hands, couldn't understand my anxiety. As usual he was completely involved with the film, this time as both leading man and co-producer.

I'd heard a great deal about the new Italian bombshell and looked forward to meeting Sophia Loren. The morning after my arrival the cast had breakfast together, and I saw her for the first time. Can this be the gorgeous Loren everyone is raving about? I asked myself, trying not to stare at what seemed to be just another pretty face. Loren's eyes were unexceptional, her mouth too wide, her figure hidden by loose clothes. When I saw her again at lunch, fully made up and dressed for her role, she looked like a different person, absolutely breathtaking. Sophie could assume beauty the same way she assumed a role, an ability she shared with many of Hollywood's most compelling female stars.

Of all the cast and crew, Duke alone remained unimpressed by her charms. He just didn't find her as interesting or attractive as Lauren Bacall or Liz Taylor. Loren was dating her future husband, Carlo Ponti, at the time, but it soon became obvious that she and Rossano Brazzi were close friends. They spent all their time off camera together.

Duke didn't approve of the apparent romance. He'd grown up in an era where boys could be boys but girls were supposed to be ladies. Duke could excuse Brazzi's behavior, even though the Italian actor was married, but he couldn't excuse Loren's. She had my unspoken sympathy, though. I'd come to realize that an actress needed three things to succeed in Hollywood—a luscious figure, a gorgeous face, and the mind of a 40-year-old accountant. Sophia came handsomely equipped with all three.

As filming drew to a close, Duke decided that he wanted me to accompany him to Rome, where the interior scenes remained to be filmed. I argued that Aissa needed me at home, but he was adamant. I didn't understand why our marriage seemed to stand between me and my maternal instincts. Duke didn't want to admit that we had a serious problem, let alone discuss it, so all I could do was hope we'd stumble across a resolution.

When we got back to Encino I found myself resenting the fact that Aissa had grown and changed while I'd been gone. A child's first step or first words should be joyful family experiences, I thought angrily, not notes to be read in a nurse's diary.

The sleepless nights I'd spent worrying about Aissa had taken their toll, leaving me irritable and on edge. When I related my complaints to a friend, she recommended a Beverly Hills physician who was noted for dealing with the nervous crises which are an occupational hazard for Hollywood wives.

"You need to get some rest," the doctor said after he examined me briefly. "A little sleep will work wonders." He jotted down a couple of prescriptions and I filled them on my way home.

I took a pill that night and slept soundly for the first time in weeks. It felt wonderful to wake up the next morning, refreshed and rested. From then on I took those pills faithfully, and they continued to work wonders, giving me a new-found confidence, and letting me sleep. Within a few months I was taking one whenever I felt nervous, upset, depressed, angry, or inadequate. This was fairly often as my youth and lack of sophistication still made me feel insecure in Duke's world of wealth, privilege, and famous, talented, and influential friends. My husband could talk to cowboys or kings with equal ease and could not understand my anxiety. When I tried to share my feelings with Duke, he would tell me how pretty and young I was, as if that solved my problems. The pills gave temporary relief from anxiety, and my dependence on them grew.

Three months after we returned from Rome Duke was due to leave for another foreign location. He'd agreed to star in *The Barbarian and the Geisha*, a John Huston film scheduled for filming in Kyoto, Japan, from early December 1957 to the end of February 1958. Knowing it would be useless to argue, I agreed to join him before Christmas. He'd never worked with Huston. This picture would require a real stretch of Duke's talent, and he counted on Huston to help him turn in a creditable performance.

He left for Japan in high spirits, anticipating a memorable experience. Within days the first of a series of ominous letters arrived in Encino. Duke reported that he'd been unable to establish any rapport with Huston, that he couldn't get a handle on Huston's character, let alone the character he was supposed to play in the film. As an actor Duke felt lost. As a man he was furious.

The Barbarian and the Geisha was a gentle story about the United States' first emissary to Japan. Huston told the press that he'd cast Duke as Ambassador Harrison Townsend because Duke was the "quintessential American." Huston added that he planned to "let loose" Duke's giant figure against a background of Japanese scenery, sets, and actors.

Duke wasn't used to working in a totally unstructured atmosphere. He'd learned his craft from directors like Ford and Hathaway, men who wouldn't dream of letting loose an actor in a single scene, let alone throughout the course of an entire production.

Duke wrote to me in desperation, "My Darling—I wish the next two weeks would fly. Take care of yourself after that flu. Hurricane weather today—no shooting.

"I have done everything but stand on my head to get near this man's [Huston's] thinking. Just have to hope and pray that he's good."

When I arrived in Japan just before Christmas, Duke, who relished the holiday, was having trouble coming up with a feeling of "peace on earth, goodwill toward men." He was just too angry. "I can't work with the son of a bitch," he said, speaking of Huston. "I ask him what's on tomorrow's shooting schedule, and he'll tell me to spend more time absorbing the beauty of the scenery and less time worrying about my part. When I tell him I can't memorize the script unless I know what we'll be shooting, the bastard says 'don't worry, we'll improvise.'"

Duke believed a director should direct. He never understood Huston's methods and complained that the man spent far too much time searching out art and not enough working on the script. "He can quote chapter and verse on the price of a goddamn piece of Japanese porcelain, but he won't tell me how he wants me to do a scene," Duke growled. "The son of a bitch can't make a good movie without his father or Bogart to carry him."

And so it went day after day as the grey winter days dragged by. A needed change arrived in the person of Liz Taylor. Taylor and her current husband, Mike Todd, were traveling through the Orient when they called us from Tokyo. "We want to come spend a few days so you can get to know Mike," Liz said, bubbling with happiness. "You're going to love him."

She was right. They arrived the next day, and their visit proved to be just the tonic needed to raise Duke's spirits. He and Mike must have been friends in another life, because they had an instant rapport. Mike was tough, humorous, honest, and outspoken, just the kind of man Duke needed after his association with the mystical, nebulous Huston. Although he didn't drink, Mike loved to party. He smoked a big black cigar while Duke relaxed with cigarettes and scotch. The two of them swapped stories by the hour.

Duke and I agreed that this time Taylor had a real winner. We'd never seen her so happy, so content. When the visit drew to a close we said goodbye reluctantly, planning to get together again as soon as we could. Fortunately we saw the Todds one more time before Mike's untimely death in an airplane accident. We were to mourn his passing.

Two weeks before *The Barbarian and the Geisha* was due to wrap, Duke told me he wouldn't mind if I went home early. I'd been feeling uneasy again, quite certain that Aissa needed me. As it turned out, she really did.

One night, shortly after my return, Blackie woke me from a deep sleep, barking frantically and scratching at the bed covers. I opened my eyes to see a few wisps of smoke hovering near the ceiling. Thinking it would help clear the air, I rushed to the windows and flung them wide before racing downstairs to wake our servants. Then I grabbed the kitchen fire extinguisher and charged back upstairs.

To my shock the wisps of smoke had become a thick, choking cloud that reached halfway down the walls. I finally had enough sense to be frightened. The house was on fire and I was alone upstairs with my baby. Smoke filled the hall as I groped toward her room. The dense cloud hadn't reached the level of her crib and she still slept soundly. I wrapped her in a blanket and, crouching, worked my way to the stairs. When I reached the front door, all four of our live-in employees were waiting for me. One of the maids, in her panic, had picked up a large vase as she fled the house, the sole treasure any of them thought to save! I'd have laughed if I hadn't been so scared.

With Blackie at my heels, I led the way next door to call for help. A rush of adrenaline had propelled me into Aissa's room and then out of the house. As it ebbed shock set in, and my knees and arms began to shake. Looking across the lawn I could see smoke billowing from the roof and the second-story windows of my home.

"How do you like one-story houses?" I asked Duke when I reached him by telephone in Kyoto several hours later. Trying to sound calm and in complete control, I went on to describe exactly what had happened. "We were lucky," I said. "The worst damage is confined to the second story, and even that isn't too bad. Blackie not only saved our lives, he saved the house too."

I didn't want Duke to worry. No matter what happened at home, he had to finish that film. If I'd learned nothing else during our marriage, I'd learned that! Duke wouldn't want anyone to say he'd run out on John Huston, no matter how valid his reason for leaving might be. But he promised to come home the minute the picture wrapped.

My husband sent me a signed check by special messenger the following day, leaving the amount to be filled in by me. The note accompanying it read, "For the girl who really has nothing to wear." It was Duke's way of saying he loved me. I laughed when I saw it. In fact I laughed until I cried.

As I finally fell into an exhausted sleep the next night, my last thought was of Aissa. What would have happened to her if I hadn't come home early? How would I ever bring myself to leave her again?

CHAPTER 17

When Duke returned from Japan two weeks after the fire, he commented that his career and our home seemed to be in equally bad shape; 1957 and 1958 had seen the release of some of his worst films, including Howard Hughes's lamentable production *Jet Pilot*. Although the critics had never appreciated Duke's work, now fans too seemed weary of his movies. Duke knew that rebuilding his career would require careful thought and planning. Meanwhile the house demanded immediate attention. An optimist by nature, Duke said the fire gave us an ideal opportunity to do some remodeling. He decided to build a screening room, his and hers dressing rooms, and an exercise room, as well as enlarging the floor space and raising the ceiling in his den so that it accommodated his height. Redoing the house was a short-term challenge that Duke, a frustrated architect and decorator at heart, relished. Changing the course of his career was going to take a little more time.

He was particularly unhappy with his last two films. Despite the fact that he was a new father and the romantic lead in my life, he no longer felt comfortable playing romantic leads on screen. His fiftieth birthday had come and gone, an age when leading men traditionally retired or moved on to character parts.

Duke knew he was too recognizable on screen to submerge the John Wayne persona beneath the veneer of character roles. He had to go on playing leads, but they would have to be roles that allowed for his thinning hair. He was an older man, and it was time he started playing one, but he hoped to be an older man with a new slant—someone women from 8 to 80 could adore. Duke knew only too well how difficult a task he'd set for himself. Good scripts were going to be very hard to find. His difficulties would be compounded by the fact that industry money men were firmly convinced a leading man over 50 was box office poison.

Duke knew he'd have to reeducate them. Other men his age talked about retiring, but he wanted to work, and working meant he would have to find a way to establish a new standard for mature actors. In the future a host of aging stars, such men as Charles Bronson, Clint Eastwood, and Paul Newman, would follow down the path that Duke prepared for them back in the fifties.

Duke's next film, *Rio Bravo*, gave him an excellent opportunity to explore the new image he hoped to create. The movie would be directed by Howard Hawks, whose westerns depended on the development of character as much as they did on action. Duke would be playing Sheriff John T. Chance, a stubborn man who thinks he's too old for romance. When Angie Dickinson falls in love with him in the film, she makes the first advances. Their relationship is told with humor and warmth rather than steamy love scenes. Dean Martin, Rick Nelson, Ward Bond, John Russell, and Walter Brennan would round out the excellent cast.

Duke left for the movie's "Old Tucson" location in May, leaving me behind to oversee the final stages of remodeling. He returned in mid-July, feeling that he'd gotten his career back on the right track. Hawk's movies were invariably high points in his career. His next picture, *Horse Soldiers*, scheduled to begin location shooting in Louisiana in October, would reunite him with John Ford. His costars would be William Holden and Constance Towers.

Horse Soldiers was a difficult picture to put together. Duke, Ford, and Holden all owned their own production companies—Batjac, Argosy, and William Holden Productions. *Horse Soldiers* would be produced by these entities as well as The Mirish Company and Mahin-Rackin Productions. The complex contracts which defined the deal required 250 pages, far longer than the average script. Compared to the legal agreements, the story, a basic Civil War shoot-em-up, was relatively simple.

We were all looking forward to the movie. Our pediatrician had told me that Aissa was old enough to travel with us. For the first time the Waynes would go on location as a family. When we moved back into our refurbished home that summer, Duke was in high spirits. His career and our marriage seemed to be back on track. But I had a secret that would soon shatter our lives.

One evening Duke invited Ward and Maisie Bond and James and Josephine Grant and other friends to watch a movie in our new screening room. I'd run out of pills that morning, and, thinking it could wait until the next day, hadn't bothered to refill my prescriptions. Halfway through the film I began to feel very sick. A clammy sweat bathed my body, and I couldn't concentrate on the movie or our friends' conversation. I excused myself and ran upstairs, hoping that no one had noticed my condition. Duke followed me immediately.

"What's the matter, Pilar?" he said, kneeling by my side.

I was terrified, sick, confused, and out of control. "I ran out of my pills today. You've got to get the druggist to refill my prescription now—tonight!"

"What the hell are you talking about?"

"I'll show you," I said, crawling out of bed to retrieve the empty pill bottles that I kept hidden in a drawer in my dressing table.

Duke snatched them from my hand and read the labels. "Who the hell gave you this crap?"

"A doctor in Beverly Hills. They're for my nerves. And they help me!" Duke had to realize how much I needed those drugs. If he really loved me, he'd get refills at once.

Duke pocketed the vials. "No!" he shouted. "They don't help you, Pilar."

I knew it was useless to argue, and, in any case, I felt too sick to try. The next day our family doctor told Duke I was very sick and suffering from an addiction to sleeping pills. "Your wife needs to be under constant supervision until she's over this crisis," he said.

"Pilar and I will conquer this ourselves," Duke replied. "I'm leaving for Louisiana in a few days, and I want her to join me." Then he took my hand, and his tone softened. "Honey, I'm going to get you through this thing. I'll be with you every minute, every step of the way. As soon as the picture wraps, we can go down to Mexico for a vacation. All you need is a little rest, a little good food."

Duke misjudged both the seriousness of my condition and my mental and physical ability to conquer the addiction. The next few days were hell. What should have been one of the happiest times in my life, preparing to take our little girl on location with us, proved to be the most difficult. When Duke left for Louisiana, I was in no condition to travel. He had to leave me behind, asking Mary St. John to watch over me.

A few days after his departure, I followed him to Louisiana with Aissa and our maids. But I barely remember making the trip. Two days after arriving on location, I began hallucinating. I was told that I tried to slash my wrists. Duke hired a private plane and sent me home with two nurses and a maid. I woke up in an Encino hospital. My first thoughts were of Aissa and Duke, who, I was told by the doctor, had been calling hourly. The doctor also told me Aissa was safe with her father. At that moment Duke called again. I told him how sorry I was and he replied, "Darling, all I want is for you to get well and hurry back to us." When I recovered I returned to my daughter and husband for a joyous reunion.

My illness was just the first in a series of disasters that occurred during the filming of *Horse Soldiers*. The $3.5 million epic was in trouble from the very start. Ford was unhappy with the script and uncomfortable associating with Marty Rackin, one of the producers. When Ford arrived on location he'd given up drinking, and, as a consequence, he was in a vile mood throughout the filming. Duke, who wasn't in the best frame of mind himself, made this movie the exception to his own self-imposed rule of not drinking while he was working. Holden, who also had a problem with alcohol, drank steadily while on location. Ford nagged and lectured Duke and Holden, miserable because he wouldn't permit himself to join their parties. But these disagreements were minor irritations compared to what lay ahead.

One day halfway through the shooting, Fred Kennedy, an aging stuntman, persuaded Ford to allow him to do a simple stunt to earn some extra Christmas money. Kennedy wanted to double William Holden in a horse fall, a trick Kennedy had probably done a thousand times. At the end of the action, Constance Towers was to rush to Holden/Kennedy's side as he lay on the ground and throw herself on him.

When Ford called for action, the brief scene appeared to go smoothly. Kennedy took the fall in the precise spot Ford had designated. Right on cue Constance ran to the downed man, throwing herself across his body. Within seconds she was on her feet again, her face a mask of horror. Kennedy was dead, his neck broken.

Duke told me that Ford couldn't seem to forget the accident and get on with his work, blaming himself for Kennedy's death. He began drinking heavily and lost interest in finishing the film. The final product didn't live up to Ford's high standards and was poorly received by the critics.

The Ford era seemed to be drawing to a close, and no one regretted it more than Duke. He returned from Louisiana saddened and disturbed by the events of the last few months. "Ford just doesn't seem to care any more," Duke explained. "Hell, he looks and acts like a beaten man."

Ford's star would rise again, he and Duke would make other movies, but they would never again share the lighthearted *esprit de corps* that made their earlier collaboration so much fun.

The world was changing, and the film industry, a mirror of the times, was changing too. Movies were beginning to reflect the nation's growing liberalism. Violence and explicit sex were becoming part of the moviemaker's stock in trade. Westerns, which had always used carefully choreographed violence, were becoming increasingly graphic in their depiction of pain. The trend concerned Duke. He believed that all the bloodletting on screen, the gratuitous sex, was bound to weaken the fiber of U.S. society. He was prepared to fight that trend with every ounce of his star power and box office appeal.

In Duke's opinion the time was ripe to film the saga of the Alamo—a story of sacrifice, courage, and devotion. The film would be his response to all the flag burners, draft dodgers, and the fainthearted who didn't believe in good, old-fashioned American virtues.

In 1959 the most critically acclaimed filmmakers were preparing to shoot movies such as *La Dolce Vita*, a story of moral decadence; *Never on Sunday*, about a prostitute; and *Elmer Gantry*, about the perversion of religion. By contrast, 1959 found Duke on the brink of making a movie about a group of men who gave their lives in the cause of freedom.

Most of Hollywood's movers and shakers thought he'd lost his mind. They looked at James Grant's script and saw no sex, no nude scenes, no decapitated bodies flying through the air. "Who the hell is going to pay to see a picture where all the heroes die?" Herbert Yates scoffed when Duke approached him in search of funding. Despite their many past successes, Jack Warner had no interest in putting money in Duke's film either. "It'll be too goddamn expensive and," he added, "I don't think the fans want to see this kind of picture anymore."

Warner was right on one count. *The Alamo* would cost more than any other movie up to that time, over $10 million—and Duke would have to mortgage our home and our future in order to complete it. But first he had to make amends at home.

I was fully recovered from my addiction when Duke and I returned from Louisiana and we were anxious to get our lives on an even keel again. Duke shared my desire, but he didn't believe in introspection, analyzing a situation or talking it to death. We'd both made mistakes and paid a price for them. As was his custom, Duke refused to spend time or energy on regrets. The past was over and done with. He didn't know how to say "I'm sorry," but he was very good at saying "I love you." In fact he said it so well and so often that we Waynes were very much the happy couple again as Duke moved ahead with plans to make *The Alamo*.

CHAPTER 18

Duke had dreamed of filming the story of the Alamo for a decade, planning, talking, and researching until, in 1959, he finally felt ready to transform that dream into celluloid reality. But first he had to find financial backing and cut a deal with a major studio for distribution of the film.

He wasn't at all discouraged by the quick negatives he'd gotten from Yates and Warner. After all, Duke reasoned, he was a very rich man himself and could come up with the seed money on his own. Duke called his own financial adviser, Bo Roos, to schedule a conference. When the two men met Duke wasted no time in coming straight to the point. "Bo," he said, "exactly how much money do I have?"

"Well, Duke," Roos delayed, "not a great deal of cash. Your money isn't sitting in the bank someplace. It's all invested; real estate, various business ventures—"Roos's voice dropped off.

"I know that," Duke answered impatiently. "Just tell me how much money I could raise if I had to."

Roos stared at the floor. "That will take a couple of weeks."

Duke left the office, feeling vaguely uncomfortable but not really worried. He and Roos had been close associates for seventeen years. In the early forties Roos had put a chunk of Duke's money into a property adjacent to Twentieth Century Fox studios. The property sold a year or two later at an enormous profit, and, from then on, Duke had complete faith in Roos's ability as a financial manager and investment counselor. "I can earn it," he told Roos at the time, "but I don't have time to worry about it after that. So I'm counting on you to handle that end of things."

Duke never kept accurate records, but he thought he'd turned millions of dollars over to Roos during their long association.

With that much money behind him, Duke didn't see how he'd
have a problem financing *The Alamo*. He returned to Roos's office two weeks later, expecting to go out for a few drinks as soon
as they completed their business.

"Well, Bo," he said after they were seated in Roos's private
office, "how much am I worth?"

Bo was evasive. "It isn't that simple, Duke."

Duke grew impatient. "For chrissake, I've given you a goddamn
fortune over the years. It's a simple question. What the hell have
you done with the money?"

Roos sagged in his chair. "It's all gone. You've got the house,
your personal possessions, and Batjac. That's all I could save."

Duke later told me he couldn't believe what he was hearing. It
seemed like a bad joke or a bad dream. He and Roos were friends,
they visited in each other's homes, drank together, talked weekly
on the phone. In all the years, Roos hadn't once said things were
going badly. How could all that money have disappeared overnight?

The answer, mismanagement, would be supplied by Duke's
attorney, Frank Belcher, after a long and painstaking investigation. Roos had put Duke's money into a series of losers, and then,
rather than cut the losses, he'd poured more and more money in
the investments. There'd been deals such as an Acapulco hotel
which stayed so full of nonpaying friends that it never made a
profit or the Culver City property that had been carried on the
books in the red for years. Duke finally gave the building to the
YMCA, but that was after he fired Roos.

Duke felt Roos had betrayed him, and that hurt even more than
the loss of all the money. As far as he was concerned, how the
money was lost didn't matter; the end result was all that counted. Despite feeling personally used and betrayed by Roos, Duke
would still have a soft spot in his heart for the man. Years later,
when Roos died, his widow called Duke and begged him to attend the funeral. I was amazed at such a request, given all that
had happened between the two men, and I was opposed to Duke's
going. But Duke felt it was the right thing for him to do, and he
went and paid his respects to Roos's family and to the memory
of their friendship.

Hoping a family member would prove to be more trustworthy,

Duke hired his son-in-law to replace Roos. When he left Roos's office that afternoon, Duke knew he'd have to get the money to make *The Alamo* someplace else. A wiser man might have delayed the project and made five or six other pictures as quickly as possible to recoup some of his losses. But Duke was never wise or practical about commitment; he was, however, stubborn, determined, and devoted to things he believed in.

In the coming months Duke would overcome all the odds against getting the picture made. His search for funding concluded successfully when he signed a multipicture deal with United Artists. Both parties to the contract walked away from the bargaining table satisfied; Duke had his money and United Artists had Duke.

He envisioned *The Alamo* as a true family effort, one that would involve all the Waynes. Son Michael and brother Bob would be working in the Batjac offices, functioning as his aides. Son Patrick would be playing Captain James Bonham, daughter Toni Wayne LaCava had a one-line speaking part, and our own Aissa, now a lively 4 year old, would make her screen debut as Angelina Dickinson. Although I hadn't been in front of a camera for years, I told Duke I wanted to be an extra.

We hadn't all been together for some time and I felt a bit nervous about the months we would spend on location. Duke, Bobby, and Michael weren't close. They would become further estranged a couple years later in 1964 when Bobby and Michael were involved in a serious automobile accident. Though both men were married, the women in the car with them weren't their wives. The Wayne family name was worthy of headlines, and several newspapers reported the incident. Duke was visibly upset when the police called us in the middle of the night to report what had happened.

Duke told me that Michael, more than any of his other children, had judged him harshly when Duke divorced Josephine. Duke suffered lifelong guilt in the aftermath of the divorce as a result. Over the years Duke had done everything he could to earn his oldest son's approval and understanding.

Once Duke learned that Michael's behavior was less than proper in his eyes, they rarely spoke, except about business. Duke had even taken to calling Michael "Khrushchev" because of the way Michael dealt with his fellow Batjac employees. But he kept Michael and Bobby on at Batjac because they were *family*, and Duke believed in keeping the family together. As family, they too would be expected to make a contribution to *The Alamo*.

In typical John Wayne style, the first picture over which Duke exercised complete artistic control was bound to be larger than life. Most men would have taken one look at the scope of the project and decided that producing it would be a full-time job. Duke regarded producers as paper pushers and intended to direct the movie and star in it too. Consequently, he surrounded himself with past associates whose work he knew, whose devotion he could count on.

James Edward Grant, Duke's favorite writer, would serve as coproducer in addition to writing the script. William Clothier, a gifted cinematographer Duke respected, would be behind the cameras. Ken Curtis was given the part of Captain Dickinson, Olive Carey would play Mrs. Dennison, Carlos Arruza (a great matador, long-time friend, and a stunning figure on horseback) would appear in the film as General Santa Ana's mounted messenger.

Duke had wanted to play Sam Houston, a supporting role rather than a starring one, but United Artists wanted to protect their investment; they wanted Duke to play one of the leads. So he cast himself as Davy Crockett, and the Houston role went to Richard Boone. Another Richard—Richard Widmark—had agreed to play James Bowie. Duke was so elated when Widmark signed the contract that Duke took a one-page ad in the *Hollywood Reporter* which read, "Welcome aboard, Dick."

The next time the two men met, Widmark stared up at Duke and said, "Tell your press agent that the name is Richard."

Duke struggled to control his temper. After all, he told himself, you're going to have to direct this man. "If I ever take another ad," he said, enunciating each word with exquisite care, "I'll remember that, Richard."

Fortunately the other pivotal role in the film, that of William Travis, was to be played by a far more agreeable man. Lawrence Harvey was a fine English actor with a Shakespearean background. With his gift for telling hilarious stories he proved a delight once we were isolated on location.

While Duke assembled the cast and crew, a replica of the Alamo and the town of San Antonio de Bexar had been going up on "Happy" Sheehan's ranch 20 miles outside of Bracketville. The location was in a remote, southwestern corner of Texas. Another producer would have been content with the false-fronted buildings that are typical of movie sets. Not Duke. He wanted real buildings, authentic exteriors, and interiors that reflected the long hours of research that thad gone into set design.

Hundreds of workers, including some Mexicans who could make real adobe brick, toiled for months to complete the buildings. In addition they built miles of asphalt road, bulldozed a dirt landing strip, dug wells, installed sewer lines. Portable generators, portable air-conditioning units, and thousands of feet of electrical cable had to be in place before the workers left and the film crew arrived. The crew brought tons of equipment with them, cameras, dollies, lights, sound equipment, portable dressing rooms and toilets, an endless list of needed supplies. And it all cost money. The picture was in financial trouble long before the cameras rolled.

Fifteen hundred horses, with corrals to hold them and wranglers to handle them, had to be on location before shooting began. A herd of longhorn cattle and 500 mules were also required. Dozens of stuntmen and hundreds of extras began pouring into Bracketville. Knowing the town of 1800 couldn't hold or feed all of them, Duke had leased Fort Clark, an abandoned nearby army base. Workers were hired to refurbish the barracks, officers' quarters, and the mess hall so that everyone could be housed and fed.

Almost everything the company would need during our stay would have to be shipped in, from cattle feed to human food, including cases of tomato juice for deodorizing Blackie, who discovered the joys of chasing skunks while on location. The Alamo was destined to be a logistical nightmare.

Somehow Duke managed to stay in control of the preproduction, but I was very concerned about his ability to function as the producer while directing and starring in the film. He was driving himself and all his associates very hard, reaching for an impossible standard of perfection.

Ford had taught him the importance of authenticity and realism, but even Ford hadn't imagined applying those standards to a picture with the *Alamo's* size and scope. Duke refused to cheat his cameras. He wouldn't dream of trying to film a hundred horses so they looked like a thousand. Instead he planned to hurl a thousand horses and riders onto the rolling hills of Texas—and to hell with the cost.

The extent of Duke's commitment to the picture amazed me. He wasn't making a movie, he was on a crusade. But, despite the constant work and worry, we'd never been happier. When we arrived in Bracketville, Duke was fully prepared for his mammoth task. He knew the script by heart—not just the scenes and the lines but the exact pages they appeared on.

Never once during the entire $3\frac{1}{2}$ months of shooting did he have to refer to the script while on the set. Like Ford, Duke carried in his mind a detailed vision of every shot. He'd figured out every camera setup, every possible take in advance. At night we reviewed the rushes together. I was so proud of Duke's work and his ability as a director.

Duke was a superb field general, in control of every detail except the escalating costs brought on by his own need for realism. The United Artists money disappeared quickly. Then Duke put together a consortium of Texas backers which included the Mc-Cullough brothers and Clint Murchison. After their money had been absorbed, Duke used Batjac and our Encino estate, all he had left in the world, as collateral for a loan.

The risks were enormous. Although Duke wasn't a religious man, he called for a brief prayer before filming began. Despite the risks, his face glowed as he readied the first shot. Duke was living his dream. In a deep baritone that echoed across the Texas hills, he said: "Roll 'em."

CHAPTER 19

Under normal circumstances there is virtually nothing to keep a visitor occupied when spending time on a movie location. Completing a complicated camera setup sometimes takes half a day. While the crew is hard at work, the actors rest in their dressing rooms, play cards, or read. When visiting a set, you soon learn to sit quietly. Any unplanned sound can be picked up by the sensitive sound equipment. A sudden move at the wrong time may break an actor's concentration, making a retake necessary.

Most directors don't welcome daily visitors. But in Bracketville the director happened to be my husband, and he welcomed my companionship and support. I fell in love with Duke all over again during the filming of *The Alamo*. I'd been concerned about how he'd react to the stress of his triple responsibilities as producer, director, and star. But I worried needlessly. Duke clearly felt at the peak of his career.

He'd always respected his directors, and now he gave the hundreds of people who worked on this film every reason to respect him. Although there were days when he used as many as twenty-six or twenty-seven different camera setups, nothing escaped his watchful eye. He seemed to be everywhere at once, correcting the way an extra sat his horse or carried his gun, rearranging props, working with the actors, praising his crew. Despite the pressure and work load, Duke's love of directing showed.

His self-control faltered just three times. The first incident occurred when John Ford arrived in Bracketville, announcing that he intended to take a little vacation there. No one believed him for a minute. Bracketville is a sleepy backwater town, not a resort, and Ford had never heard of it until Duke chose it as the

143

location for his film. Obviously, Ford wasn't on the scene for rest and relaxation. The day after he arrived Ford showed up on the set in time for the first setup, and he spent the entire day looking over Duke's shoulder, acting like a "back-seat" driver.

Duke loved Ford and would have been delighted to see him under any other circumstances, but this was Duke's first job as a director. He knew Ford's presence in Bracketville was bound to start the rumor that Ford was the undercover director of the film. Duke confessed that he felt a little like a young man who goes into the family business, only to have his father supervising every move. Ford continued to appear on the set every day, all day, until Duke felt certain that his own authority and credibility were slipping. Something would have to be done before *The Alamo* became Ford's picture.

Duke couldn't bring himself to ask Ford to leave. He kept remembering how the director looked when they'd said goodbye at the end of *Horse Soldiers*. At the time Duke had been certain that Ford would never again be interested in making pictures. Ford's fascination with *The Alamo* seemed to be giving him a new lease on life. Duke didn't want to discourage that. The best solution involved finding an alternative way to keep Ford busy, one that would allow Ford to think he was making an important contribution to the film. So Duke decided to ask Ford if he would mind directing some second-unit scenes.

Second-unit scenes usually involve action and extras, rather than principal players, and they are often directed by experienced stunt coordinators. Duke already had Cliff Lyons, an ex-stuntman and top second-unit director, hard at work. Convincing Ford that another second unit was required would take all of Duke's skills as a performer. He had to be absolutely convincing if he wanted to save Ford's feelings and his sense of self-worth.

No matter what it cost in time, effort, or money, Duke was determined not to hurt his friend. So he asked James Grant to write some new action scenes and then turned that portion of the script over to Ford, telling Ford that Lyons couldn't complete all the second-unit scenes. Ford immediately agreed to shoot the sequences. Later he was quite surprised when his footage wound up on the cutting room floor. No one other than James Grant knew that Duke never intended to use the film Ford exposed, that he was willing to go to the extra expense of shooting it to save their thirty-year friendship.

Duke's other problems during the filming were not so easily solved. Richard Widmark continued to stand at the head of the list. Widmark was a difficult man whose scratchy personality was not unlike a tweed jacket, serviceable but uncomfortable. The day Widmark arrived in Bracketville he began to challenge Duke's authority. Many actors make a habit of questioning or defying their directors. Duke had seen these men in action before and often wondered how he'd deal with the problem himself. Some directors out shouted defiant actors; others used patience and understanding. Duke tried patience and understanding first, because he respected Widmark's talent.

But Widmark seemed to interpret Duke's patience as a sign of weakness. He kept on arguing with Duke in front of the rest of the cast and crew. Predictably, the day came when Duke's patience ran out. I wasn't on the set at the time, but other people who were told me that Widmark and Duke had a violent confrontation and that Duke threw the smaller man against a wall.

Everyone worried about how they'd work together from then on, and a few pessimists even predicted that Widmark would walk out on the picture. They didn't understand Duke's or Widmark's professionalism. Whatever their differences, they would finish the picture together.

Duke's third test came as he set out to direct our daughter. Aissa was playing Ken Curtis's little girl in the film, the only child to be shut up in the Alamo before the arrival of the Mexican army. Her major scene as Angelina Dickinson would be a birthday party.

Aissa wasn't a professional child star—she had no acting experience. Although she'd been on locations with us before, she was far too young, at 4 years old, to comprehend exactly what was happening. I was afraid she might not understand what acting meant, that she might think she was having an actual birthday party.

Most directors dread working with children or animals, both of whom can be unpredictable or uncooperative. What, I worried, would Duke, as her director, do if Aissa forgot her lines, giggled at the wrong time, or simply forgot she was making a movie and called him Daddy?

He was a perfectionist who expected everyone, from the grips and gaffers to the stars, to do their job. How would he react if his tiny daughter and favorite child failed to do hers? My worst fears were realized midway through the first take. Aissa stopped the entire take by running to her father's side, asking, "Did I do right, Daddy?"

She took everyone by surprise, including her father. He stared at her for a moment, and then it was clear that he'd forgotten about being the director of a multimillion-dollar epic. He'd forgotten everything except being a father. The action stopped while his giant figure bent down to hug her small one. "You did just fine, honey," Duke said, picking her up and carrying her back to her place on the set.

Duke couldn't resist Aissa. She was a love child in every sense of the word, a gift that had come to him when other men his age are concentrating on grandchildren, and he lavished affection and attention on her. When I complained that she was getting spoiled or worried about the long-range effect of his indulgence, Duke would say, "I can spoil her—but you better not."

Duke's attitude didn't change just because Aissa was working for him. After that first interruption she got through all her scenes without too much difficulty, but after every take she'd run to her father for a kiss and a pat on the head. No one on the set was surprised to see Duke roughly wipe aside an occasional sentimental tear as he directed his little girl.

I have nothing but happy memories of filming in Bracketville. My daughter was with me, my husband was finally seeing his dream come true, and all the Waynes seemed to be growing closer. Toni LaCava came to stay with us for a few days during the filming, and she and I were becoming friends. We were close enough in age to have things in common, not the least of which was loving Duke.

In Bracketville we shared one hilarious day on the set working as extras, playing women who were permitted to leave the Alamo during the siege. That morning Duke directed Patrick, Toni, Aissa, and me in the same scene, and we all had fun. Afterward I felt certain my problems as a stepmother were behind me.

Duke wanted to finish the picture by mid-December so that his cast and crew could be home for the holidays. Two years before we'd spent a lonely Christmas in Kyoto, and the following year Duke had been on location with *Horse Soldiers* during the holidays. He knew only too well how lonely the season could be when spent away from family and friends.

It was a triumphant John Wayne who shouted "Cut" one last time on December 15, 1959, in time to send everyone home for Christmas. He'd finished the job he set out to do so many years ago, but the cost had been high. Duke weighed 30 pounds less than he had when we arrived in Bracketville. His smoking had increased from a three- to a five-pack-a-day habit, he'd mortgaged our house and his own film company, and the job wasn't finished.

The cast and crew returned to California to celebrate the holidays. Duke returned to complete his movie. He'd exposed over 500,000 feet of film on location, and they needed to be edited, a job Duke intended to supervise. Dimitri Tiompkin, who'd done the *Red River* score, went to work scoring the film, surprised to learn that Duke wanted to work closely with him. Every last detail of the movie would bear the stamp of my husband's personality.

During the postproduction phase, Duke set publicist Russell Birdwell to work to build an audience for the movie. Birdwell, who'd orchestrated the publicity campaign for *Gone with the Wind,* was regarded as the best in the business. Three months before the picture's October 24, 1960, premiere, Birdwell took a three-page, $200,000 color spread in *Life Magazine* which seemed to be making comparison between this film and the 1960 presidential campaign: "There were no ghostwriters at the Alamo!" the ad read. "Only men."

Duke was hoping to draw America's attention to the fact that candidates were becoming a great deal like actors in that they made a practice of hiring speechwriters. By taking that ad Duke hoped to remind the public of the time when U.S. politicians composed their own words, speaking their minds without help from professionals.

There was nothing inherently wrong with Duke's idea. From the beginning he'd conceived *The Alamo* as a way of reawakening the country's patriotism. But Duke forgot an important principle of filmmaking—people don't go to the movies to be lectured, they go to be entertained. Tying his film to politics was the worst thing Duke could have done. After seeing *The Alamo*, Sam Goldwyn is reported to have commented, "If Duke wanted to send a message, he should have used Western Union."

A few of Duke's peers rose to defend the film. George Stevens, one of Hollywood's most respected directors, said, "When the roll call of the great ones is made, *The Alamo* will be among those few by which the films of the future will be measured."

Ford added the weight of his own approval, saying "It's the greatest picture I've ever seen. It will last forever—run forever." Ford was partially right—the film still runs periodically on television where it has always been an audience favorite.

The Alamo premiered in San Antonio with the governor, the mayor, and a host of dignitaries in attendance. Texans loved the story, as did most Americans. The London premiere was attended by Princess Margaret, who claimed she didn't know which she enjoyed more, meeting Duke or seeing the movie. Several British critics praised Duke's efforts, calling the picture a genuine epic in the same category as the classic, *The Seven Samurai*.

Although fans lined up to see *The Alamo*, U.S. critics did everything in their power to ensure that the picture would fail. They seemed to be offended by its sentimentality, its flag-waving patriotism. The influential Bosley Crowther called it, "just another beleaguered western." John Cutts, in cruel mimicry of Ford's praise, wrote, "May I humbly suggest to Mr. Ford that the film only seems to last forever."

For once Duke couldn't conceal his dismay over the critics' attacks. He'd stripped his soul bare in this film, held his own deepest convictions up to public scrutiny. Duke's sentimentality, his love of the United States, his firm belief that people must be independent if they hope to be free, were the "through line" in every scene. When, as Davy Crockett, Duke speaks of the Texan's struggle to create a republic, the lines come from his heart as he says, "It means people can live free, talk free, go or come, buy or sell, be drunk or sober, however they choose."

Those sentimental, simple words spelled out Duke's dreams, his hopes for the United States. He wanted the country and its people to be as strong, as independent, and as ornery as those men who chose to give their lives in the Alamo.

I still get goosebumps, watching one of the last scenes before the climactic battle. It is the one where the parson turns to Davy Crockett and says, "You never pray, do you?"

As Crockett, Duke's voice has a husky sadness when he answers, "I never found the time." That single line says so much about Duke the man—not the actor. He was a doer who rarely found the time to pray. But *The Alamo* would need his prayers if he was going to recoup his enormous investment, and time was running out.

The annual Oscars were approaching, and Duke wanted to see his film reap a few nominations. Although he honestly didn't care if his work as the director received recognition, he hoped William Clothier's cinematography, Dimitri Tiompkin's score, Widmark's performance, and James Grant's script would get the attention they merited. In hopes of attracting that attention, Duke put Birdwell back to work.

Some marvelous films were released in 1960. *The Alamo* would have to compete for Oscar nominations with epics such as *Spartacus* and *Exodus* as well as more intimate films such as *Never on Sunday* and *The Apartment*. Duke made a second public relations error by allowing Birdwell to try and convince the Academy's voting membership that a vote for *The Alamo* was a vote for the U.S. way of life.

When a reporter asked Duke about his film's Oscar chances, Duke reinforced the error by saying, "This is not the first time the *Alamo* has been the underdog. We need defenders today just as they did one hundred and twenty-five years ago."

The critics began to attack the movie's overblown publicity campaign. Duke, having made a film about a battle that altered the course of U.S. history, now found himself in a battle of words that demeaned his reasons for making the film in the first place.

The struggle took place at cocktail parties, over dinner, and in studio board rooms. Everyone had something to say about *The Alamo*. Duke was particularly incensed when Darryl Zanuck gave out the following quote: "I have great affection for Duke Wayne, but what right has he to write, direct, and produce a motion picture? Everyone is becoming a corporation. Look at poor old Duke.

He's never going to see a nickel for his film and he put all his money into finishing *The Alamo*."

I don't know what bothered Duke more—being called old or poor. He responded immediately. "Please inform Zanuck that as far as "old Duke" and his picture are concerned—which has, by the way, made $2 million playing in just thirteen theaters and has ten thousand more theater dates to play—that we're doing just fine!"

In private Duke was a little more graphic. "It's s.o.b.'s like Zanuck that made me become a producer," he said. "Who the hell does he think he is, asking what right I have to make a picture? What right does he have to make one?"

Despite all the sound and fury, *The Alamo* received six Oscar nominations. They were for best sound, best song, best cinematography, and best score, and Chill Wills was nominated for best supporting actor. Duke was thrilled when the picture received the highest accolade of all. It was nominated as one of the year's best pictures.

But Duke's hopes of winning Oscars were dashed when Chill Wills began, in his own behalf, one of the most tasteless ad campaigns in the history of the awards. Wills took a full page in the *Hollywood Reporter* with a picture of the entire cast and crew standing in front of Duke's replica of the Alamo. The body of the ad read, "We of the Alamo cast are praying—harder than the real Texans prayed for their lives in the real Alamo—for Chill Wills to win the Oscar. Cousin Chill's acting was great!" The copy was signed, "Your Alamo cousins."

Duke felt compelled to put a denial in both the *Reporter* and *Variety*. The denial said, in part, "No one in the Batjac organization or in the Russell Birdwell office has been a party to his (Wills) advertising. I refrain from using stronger language because I am sure his (Wills) intentions were not as bad as his taste. Signed, John Wayne."

Duke wasn't surprised on Oscar night when *The Alamo* went down in defeat. The movie's only Oscar came in the category of best sound.

Eventually, thanks to worldwide release, *The Alamo* would earn an enormous profit, but by then Duke would no longer have a financial interest in the film. He was forced to sell his share of the movie to United Artists to pay back the money he'd borrowed to complete the film. Although Duke didn't make any profit from all his work, he had the satisfaction of having made a dream come true. And, after the deal with United Artists was finished, he could sleep better at night knowing we were solvent again.

Remarkably, Duke never voiced a single complaint about the way things turned out. He'd done his best and shown the world what was in his heart. Besides, he was too busy to spend time looking back and thinking "if only." Duke had agreed to do two films in 1961. The first, Henry Hathaway's *North to Alaska,* costarring Stewart Granger and Capucine, was a lighthearted comedy adventure. Duke threw himself into his part with zest and good humor. It's obvious, watching the picture today, that he was having a good time.

His next film, *The Comancheros,* marked the first time that his script didn't feature a romance for the character he was playing. This pleasant duty fell to his costar, Stuart Whitman, who romanced Ina Balin in the movie, who, by the way, played a character named Pilar.

Duke felt particularly pleased with *The Comancheros,* because it gave him an opportunity to concentrate on his new screen image. It was this image of mature and enduring strength that would make him a legend.

CHAPTER 20

Duke became a star during the forties, in an age of giants. Back then his peers included Spencer Tracy, Humphrey Bogart, Clark Gable, Gary Cooper, Tyrone Power, and Errol Flynn. By the sixties, death and retirement had decimated the ranks of his closest friends. Movie marquees now bore names like Newman, Redford, McQueen, and Eastwood. My husband's career and longevity linked Hollywood's golden age to the present and the future.

Grant Withers, the first of Duke's friends to go, died in 1959, while Duke was heavily involved in the preproduction of *The Alamo*. Withers, one of the actors who'd been a part of the Young Men's Purity, Total Abstinence and Yachting Association, took his own life. He'd become a tragic figure, an alcoholic who failed at many reform attempts during the last few years of his life. Defeated by his addiction, he'd washed down an overdose of sleeping pills with the contents of a bottle of vodka. His farewell note begged his friends "to forgive me for letting you down."

Duke was shaken when he read those words. This was one time in his life when he found himself looking back and thinking, "if only." He'd been party to a lot of Withers's drinking in the old days, when it had all seemed like such harmless fun. He'd never anticipated that any of his friends would pay so high a price for those drunken nights when all of them were the scourge of Mazatlan bars, laughing and consuming tequila until even the tolerant Mexicans wearied of all their partying.

Duke was at work when he learned of Withers's suicide. He came home early, terribly shaken, and later that night he sobbed in my arms as he recalled thirty years of friendship. There'd been a time when Duke and Josephine and Grant and his wife, Loretta Young, had been an inseparable foursome. "Sure Grant drank a little too much, even then," Duke remembered, "but what the hell, so did half of Hollywood. I guess I should have tried to stop him, but I didn't think he was hurting anybody, certainly not himself." Duke never fully grasped the fact that other people didn't have his capacity for or tolerance of alcohol.

He had a hard time coming to terms with Withers's death. But Duke was a strong man. He shed his private tears and went back to work, unaware that greater sadness lay ahead. In 1960, shortly after the premiere of *The Alamo*, Mary Lou Bond called early one evening with devastating news. Her husband, Ward, had just suffered a fatal heart attack.

Withers's death had been hard to take, and losing Bond, too, was unthinkable. Ward was only 55, a year or two older than Duke. After years of playing character roles, Bond had finally achieved an enormous and deserved success as the star of the top-rated television series, *Wagon Train*. Duke felt that fate had played a cruel trick on a very good man.

We stayed up late that night while Duke talked about the three decades he and Bond shared, from the day Duke tried to throw Bond off that Annapolis-bound train to the last time they'd worked together just a few months earlier. Ford had agreed to direct one of Bond's *Wagon Train* episodes, and Duke, breaking his self-imposed rule against appearing on television, agreed to do a brief guest appearance as Civil War hero General Sherman.

"They're going to bill me as Michael Morris," Duke told me. "I'll be on and off the screen so damn fast that the audience will go crazy, wondering if that was really John Wayne."

The taping had been a happy occasion, a chance to relive the camaraderie that Duke, Ford, and Bond enjoyed as younger men. The segment was scheduled for air time later that year, and they planned to watch it together. None of them could have foreseen that the screening would take place after Bond's death. There was no laughter in our home on November 25, 1960, three short weeks after Ward's funeral, as Duke and I watched Ward's last performance.

"There will never be another Ward Bond," Duke said sadly at

the end of the show. "I remember telling him, a hell of a long time ago, that he was too damn ugly to be a movie star. But I was wrong, Pilar. He was beautiful where it counted—on the inside."

Duke had been able to ignore the implications of Withers's death to a certain extent, but he couldn't ignore Bond's passing. For the first time in his life Duke faced his own mortality, and one more death would shatter Duke in the coming months. Beverly Barnett, who'd been Duke's publicist for a couple of decades, died in the spring of 1961. This series of bereavements hurt Duke deeply, and he was unable to be comforted for months. John Ford reacted to the tragedies by retreating into the religion of his childhood, seeking solace within the Catholic church, but there was no easy path to acceptance for John Wayne. When comfort finally came, it was in a very small package.

I began to suspect I might be pregnant during the filming of *The Comancheros*, but my queasy discomfort was eclipsed by the very real illness which afflicted the picture's aging director, Michael Curtiz. Curtiz was so sick that Duke often filled in for him on the set, directing the lighthearted comedy-adventure so deftly that no one would ever realize it wasn't Curtiz's work.

The film marked a reunion with some of the participants in *The Alamo*. Once again, William Clothier was responsible for the cinematography while Cliff Lyons directed the second-unit scenes in addition to coordinating the stunts. Patrick and Aissa had parts in this film as well. Despite our concern for Curtiz, we were a congenial bunch on location.

By the end of the shooting I felt sure that I was pregnant. But in view of three miscarriages I'd had over the six years since Aissa's birth, I didn't want to raise Duke's hopes until we returned to Encino where my obstetrician, Dr. Mitchelson, could give me a thorough examination.

Back home my pregnancy was confirmed and this time the doctor thought I'd have no difficulty carrying the baby to term. I was elated to have conceived again. And after the loss of so many close friends I couldn't have given Duke better news. Life would go on. The anticipation of a new baby lifted his spirits immensely. He felt like a young man again with his whole life ahead of him. Duke escaped from the recent tragedies by concentrating on Aissa and the unborn baby. They were a joy that kept him young in spirit and firmly tied to the future rather than the past. It was a renewed John Wayne who prepared to film his next picture, another Ford vehicle titled, *The Man Who Shot Liberty Valance*.

Reporters often asked Duke if the difference in our ages created any problems. I've never forgotten Duke chuckling as he replied, "The difference in our ages is not a problem! And if it ever gets to be one, I'll just have to find a younger woman." He liked the comment so well that he repeated it every time someone asked him that particular question.

To be truthful I'd never even thought about the age difference until Duke's friends started dying. And then I only thought about it because I couldn't bear the idea of something happening to Duke too. But he was so full of vitality and enthusiasm as we made ready for the baby that I put all considerations of age aside.

Duke and I were hoping for a boy to make our family complete, and I wanted to name him Michael after Duke, my brother, my father who'd died when I was in my early teens, and after Duke's oldest son. Duke understood my reasons for choosing the name. "But I'll have to discuss it with my Michael first," he said. "If he doesn't object, it's fine with me."

In a few days Duke told me that Michael had objected at great length. "He feels that Michael is a Wayne family name," Duke explained.

"But this baby will be a Wayne too," I objected.

"Hell, you know what I mean," Duke interrupted. "Gretchen is pregnant too, and they want to call their baby Michael. It would just be too damn confusing to have three Michaels in the same family."

I couldn't argue with that kind of logic. We still hadn't picked a boy's name as my due date drew closer, and this time I didn't have any sudden inspirations like the one which had led to naming Aissa.

One night, two weeks before the baby's predicted arrival, Duke and I were watching *The Searchers* on television. It was one of our favorite films, and seeing it again brought back a lot of happy

memories. I was completely absorbed in Duke's portrayal of the
obsessed Ethan Edwards when the perfect name popped into my
head. If we had a son we'd name him John Ethan Wayne and call
him Ethan. That way he would be named for both his father and
one of his father's favorite roles.

When I told Duke my idea he was enthusiastic. "I love it. John
Ethan Wayne, J. E. W. We'll have our own little jew in the family," he said with a grin.

It proved to be a timely decision. I went into labor an hour
later, and our son was born at six the following morning on February 22, 1962. Duke was ecstatic about Ethan. He said proudly
over and over to me and anyone who would listen, "Now we
have one of each." Duke sounded just like a little boy himself,
thrilled at having been given a new gift.

In the Wayne's topsy-turvy family, Duke now had two grandchildren—Michael's Alicia and Toni's Anita—who were older
than Ethan. Duke was completely absorbed by Aissa and Ethan
instead of doting on his grandchildren like other men his age.
Being a good father, in the limited time he had available for family life, was far more important to him than being a grandfather.
He lived for those two kids.

Duke's older children never accepted his priorities, and I
sympathize with their feelings to a degree. We tried hard to act
like one big happy family, but it didn't always work. I feel that
Michael and Duke never completely overcame their differences
although Duke relied on Michael more and more at Batjac. Toni
would draw close one minute, but in the next I would feel she
was distant again. Patrick was the friendliest of them all. Michael's beautiful blonde wife, Gretchen, totally accepted me and
my children. Like me, she was a Wayne by marriage rather than
birth.

When Melinda was planning her wedding to attorney Gregory
Munoz, all the old antipathies rose to the surface again. Aissa,
who loved and admired Melinda, had her heart set on being a
flower girl. I didn't think it was my place to talk to Melinda about
her wedding plans, but I told Aissa it would be all right if she
did.

I wasn't present during their conversation, and Aissa wasn't willing to talk about it afterward. Someone else who heard what happened told me that when Aissa told Melinda how much she wanted to be in the wedding, Melinda said, "That's impossible. Hasn't anyone told you that you're not my real sister?" Melinda went on to explain her personal belief that Duke and I weren't married in the eyes of God.

The conversation devastated Aissa and infuriated me. Duke had always emphasized the fact that his first and second families were brothers and sisters. They were all his children, and he expected them to love and care for one another.

The incident hurt Aissa so deeply that she never mentioned it or the wedding again. This time I wasn't surprised when I wasn't invited to the ceremony or the reception afterward. My anger made me want to tell Duke I would no longer have anything to do with his older children. But concern for his feelings made me hold my tongue. No matter how they treated me I wouldn't permit myself to be that cruel. Michael, Patrick, Toni, and Melinda would always be part of my husband's family and that made them part of mine.

Duke was so busy in the early sixties that we seldom had to confront the problems of blending two families. He was in great demand, professionally and socially.

Duke didn't belong to any of the groups, such as Sinatra's Rat Pack, that dotted the Hollywood social scene. We lived in Encino because he preferred a quiet life. Although he never chose his friends on the basis of their success in the film industry, there was one stellar event he wouldn't dream of missing.

SHARE had been founded by a group of Hollywood women who wanted to raise money for handicapped children. Their annual fund-raiser, the Boomtown party, was Duke's idea of a real wingding. The event had a western theme, and no one in pictures looked better or felt more comfortable in a cowboy costume than Duke. The evening's climax was a floor show starring the wives of producers, directors, and actors as well as stars such as Janet Leigh, Jeanne Mancini, Lucille Ball, Neile McQueen, and Cyd Charisse.

I wanted to be part of the show too, but Duke put his foot down when I suggested it. "Honey," he said, "I don't want you away from home." I should have anticipated his reaction. Duke was a jealous husband who monitored the length of my skirts, the depth of my décolletage, and the amount of time I spent talking to other men.

In those days Frank Sinatra was SHARE's angel. He came to all the parties, bringing other Rat Pack members. Dean Martin, Joey Bishop, Sammy Davis, Jr., and Sinatra could be relied on to take the stage some time during the evening, and they never failed to bring the house down.

A talent auction was another popular feature of the party. The master of ceremony might start by asking, "What am I bid for five minutes of Gene Kelly dancing?" I'll never forget one particular evening when Sammy Davis, Jr. was the emcee. Someone in the audience shouted, "I'll pay a thousand dollars to hear John Wayne sing 'The Shadow of Your Smile.'"

Duke promptly responded, "I'll pay two thousand if I don't have to."

Then Steve McQueen was on his feet. "I've got five thousand bucks that says you're going to do it, Duke."

Duke knew a setup when he saw one. He rose to his full height and bowed in Steve's direction before making his way to the stage. Duke wobbled and weaved in a perfect exaggeration of his own rolling gait as he staggered through the audience. By the time he took the mike everyone was rocking with laughter. Duke kept up his drunk act, almost flattening Sammy Davis, who struggled to support him while Duke warbled "The Shadow of Your Smile" in a dreadful, off-key monotone.

On our way home that night, Duke had an urgent need to use the men's room. He told our driver to stop at the next bar or restaurant. We pulled up in front of a run-down beer hall, and Duke uncoiled from the back seat. He strode through the establishment's front door and disappeared from my view.

Duke had dressed for the evening with special care. He wore silver-spurred boots, a matched pair of pearl-handled six-guns holstered snug against his hips, and a well-worn Stetson. He told me the men at the bar stared wide-eyed as he appeared in their midst. The only sound in the room was the k-ching, k-ching of his spurs as he strode to the restroom. When he emerged a few minutes later, the bar was still enveloped in silence. No one spoke as Duke walked back out the door, k-ching, k-chinging all the way.

Duke got back in our limousine and exploded into laughter. After describing the scene he asked, "What the hell do you suppose those guys will tell their wives?" And then, being Duke, he went back into the bar and bought those men a round of drinks.

The sixties saw a series of films which featured a glittering lineup of stars. Duke would appear in three of them during the decade. When Zanuck called from Europe in 1962 to offer Duke his choice of roles in *The Longest Day,* Duke was still smarting from Zanuck's reference to "poor old Duke." "I'm really not interested in doing a picture," Duke told the producer. "Pilar and I are thinking of taking a vacation."

Zanuck simply couldn't take no for an answer. He called the next day and the day after, and each time he called he raised the salary he was willing to pay for Duke's services. When his offer reached $250,000, "poor old Duke" finally agreed to appear in the picture. "What the hell," Duke said, grinning with satisfaction after the negotiations were concluded. "It might be highway robbery, but it serves the bastard right."

In 1963, after completing *Hatari,* Duke reprised his *Wagon Train* appearance as General Sherman. He played the role again in a John Ford-directed segment of the movie *How the West Was Won.* The small part paid $25,000, the customary salary for cameo roles but a tiny figure compared to the $600,000 or more that Duke was receiving for starring roles. However, he felt the chance to work with Ford in another western was more important than any salary considerations. The film would be the last western he and Ford would make.

Star-studded sagas such as *How the West Was Won* and *The Longest Day* were supposed to lure moviegoers away from their television sets and back into the theaters. Duke was in such demand that he could have worked in a half-dozen such films, but he decided to do just one more, George Stevens' *The Greatest Story Ever Told.*

Duke hadn't fared too badly in his first two cameo appearances. He wouldn't be as lucky with the last. Cast as the centurion who supervised the Crucifixion, Duke was far too recognizably "good old John Wayne," to be accepted in a Roman soldier's armor and toga. In Duke's final sequence, immediately following the death of Christ, Duke was to look up at the cross and say, "Truly, this man was the son of God."

Stevens was unhappy with Duke's delivery on the first take. Looking at Duke he said, "Put a little more awe into the line." Duke grinned, stared up at the cross and drawled in his best Wayne style, "Aaaw, truly this man was the son of God."

Throughout the sixties Duke's popularity continued to grow. While other filmmakers were spicing their pictures with sexually explicit scenes and graphic violence, Duke went right on making the kind of old-fashioned movies he'd been making all his life. The critics began to write about Duke as if he'd become the dinosaur of the film industry rather than its most successful star. In a *Saturday Evening Post* profile titled, "The Woes of Box Office King John Wayne," Dean Jennings wrote, "John Wayne is still tenaciously playing heroic leads in action pictures because he needs the money."

Jennings made a serious miscalculation. Box office kings seldom need money, and this one in particular was doing just fine financially, thanks to men like Zanuck. The steady stream of work had put Duke in a sound financial position again, a fact he celebrated by buying a magnificent new toy.

We had owned the *Nor'wester* since the early days of our marriage, but, at 75 feet, it wasn't the boat of Duke's dreams. He'd been looking for a new yacht when a friend called to tell him that *The Wild Goose,* a ship we knew and liked, was for sale.

The *Goose* was no ordinary boat. She was 136 feet of rebuilt mine sweeper with the best engines and navigational equipment. Her accommodations included a luxurious master suite, three guest staterooms with their own baths, a salon, a 60-foot afterdeck for sunning and relaxing, a dining room that could seat ten in comfort, a well-equipped galley, a liquor locker and bar, and crew's quarters that could accommodate eight. The minute Duke heard she was for sale he had to have her. Once the papers were signed he set about a remodeling job that would make her even more luxurious, paneling the main salon in a warm oak as well as installing a wood-burning fireplace and projection equipment.

Yachting was a traditional Hollywood pastime. Such stars as Errol Flynn, Dick Powell, Humphrey Bogart, and Clark Gable used boats to escape the public eye. Like them, Duke couldn't go out in public without being mobbed. Although he was just plain Duke to family and friends, he'd become the uncrowned king of the movie industry. The *Goose* became his refuge from the fans and the press who surrounded his every public appearance.

I don't think anyone in the nation, not even the president, was as well-known as Duke. In the sixties a few Republican party power brokers, hoping to capitalize on his popularity and well-documented conservatism, approached Duke about running on the national ticket. He thought the whole idea was pretty funny: "I can't afford the cut in pay. Besides," he added, "who in the world would vote for an actor?"

CHAPTER 21

Duke never accepted the offer to run for national office, but he did visit the White House several times, and some people still think he would have made a good public servant. In November 1985 President Ronald Reagan told reporters that his dream cabinet would have included John Wayne as secretary of state.

In the sixties when the press learned that Republican party leaders had talked to Duke, reporters hounded Duke for a scoop. When questioned, he gave them the kind of straightforward answer that is rarely associated with politicians.

"Is it true you've been asked to run for the presidency?" they asked.

"Bullshit!" Duke replied.

"Come on, Duke. Are you going to run? Give us a useable quote."

"I just did," Duke replied, keeping a straight face. "You can quote me. Bullshit!"

The next day one of the papers printed the following: "When Mr. Wayne was questioned about the possibility of running for national office he replied, 'B_____t.'" For once, Duke wasn't misquoted.

Always outspoken, often in the most colorful terms, Duke kept a high profile when it came to his own ideas. He had a low opinion of politics and most politicians, which didn't prevent presidents from wanting to meet him. He paid visits to the White House during the Roosevelt, Truman, and Eisenhower administrations before we married. Our first joint invitation to the Johnson White House came through Lynda Bird Johnson, who we met in Acapulco.

Duke and I took a yearly cruise to Acapulco, first in the *Nor-'wester* and then in the *Goose*. The trip, a family tradition, was made in the company of a few close friends and our children. Duke treasured the serenity of those vacations, and, although Acapulco was a famous resort, he preferred not to take part in the social life of the U.S. colony.

One night at a party in Beverly Hills we were introduced to Merle Oberon, who'd become the uncrowned queen of Acapulco's jet set. Oberon was a mystery woman of sorts. Born in Tasmania, her background was a publicist's dream or nightmare, depending on which Oberon history you believed. Alexander Korda, the most powerful figure in the British film industry, had launched Oberon's career and, in return, she'd married him.

Despite her exotic beauty, she'd never been popular with U.S. audiences. Retirement and a second marriage to an international businessman took her down to Acapulco, where she became known as an extraordinarily accomplished hostess with a keen eye for who was who.

With that background, Duke and I were surprised when she turned out to be warm and friendly. "I always see your boat in the harbor when you're in Acapulco," she said after we were introduced. "The next time you come down my way you must visit."

Her invitation didn't sound like the usual "we must get together sometime" cocktail party chatter, so the next time we were in Acapulco, Duke gave Oberon a call. From then on we visited whenever we were in town. We never knew who we would meet at her villa. On our second or third visit Oberon introduced us to Lynda Bird Johnson and her beau at the time, the actor George Hamilton. Duke wasn't very fond of Johnson's father's politics, but he liked her immediately. She had a down-home, Texas charm coupled with a sincere interest in people.

Lunches at Oberon's were usually served around the pool. Afterward her visitors would laze away the afternoon, talking or playing cards. Aissa and Ethan were always welcome at these informal meals, and they usually played with Oberon's adopted children, Bruno and Francesca, when they finished eating. Our children were seasoned travelers by then and took part in most of our activities. Since we spent so much time on our boat, they'd learned to swim almost before they could walk.

One afternoon while we lunched with Johnson, Hamilton, and Oberon, 3-year-old Ethan, bored with the adults, suddenly left the table and dived into the pool. He was a good swimmer, but Johnson had no way of knowing that. Before anyone could say a word she was on her feet, diving after Ethan. Seconds later she hauled a very irate little boy to the edge of the pool, where Duke reached down and lifted the two of them to the deck.

Before she jumped into the water Johnson had been wearing an attractive paper dress. They were a new fad, one doomed to failure because the dresses dissolved in water. Johnson wore nothing other than her underwear when Duke lifted her out of the pool. Four secret service men ran to her aid immediately. Armed with guns rather than spare dresses, they weren't much help.

Ethan took one disgusted look at his would-be rescuer and turned to his father. "Daddy," he said, "why did that crazy naked lady jump on me?"

A few months later we received a formal White House invitation to a dinner in honor of the king and queen of Thailand. The accompanying note read, "I hope you can join us. Tell your adorable son I promise not to throw myself at him again." It was signed "Lynda Johnson."

I was thrilled at the thought of attending, but Duke had reservations. He read the invitation a few times and then shook his head, saying, "I can't go, Pilar. I'm a Republican!"

"I'm sure the Johnsons know that," I replied. Duke's party loyalty was no secret. He even kept a framed portrait of Senator Hubert Humphrey hanging over the toilet in the guest bathroom, inscribed, "Dear Duke, thanks for your continued support." This time I made up my mind that my husband would have to put his personal prejudices aside. "Duke Wayne," I said, "I don't care what you are. We are going!"

During our flight to Washington I couldn't stop talking about the invitation. "Who do you think we'll be seated with?" I asked.

"Don't get your hopes up," Duke replied. "They probably just asked us because Lynda insisted. Hell. Everyone knows what I think of the Democrats. We'll probably be seated behind a potted palm."

Nothing Duke had told me prepared me for the pageantry when we arrived at the White House the next evening. Limousine after limousine pulled up under a brilliantly lit portico, discharging passengers whose faces appeared on the front page of newspapers.

I had an enormous lump in my throat when we were escorted to a large reception room where cocktails were being served. The United States of America is one of the few places on the face of the earth where people like Duke and me, an Iowa farm boy and an immigrant from Peru, can have the kind of life we'd had and the kind of success that results in an invitation to dinner at the White House. I know Duke shared my feelings, because he held my hand tightly and actually smiled back at all those Democrats.

Shortly after we arrived, we heard a drum roll which preceded the sound of a military band playing "Hail to the Chief." Then the Johnsons made their entrance accompanied by the king and queen of Thailand. The four of them stood in a receiving line while all the guests filed past. When introduced to the president, I was surprised to find myself looking up at a man who was as tall as my husband. After the formal reception, President Johnson joined us as we stood talking to his daughter Lynda.

"I'm quite a fan of yours," he told Duke, "and every now and then, when I'm back home in Texas wearing boots and a Stetson, someone mistakes me for you. Seeing you again, I must say I'm flattered. Perhaps, if they ever make a movie about my life, you'd consider playing me."

Dinner was served in the main ballroom. The guests were escorted to their seats by uniformed aides while forty violinists played music by Lerner and Loew. The table service, with its impressive presidential seal, sparkled in the light of antique crystal chandeliers. I was surprised to find myself seated at a prominent table, and even more surprised when two seats across from me stayed empty after everyone was seated. I was wondering who'd be foolish enough to miss the evening when President Johnson walked up to the chairs and seated Queen Sirikit in one of them, taking the other himself.

My pulse rate doubled immediately, and butterflies fluttered in my stomach. What in the world do you talk to a president about? I asked myself. Henry Ford II, a gentleman I knew, sat next to me, but he was already engrossed in conversation. I glanced at Queen Sirikit in the vain hope that she might start the conversation. She smiled back at me, but I soon learned that Sirikit didn't speak English. She wouldn't say a thing throughout the five-course meal.

Then I remembered that Lyndon Johnson had recently become a grandfather. I may not have known much about international events, but babies were my forte, so I asked him about his first grandchild, and I didn't have to worry about introducing another topic for the rest of the meal. Feeling that I'd acquitted myself like an experienced diplomat, I was still floating when Duke and I returned to our hotel suite.

We were to visit the White House again several years later on the occasion of the return of the Vietnam POWs. Duke and other celebrities who'd been asked to provide the entertainment for the evening had all spent time in Vietnam touring with the USO. Duke had spent a month there in 1967. If it had been up to Duke, every returning Vietnam veteran would have had a tickertape parade.

President Nixon sent Air Force One to Los Angeles to pick us up. Celebrities on board included Bob and Dolores Hope, Jimmy and Gloria Stewart, Edgar and Frances Bergen, and Connie Francis.

Duke and I were used to flying first-class, but we'd never seen anything as luxurious as that plane. Each couple had a private sitting room-bedroom with its own bath. We'd never seen a telephone on a plane before, but this one had several, and we couldn't resist calling a few friends and asking, "Guess where we are?"

So many people had been invited to the reception that it was held in a large tent on the White House lawn. Bob Hope was the master of ceremonies, with the tough job of lightening up a very solemn occasion. I couldn't imagine how he'd get us laughing, but Bob rose to the challenge. He opened his monologue by saying, "Well, what do you know? Here I am talking to a captive audience."

Duke made a short speech next. His brief words were touching, but the tears in his eyes said it all.

CHAPTER 22

Duke loved the ocean, and most of our family vacations were spent aboard the *Nor'wester* and the *Goose*. Though Duke is best remembered for westerns, he made thirteen films where the major action sequences take place at sea. In a way, because he first came to John Ford's notice during the filming of *Submarine*, Duke owed his entire career to the sea.

One of the funniest episodes of his career took place on a U.S. Navy ship during the filming of John Ford's *Wings of Eagles*. As the Navy pilot, Spig Wead, Duke had a brief glimpse of the life he might have known if his dream of going to the U.S. Naval Academy had become a reality.

Part of the filming was actually done aboard Navy destroyers. Ford had served in the Navy during World War II and enjoyed acting the salty old sea dog for my somewhat envious husband. Halfway through the shooting Ford asked Duke if he'd be willing to ride a bosun's chair during a sequence that had been slated to be carried out by a stuntman. Duke knew Ford was challenging him. If he refused he'd never live it down. The shot called for Duke to ride the bosun's chair from one destroyer to the other while both ships were under way. Duke decided it didn't sound too difficult—what the hell, it might even be fun.

Ford was delighted to hear Duke agree so readily, because he knew something Duke didn't—John Wayne was in for the ride of his life! He would be sitting in a fragile chair suspended on a cable between two ships as they raced across a heaving ocean. Regular Navy officers had been known to grow pale at the thought of making such a transfer. Ford concealed his glee as he watched two seamen strap Duke in the chair.

Duke looked at the fragile rigging, and suddenly the other ship seemed a hell of a long way off. But Ford was acting so matter of fact that Duke didn't dare express a single doubt. He gave everyone a big grin and a thumbs-up sign, and the terrifying crossing was under way. Duke knew that every eye was on him, to say nothing of the camera. Look confident, he commanded himself. You're an actor. Pretend you're having the time of your life! After what seemed like an eternity, he reached the other ship. He told me his knees shook as he was helped from the chair.

The next day Duke received the following message from the Navy Department: "Dear Mr. Wayne—We are pleased to record this latest addition to naval lore. To the immortal expression, 'damn the torpedoes, full speed ahead,' we now add your own memorable words, 'get me out of this son of a bitch.'"

In Duke's sea stories he played everything from a deckhand to an officer. After playing a captain in *In Harm's Way* in 1964, Duke retired from the celluloid navy forever. From then on all his sailing would be on the *Goose*, his dream ship.

Our first trips in the *Goose* were relatively easy excursions, up and down the Baja coast. But Duke was anxious to put his ship to the ultimate challenge, a transatlantic crossing. The perfect opportunity came when one of his favorite directors, Henry Hathaway, offered him a role in *Circus World*, a film Hathaway planned to shoot in Spain.

Duke and I had made two Atlantic crossings in huge liners. This time he planned to cross the Atlantic aboard the *Goose*. He organized the voyage with the same care and attention to detail that he put into the preproduction of *The Alamo*. We would be away from home for a whole year or more. The trip would begin with the now familiar voyage down the Baja coast to Acapulco. We'd spend a week or two there, visit Merle Oberon, and then head down the Mexican coast and on to Panama to visit Duke's old friends and business partners the Arias brothers.

From the Canal we sailed across the Gulf of Mexico to San Blas Island and then on to Bermuda. The children and I would disembark there because Duke considered the next leg of the trip too risky for women and children. With an augmented crew of eight he planned to take the *Goose* straight across the Atlantic, six days of steady steaming. The children and I would wait until we heard he'd made the crossing safely, and then we'd rejoin the *Goose* on the Portuguese coast.

I spent five days sitting by the phone hoping to hear word of my husband, praying that all would be well. The *Goose* wasn't a small ship, but there was an element of danger in taking her across the Atlantic in the spring. On the fifth day the phone finally rang. I'll never forget Duke's cheerful voice calling from the Azores. It was such a relief to talk to him again, to know that he and the crew were safe.

Two weeks later, flying over Lisbon's harbor, I saw the *Goose* far beneath us, a tiny white speck in a turquoise sea. That small speck would be home for the next few months. Duke met us at the airport, still exhilarated from his Atlantic crossing. For once in his life he hadn't just played the part of an intrepid sea captain, he'd actually lived it. The dangerous crossing proved to be the high point of the months he spent aboard the *Goose*.

We planned to sail along the Portuguese and Spanish coasts, through the Straits of Gibraltar and on to Palma De Mallorca, a mountainous island several hundred miles from Barcelona. Skip Hathaway, Henry's wife, would be with us during that part of the voyage as well as our dear friends, Marjorie and Ralph Wingfield. Duke, who enjoyed company, had made plans for friends to join us in almost every port he planned to visit. William and Ardis Holden were scheduled to meet us in Mallorca. They were to be with us for two weeks while we sailed around the island, stopping in various ports along the way.

Duke's friendship with Bill Holden began during their early years in Hollywood. They had the same agent, Charlie Feldman, and they'd partied together often in their youth. For the last few years Holden had been spending most of his time in Africa, where he had a part interest in the Mount Kenya Safari Club in Nairobi. We hadn't seen Bill since Duke made *Hatari* in Tanganyika, and we looked forward to a marvelous reunion. Duke planned to play cards with Bill while I explored the shops with Ardis. The last thing we expected was to be burdened with a couple who quarreled all the time.

Shortly after the Holdens joined us, it became apparent to Duke and me that they were in the midst of a marital crisis. They either fought like the worst of enemies or treated one another with an icy politeness that made everyone uncomfortable. Bill, who'd always been a heavy drinker, made an all-out effort to drown his current sorrows. He began his mornings with Bloody Marys and drank steadily throughout the day. Duke, to be a good host, often joined him.

Unless you really knew Duke, it was hard to tell when he'd been drinking. He didn't become morose or argumentative. In fact, he was a happy drunk who laughed easily and often. Bill held his liquor equally well, but the more he drank, the more he and Ardis fought. Their constant bickering became a burden. We were enjoying a second honeymoon, a period of our marriage when we were completely in tune with one another, and our happiness played an incongruous counterpoint to the Holdens' deteriorating relationship. Duke and I were both relieved, if a bit saddened, when they flew back to Africa.

We weren't alone very long. While we moored in Monte Carlo, Grace Kelly, David Niven, and Aristotle Onassis joined us on the Goose. I'd met Niven and Kelly before, but Onassis' visit was completely unexpected. Despite his ordinary appearance, Onassis was a compelling personality. After spending a little time with him it wasn't hard to understand why a woman such as Maria Callas had found him irresistible. His dark eyes would gaze at you with hypnotic intensity while he concentrated on your every word—five minutes with Ari Onassis made you think you were the most brilliant conversationalist in the world.

Onassis insisted that he have a chance to return our hospitality, and he was the kind of man one didn't refuse. Duke and I were anxious to see the fabled Christina, a yacht so huge that she made our own Goose look like a bathtub toy. When we stayed on the Christina a few days later, we discovered that her guest staterooms were larger than the master suite on the Goose. Our bathroom had marble-covered walls and malachite fixtures. Onassis told us that he kept stewards on call twenty-four hours a day to see to his guests' needs. Duke took a perverse pleasure in ringing for champagne at midnight and sandwiches at two in the morning. But Onassis hadn't exaggerated the care his guests received.

Duke loved unexpected visitors. During this phase of our trip,

Henry Ford II, my former White House dinner companion, and his wife, also popped in to say hello. When we sailed to Porto Fino on the Italian Riviera, Jack Hawkins, an English actor, simply walked aboard one day and introduced himself. He and Duke hit it off so well that Duke insisted that Hawkins stay with us for a while. Hawkins was another of those charming Englishmen, like Lawrence Harvey, with an abundance of amusing stories and an ability to hold his liquor—a requisite when cruising with Duke.

Our most unusual surprise visitor literally swam to the *Goose's* side when we were moored in the harbor at Acapulco on our way home. He climbed up to the deck, saying, "Mr. Wayne, I hope you don't mind, but I've always been a fan of yours and I couldn't think of any other way to meet you." The intrepid frogman was astronaut Buzz Aldrin, the second man to walk on the moon.

Our vacation came to an end in Porto Fino when Henry Hathaway sent word that *Circus World* was ready to go before the cameras. We flew straight to Madrid, where we'd already rented a villa belonging to Ava Gardner. She'd shared this home with Frank Sinatra during their well publicized, stormy love affair, and the neighbors still talked about the two of them and their noisy disagreements. I wasn't surprised to hear about Sinatra's violent temper. Duke had experienced problems with the volatile singer in the past. Back in 1960, when Sinatra was one of Hollywood's most outspoken supporters of liberal causes and Democratic party candidates, he hired Albert Maltz, one of the infamous "Hollywood Ten" to write a screenplay. The script in question was *The Execution of Private Slovik*, a tragic story which showed the U.S. military in an unfavorable light. Duke was furious when he learned that Frank had chosen Maltz to write a screenplay about one of the saddest episodes in U.S. military history.

The Maltz affair soon became a battleground for liberals and conservatives, and Duke was in the thick of it. The papers quoted him saying, "I wonder how Sinatra's crony, Senator John Kennedy, feels about Sinatra hiring such a man? I'd like to know Kennedy's attitude, because he's the one who is making plans to run the administrative government of our country."

Faced by the growing tumult, Sinatra backed down, paying Maltz a reported $75,000 not to write the screenplay. The next time Sinatra saw us was at a charity benefit. He had been drinking heavily and was obviously looking for a fight. He walked up to Duke, snarling, "You seem to disagree with me."

Duke had no intention of letting Sinatra provoke a fight. "Take it easy," Duke said. "We can talk about this later on."

"What's wrong with right now?" Sinatra really seemed to be looking for trouble but a few of his friends pulled him away just in time.

Gardner's villa was barely livable, which may have contributed to Sinatra's irritability when he shared it with her. The rooms were cold and drafty, not an ideal situation for our two small children, the kitchen and bathrooms were inadequate, and the pool was unheated and dirty. Melinda, the youngest of Duke's first family, and Peggy Hunt, Patrick Wayne's socialite fiancée, joined us within a few weeks. This was to be a last vacation for the two girls, one final fling before they settled into married life.

I was happy to have their company because Duke was working from first to last light on *Circus World*. He'd made several Hathaway pictures by then, including *North to Alaska* and *Legend of the Lost*. Hathaway was a fine director, but he worked his cast and crew very hard. He particularly enjoyed challenging Duke with the physical aspects of a part. When Duke worked in a Hathaway film I knew he'd come home late, have a quick dinner, and fall asleep.

The picture was proving to be a disappointment. It was Duke's first film with Rita Hayward, and he soon swore it would be his last. She habitually arrived on the set late, her lines unmemorized, her moods mercurial. Dining out with her in public turned out to be a mistake too. We were sorry to observe that Rita couldn't handle alcohol, not even half a glass of wine, without becoming belligerent. Later in her life this talented beauty would tragically develop Alzheimer's disease.

Circus World seemed to be a shining example of the Murphy's law. If anything could go wrong it did! The script was an ongoing problem. Minor accidents and language difficulties with the Spanish crew were an everyday occurrence.

In the midst of filming we learned that John Kennedy had been assassinated in Dallas. Although Duke abhorred Kennedy's politics, losing such a young, vital president was a terrible shock. Our Ethan and the Kennedy's John-John were close in age, as were Caroline Kennedy and Aissa. The picture of those two fatherless children clinging to their mother during their father's funeral brought tears to our eyes. We got word from friends at home that the entire nation had come to a stop as the sad events unfolded on television.

We struggled to go on with our work. The movie was slated to have a spectacular climax, a frightening scene where the big top would catch on fire and Duke, as Matt Masters, would lead the fight against the flames. What actually happened was more dramatic than the scriptwriter could have anticipated.

Hathaway didn't want Duke to use a double although the sequence would take five days to shoot. When I voiced my concern about what sounded like rather dangerous work, Duke said, "Hell, Pilar, it's my job. It's what I get paid for." Duke had never backed away from any of the dangerous sequences in his various roles. He trusted his directors and stunt coordinators, certain they wouldn't put him in a situation they couldn't control. This fire sequence had been carefully plotted. Duke wore fireproof garments under his costume, working close to the flames, in the smoke hour after hour. He came home at night, exhausted, barely able to eat a decent meal before falling into bed, but he coughed so hard after he lay down that he couldn't really rest.

"Please tell Henry that you have to use a double," I said when neither of us could sleep.

"Don't worry, honey," Duke replied, "I'll be fine once the fire scene is finished."

The last day of shooting Duke was armed with an axe and, as Matt Masters, had to create a firebreak to save the circus animals. Despite all the crew's precautions the carefully planned fire got out of control, creeping closer and closer as Duke swung his axe tirelessly. He stayed in the midst of the growing inferno, his vision obscured by choking smoke, unaware that everyone else had fled. He didn't want to go through the smoky torture of another take, so he stayed where he was, waiting to hear Henry shout "Cut."

Duke didn't leave the burning set until the flames singed his hair. Emerging from the smoke, he realized the set was deserted. In a fury, he threw his axe across the sound stage. He'd been eating smoke, choking on the stuff, and the cameraman hadn't even been there to film the action.

I was shocked by Duke's condition when he got home that night. His eyes were red-rimmed, and he could barely tell me, between prolonged coughing spasms, what had gone wrong. I insisted that he go straight to bed.

At that moment, I couldn't wait to get away from the picture and the villa. Disaster seemed to cling to both of them. We'd had our own household accident a few days earlier. Ethan had sat on one of the space heaters I used to keep those drafty rooms warm, and he'd gotten a nasty burn. He was still in diapers, and every time he got wet those burns really hurt.

Unlike Ethan, Duke didn't complain. I didn't think his problem would be much more serious than his son's. But he coughed nonstop that first night. By morning I felt sure he had to be bringing up blood along with phlegm. But it never occurred to us to look beyond the events of the last few days for the cause of his illness, since anyone would have coughed from the work he'd been doing. Duke was too big and strong to be seriously ill—at least that's what I told myself.

When the exterior shooting was finished, we moved on to London for the filming of the interior scenes. The cold, damp weather didn't agree with Duke, and his hacking cough continued throughout our stay. I began to nag him, something I'd never done before.

"You've got to see a doctor," I insisted day after day.

"I'll be fine," he said, "as soon as we get out of this damn climate."

His health did seem to improve when we left England to fly to Acapulco, where we rejoined the *Goose* which had sailed on ahead of us. Duke needed a peaceful, sun-filled voyage home, a time to rest and regain his strength. But a tragic accident occurred off the Mexican coast. Duke had done everything possible to ensure a safe voyage for everyone. No one could have foreseen three of our crew trying to row out to the *Goose* with too much tequila under their belts. Their dinghy capsized, and all three drowned.

Duke felt responsible. He wouldn't listen when people told him the whole thing was an accident. The tragedy cast a pall over the final leg of our trip. When we got home to Encino, Duke needed a rest. I longed to put him in bed for a few days, but he'd already signed to star opposite Pat Neal in *In Harm's Way*. The picture would be made in Hawaii, and we were scheduled to leave immediately.

Neal and Duke had worked together in 1951, starring in *Operation Pacific*. She was the kind of quietly confident woman he liked most as a costar, and they had chemistry on screen. Neal and her husband, the writer Roald Dahl, were amusing and entertaining companions on location. Kirk Douglas, another of Duke's favorite costars, would play Duke's antagonist in this film. Kirk's intense, barely controlled energy served as a perfect foil for Duke's calm, steadfast manner. *In Harm's Way* had all the ingredients for an excellent film, including a gifted director, Otto Preminger. And we had every reason to be happy in one of our favorite places with some of our favorite people. But Duke's coughing continued. It began to interrupt the shooting, and soon everyone was aware of his deteriorating health—everyone but him. He refused to see a doctor while we were on the island. I'd been praying that Hawaii's temperate climate would restore Duke's health. Instead his cough grew worse.

"You've got to see a doctor," I insisted, again and again.

Duke finally agreed. "I'll check into Scripps as soon as we get back." he promised.

He made an annual trip to the Scripps Clinic in La Jolla to qualify for the expensive insurance that movie companies carry on their stars. Now we moved the checkup date forward a few months.

I always went with him during these stays. He insisted on having twin beds in his room so we could be together. Duke was like a little boy about his checkups, demanding that I have every test he did. I used to hate those checkups; there wasn't a reason in the world for me to submit to all that poking and prodding. However, by the time we left Hawaii, I could hardly wait to get to the clinic.

No matter how he tried to conceal his condition, I knew Duke was very sick. On the second day at Scripps I returned from one of my own tests to find him already in our room, sitting on one of the beds.

"I've got a little problem," he said, refusing to meet my eyes. "The doc says I've got a spot on my lung. But don't worry, honey. He thinks it's just valley fever."

Duke was a terrible liar. Choking back tears, I said, "What are they going to do?"

His voice was a hoarse monotone as he answered. "I'm scheduled for exploratory surgery in a few days, at Good Samaritan Hospital."

CHAPTER 23

Duke and I had two weeks between his diagnostic visit to the Scripps Clinic and his scheduled surgery at Good Samaritan, two weeks to prepare ourselves for what lay ahead. Despite Duke's use of euphemisms such as valley fever, I knew he faced a far more serious illness. Neither of us was able to say the word "cancer" because, back in 1964, a diagnosis of lung cancer was a virtual death sentence.

Duke was 57 years old at the time, but he looked and acted at least ten years younger. He had a 2-year-old son and an 8-year-old daughter, and he adored both of them. They'd given him a feeling of being young again. After years of struggle, he'd established a unique place for himself in the annals of American film. We were happy as a couple and a family. What kind of God, I asked myself, would jeopardize a man's life just as he came to know true happiness?

Duke was a pragmatic man who regarded organized religion as little more than mumbo jumbo. He believed in a God he could talk to any time, any place. Duke didn't pray in the usual sense. Instead, he seemed to strike bargains with God.

After we married I heard him say, "Lord, I'll settle for just five more happy years." By the time we had Aissa and Ethan, Duke was upping the ante and trying for an additional ten. I wouldn't allow myself to believe that God wouldn't grant them.

As far as Duke was concerned, the issue never seemed to be in doubt. He intended to win this fight. He never made any of the cautious preparations other men make when faced with a life-threatening illness. He never had his lawyer make special trips to the house, never spoke to me about any final arrangements,

The Waynes and the Reagans.

With Pilar, meeting Princess Margaret at the London premiere of *The Alamo*.

Arriving at the 1958 Academy Award presentations in Hollywood. (AP/Wide World Photos)

The family man, with daughter Aissa and Pilar, just after son
Ethan's birth. (Joseph Bell)

With son Ethan on location.

With Ethan, Marisa and friend.

With daughter Marisa at USC campus in L.A., where Duke threw out the first ball during celebrity baseball game. (Galella)

Wayne family portrait.

On deck of the beloved *Goose*.

With brother, Bob, and Pilar's dog, Blackie.

In Berlin, 1956, for German premiere
of the *The Conqueror*. (AP/Wide World
Photos)

In Rome, 1956, with Sophia Loren in a shooting gallery. (AP/Wide
World Photos)

With friend Andy De-
vine (left), and Ernie
Saftig (right).

With Jane Wyman,
1952.

With William Holden and Althea Gibson, 1958, upon her selection for second straight year as female athlete of the year in annual AP poll. (AP/Wide World Photos)

With Barbara Stanwyck after she presented him and producer A. C. Lyles with the Golden Spurs Award at Paramount Studios, 1966. (AP/Wide World Photos)

With Bogie, Betty and son on location in San Raphael, California, during filming of *Blood Alley*.

Receiving Cecil B. De-Mille award from Dean Martin in 1966 for outstanding contributions to the entertainment industry. (AP/Wide World Photos)

In 1967, visiting Vietnam casualty patients at U.S. Army Hospital on Okinawa. (AP/Wide World Photos)

At 1971 Golden Globe
Awards with Joan
Crawford. (Galella)

With Myrna Loy and
Robert Young at "A
Tribute to Joan Craw-
ford" in 1977. (Galella)

With Loretta Young.
(Galella)

With Gloria and Jimmy Stewart at "All-Star Tribute to Jimmy
Stewart" in 1977. (AP/Wide World Photos)

The Academy
Awards, 1975.
(Galella)

In March 1978, with Peter and Henry Fonda at tribute in honor
of Henry at the American Film Institute. (Galella)

Receiving Oscar for *True Grit*, 1970. (AP/Wide World Photos)

With Barbra after she presented Oscar to Duke. (AP/Wide World Photos)

True Grit.

didn't try to see any of his closest friends to say goodbye. Other than staying a little closer to home, it was business as usual.

His closest associates worried far more than Duke. His agent, Charlie Feldman, his son Michael, and his son-in-law, Don La-Cava, were all concerned about the immediate future. They urged my husband to hide the true reason for his hospitalization in order to protect Duke's career.

"You'll never work again once the studios hear you've got cancer," Feldman warned. At the time cancer was talked about only in hushed tones.

"If I still have cancer after the operation," Duke replied with a touch of irony, "it won't matter." His instincts told him to be honest—with the press, with his fans, with his potential employers, but the panic he saw in the other men's eyes began to get to him. It would be a hell of a joke if he lived through the operation and never worked again. Deep down, Duke wasn't sure he'd want to go on living if he couldn't go on working. Making movies was more necessary to his well-being than an arm or a leg—or a lung. He could live without the lung if he had to, but he couldn't live without his work.

"All right," he agreed, looking at Feldman. "We'll do it your way. But what the hell do we tell the press when they find out I'm in the hospital?"

"Let's say you're being treated for an old football injury," Feldman suggested.

Duke agreed, though he felt uncomfortable with the lie. He'd been trapped by his own growing legend. John Wayne, the movie hero, was strong, invincible, immune to the slings and arrows of outrageous fortune. He wanted his fans and the studios to continue thinking of him that way.

Duke still led the list of box office draws, but the roles he was offered were becoming more stereotyped, more tailored to fit the image he'd spent so much time and energy developing. John Wayne, cancer victim, might never work again. The illness could destroy his credibility as an indestructible hero. Faced with a choice between reality and his image, he reluctantly chose the image. I felt uncomfortable with his decision. I'm a very bad liar, and I'd be the one facing the press, telling lies while he recuperated. But I didn't dare argue with him during his last week at home.

He tried to conceal his apprehension, unwilling or unable to share his anxiety. Late one night he finally confessed that his constant coughing reawakened childhood memories of hearing his tubercular father cough in the stillness of a desert night. To be ill was torture for such a physical man. To have the illness remind him of such an unhappy period of his life seemed doubly cruel.

His smoking had been heavy before, but now it intensified. I never saw him without a cigarette in his hand. He was constantly on the go, playing bridge, screening films he wanted to see, spending time with the children, working on the script for a television spot he planned to do for Senator Goldwater's presidential campaign, streaking through the days in a race against the clock.

Duke filled every minute as if keeping busy would keep us from thinking about what lay ahead. We talked about the weather, the children, what to have for dinner, anything and everything except what was uppermost on both our minds. I waited for him to say something, anything that would permit us to lighten the burden by sharing it.

The lack of genuine communication intensified my fear, forcing me to confront the fact that Duke and I had never communicated about things that really bothered us. Our life had been lived at such a frantic pace that it had been enough to talk about events rather than feelings. Waiting for the surgery, an event we couldn't discuss, we talked about small things. Duke kept the door to his deepest feelings carefully closed.

My nights became filled with terrible dreams. I saw Duke dead, my children fatherless. I'd wake bathed in an icy sweat, wishing I could fall on my knees and beg God to spare him. I could conquer the world with Duke at my side—without him I was nothing. I'd never tried to make a life for myself or even imagined one without him. If anything, I loved him more, knowing his faults. Duke's tough exterior concealed a gentle inner core, a powerful need for love and approval. I couldn't bear the thought of losing him.

By the time we walked through Good Samaritan's doors my nerves were raw. Duke laughed and joked with the staff, and I smiled steadily. Few people knew what Duke faced. He'd insisted on shielding his mother from the truth. She'd been told the valley fever story. Mary St. John, Charlie Feldman, and a few Batjac employees were the only nonfamily to know the real reason Duke was checking into the hospital.

The morning of the operation, Michael, Patrick, Melinda, and Toni gathered in Duke's room. I'd stayed the night before, watching Duke sleep with the help of a sedative. Suddenly he no longer seemed to belong to me. Nurses came in and out of the room, checking him. The surgeon stopped by early in the morning. They surrounded Duke with the possessive cloak of hospital care. His well-being, his life, was in their hands, not mine.

Duke was taken to surgery on the morning of September 17, 1964. He waved a groggy goodbye from the gurney, still very much John Wayne. Feeling a desperate need for another woman's understanding and companionship, I was about to ask Toni to stay with me during the surgery when Michael said that he would keep the vigil. I wasn't comfortable in his presence, and throughout that horrible day I felt as if I ought to be playing hostess, when what I wanted to do was pace the floor, weep, chew my nails, or pull my hair if I chose. I felt as if my insides were being ripped apart.

Michael managed to keep up a constant stream of soothing remarks, which I barely heard. I'd been thinking about what Duke would want me to do if he didn't make it. After Ward Bond's funeral, Duke told me he wanted to be cremated when his time came, his ashes scattered in the sea by Catalina Island. "I hate funerals," he'd said, having just gone through the pain of eulogizing his best friend. The service for Ward Bond had been long and sorrowful. "When I die I want you to take all my friends to the house and have one hell of a party for me. I didn't have the guts to cremate my father the way he wanted. Don't be like me, Pilar."

Duke's words were still on my mind when Michael touched my arm. "I've tried everything I can think of to take your mind off the operation," he said, "but you're not really with me, are you?"

My heart and soul were in the operating room with Duke. Every muscle in my body ached with tension. Time passed so slowly that I began to think all the clocks had stopped. Morning had drifted into a bright sun-filled afternoon before the doctor finally came into the room where we waited. By then Duke's other children had returned, although I'd hardly been aware of their arrival.

"Mrs. Wayne," the doctor said, coming to my side, "your husband came through the surgery very well. We found a large tumor on his left lung and had to remove it with the lung."

Duke, who was such a physical man, would wake up to find he had just one lung. "And the cancer," I said, my voice sounding far too loud in the quiet waiting room, "is he cured?"

"Well, we can't be sure," Dr. Jones said. "These things aren't cut and dried. I removed all the cancer, but we can't call it a cure for five years. If the cancer doesn't recur, there's no reason why your husband can't live a relatively normal life."

I wanted to scream. How could they say Duke would be the same when they cut him up like that? Did the doctor really believe an active man, an actor who still did so many of his own stunts, would be able to go on with just one lung? "When can I see him?" I asked.

"Right now," the doctor answered, taking my arm. "But your husband is still unconscious. He's heavily sedated and on oxygen. Don't be alarmed by his appearance, Mrs. Wayne. He's had a very difficult day, but he came through it in good shape."

Duke was in intensive care, his body hooked to machines. An intravenous unit hung suspended near the head of his bed, and a clear fluid trickled down a long tube through a needle and into his arm. His heart was being monitored, and I could watch the slow, rhythmic blip on a screen. His chest was heavily bandaged, his skin so pale that it seemed as white as the ivory layers of gauze and tape that circled his entire torso.

He lay unmoving and blessedly unaware. His breathing sounded labored, far worse than it had before the operation. Tears flooded my eyes. God, poor Duke. He looked shrunken, as vulnerable and helpless as a child.

The doctor assured me that Duke would be all right, but I knew he didn't understand Duke's definition of "all right." Duke hated aging, hated anything that placed limitations on his ability to live life on his own terms. At 50 his hair had grown thin, and he'd submitted to the indignity of wearing toupees. Lately, the studio had been urging him to consider plastic surgery. But these were small things, merely cosmetic. How would Duke feel about himself when he woke up and realized he was missing most of one lung and two ribs? How would he handle the weeks of recuperation? If I knew my husband, he would hate every minute. Patience wasn't one of his virtues.

He woke up hours later, and I told him the operation had been a complete success. "Don't worry, sweetheart, they got it all," I assured him. "You're going to be fine."

He tried to smile, but a spasm of coughing shook his body, and the smile changed into an agonized grimace. Duke continued to cough off and on all through that day and the next, and each time pain tore through him. He had a 2-foot-long incision encircling his left side. The slightest movement was agonizing, the coughing was murderous. Instead of gathering strength, Duke grew worse.

The day following the operation, Duke began to swell as if his body and face were a balloon being slowly inflated by a mysterious pump. By the third day his right eyelid had grown so distended that it covered both eyes and part of his face. I had to gently push the mass aside to let him see me.

Fortunately, drugs spared him from knowing how monstrous he looked. He later told me that in his brief moments of self-awareness, he was convinced his kidneys had failed, and that meant inevitable death.

Duke's appearance didn't bother me half as much as not knowing what caused the edema. The doctor would come into Duke's room, trailing consultants, and they would look at my husband, prodding and poking and shaking their heads. I was frantic for answers, but they had none to offer.

While Duke lay in the hospital, looking and sounding as if each hour might be his last, we learned that his brother, Bobby, also a heavy smoker, had lung cancer too.

The days were a torture, the nights worse. Duke floated in and out of consciousness while the doctors waited for the swelling to go down or worsen before they decided what to do. Meanwhile I had two small children at home who needed me and a husband I couldn't leave for fear he'd die while I was gone. The few times I dared step out of the hospital the press waited for me, wanting to know what was really wrong with John Wayne.

Someone had leaked word that Duke had thoracic surgery, and finally one reporter asked if my husband had cancer.

"No, he doesn't!" I replied. I almost choked on the words.

The days had begun to blur into each other, so I'm not sure if it was the fourth or fifth one following the initial operation when the doctors decided on a second exploratory operation. This time John Ford kept the vigil by my side. He'd flown in from Hawaii, where he spent most of his time, as soon as he heard Duke was ill, but he hadn't known the serious nature of Duke's illness until he arrived in California.

Duke, worried about Ford's mental condition, had chosen not to tell him the truth. Ford's last big picture, *Cheyenne Autumn*, a film on which Ford lavished two years of work, had been a major flop at the box office. Word was out that Ford "no longer had it," and Ford was devastated by the last in a string of failures. He was an old man in ill health, still reeling from the loss of Ward Bond. When he heard that Duke was going into the hospital, he called Batjac to find out "what the hell was going on." He then took the next plane to Los Angeles and came straight to the hospital.

I hadn't seen Ford for months, and his physical deterioration shocked me. He looked far older than his sixty-eight years. Never an elegant or attractive man, he wore rumpled and dirty clothes that looked as if he'd lived in them for days. In a moment of bravado, Ford told me, "he was rich enough to dress any way he damn well pleased." He'd also developed the nervous habit of sucking on the edge of a handkerchief. I wanted to weep for him, hating to see the cutting edge of his genius dulled by the frailties of old age.

His last picture with Duke, *Donovan's Reef,* completed in 1963, had been a saddening experience for all the participants. The picture was intended to play as a lighthearted comedy, but Ford had lost the gift of making audiences laugh. Clearly, he no longer had the heart for it. During the shooting, Duke's costar, Lee Marvin, so strong and durable on screen, was in the grip of unknown demons and was drinking heavily. Though he never let it interfere with his performance, alcoholism plagued him for many

years. Later he would face this problem down with his characteristic strength, and is today completely cured.

Donovan's Reef was a far cry from Duke's and Ford's glory
days, an anticlimax to their long collaboration.

During the many hours Ford spent with me at Good Samaritan, he talked about the past, dwelling on his fondest memories,
talking of his pride in Duke and their earlier work together.

"He is like a son to me," Ford said, his voice breaking. Then
concern for me seemed to overcome his grief, and he'd talk about
the future when he hoped to work with Duke again. That cantankerous old man, who'd been so kind to me for so many years,
tried to give me what little strength he had left. But he couldn't
hide the fear in his eyes any more than I could mask the terror
in mine.

We both knew the glory days were gone. The Ford bunch had
ceased to exist. Neither of us realized that the Duke we'd both
known and loved had ceased to exist too. He'd reappear for weeks
or months at a time, but he'd never be back to stay. The operation had changed him forever.

CHAPTER 24

Duke's second exploratory operation was another slice of hell for those of us waiting for word of his condition. The doctors had been so uncommunicative that we didn't know what to expect. This time the doctor emerged from surgery with a smile on his face. "We've found the source of the swelling," he announced triumphantly. Apparently Duke's constant coughing had torn open some stitches permitting air to escape from his mutilated lung into the surrounding tissue.

I didn't share the doctor's happiness. My husband wasn't a hem in a dress to be sewn and resewn. Before surgery the doctors had discussed possible complications but I hadn't expected such serious problems.

All I could see was that Duke was even weaker, his resources completely drained after the second surgery. He was a strong man, but he wasn't a superman. Two major operations within one week had taken him to death's door. The doctors told me recuperation would take six months to a year.

I could just imagine what Duke would have to say about that. He'd never taken six months off in his entire life and never been sick more than a few days at a time. He had a bad back from too many horse falls and fight scenes and a chronic inner ear problem from the underwater sequences in *Reap the Wild Wind*. These problems flared up occasionally, and Duke would go to bed reluctantly, for a day or two. After two major operations he faced several months as a semi-invalid, followed by a long recuperation.

He hated the hospital, the odor of illness, the lack of privacy, the feeling of being imprisoned in a body he no longer controlled. He'd always had an aversion to being touched by strangers, an aversion so strong that he'd employed his own makeup man as soon as he could afford it. In the hospital a series of strangers were responsible for his care, supervising his most intimate bodily functions. Furious at being touched by women he didn't know, he began fighting his nurses as he came out of the anesthetic. In the days to come he would throw things at them, swear at them, and demand that I take over most of the chores of his care.

At first he was in so much pain that the doctors kept him heavily sedated. But Duke was going to have to live with that pain for months, so the drugs were slowly withdrawn. Nothing the doctors said prepared us for what lay ahead. The first time I saw his torso stripped of bandages I could barely hide my horror. He looked as if he'd almost been cut in half. An enormous scar curved around the left side of his body, from his breast bone to his spine. His diaphragm indented where two of his ribs had been removed.

Duke wasn't an easy or cooperative patient. He wanted me with him constantly, but I couldn't go on ignoring our children back home. They'd been told their Daddy was sick, and Aissa, at eight, was old enough to be worried. The longer I stayed away the more upset she became. Once a day I'd slip from Duke's room while he slept and race for our house in Encino. It seemed I'd hardly get through the front door when the phone would ring and one of Duke's nurses would ask to speak to me. The message was always the same: "Mr. Wayne is awake and he's asking for 'Mom' again."

Duke had never called me "Mother" or "Mom," as other husbands do after their wives have children. He'd always addressed me as "Pilar," "sweetheart," "honey," or by some other equally affectionate name. But in the aftermath of the surgery he called me "Mom"—a pretty good indication of how weak and helpless he felt. I'd always been the dependent one in our marriage. Those weeks of being "Mom" were the most difficult of my life. The better Duke felt, the more irascible he became. He reacted to the loss of a lung the way other men react to an amputation. His initial emotions were anger and denial. Duke didn't pride himself on his intellect or his acting talent—he thought of himself as an athlete, an intensely physical man. He took for granted having the vitality to work all day, party all night, and go back to work the next day without feeling weary. He'd truly been an iron man before having cancer.

I tried to tell him he ought to be grateful to be alive, but that just made him angrier. He'd hoped the operation would cure him. Instead he felt worse. His cough had been a problem before going into the hospital. It was traumatic afterward. He felt as if he was choking on phlegm; breathing was a constant and painful struggle. To add to all those physical problems, he was undergoing withdrawal from his five-pack-a-day cigarette habit.

While Duke began the slow path to recovery, my mental and physical condition deteriorated. I'd been getting catnaps and snatching meals ever since Duke entered the hospital. Trying to be Duke's wife and nurse, take care of my children, as well as deal with the press put me under tremendous pressure. At some point during the weeks Duke spent in the hospital I began to come apart. I'd always imagined that a nervous breakdown would be quite dramatic. Mine was quiet and self-contained, and I just barely continued to function.

Duke mended slowly. One day the intravenous line was removed from his arm, and he ate his first meal since the operation. Then his color improved. He progressed from lying propped up to sitting in a chair, to taking short walks in the hallway. The disfiguring swelling disappeared. Three weeks after hospital admission, Duke was told he could continue recuperating at home.

True to form, he immediately established the rules for his convalescence. "I don't want any nurses," he declared. "Nobody is going to touch me except my wife!"

The day of his scheduled departure he dressed slowly, not allowing anyone to help. I know he hated being taken from the room in a wheelchair, but the simple act of putting on clothes had sapped his meager store of energy. He sat slumped, his breath ragged, while one of the staff wheeled him to the elevator which would take us down to the lobby. On the way down we were told that a large crowd of reporters was waiting to see him. The rumor that he had cancer had spread all over town, and we knew the press would be alert for any visible evidence of a serious operation. At the time Duke was still determined to keep his illness a secret. Nevertheless, I was amazed when he managed to stand up before we reached the ground floor.

"Get that damn thing out of my way," he muttered, kicking the wheelchair behind him.

The elevator door whooshed open to reveal Duke, standing straight and proud, looking as if he'd had a two-week vacation.

"Nice of you fellows to pay me a visit," he drawled, stepped forward briskly and reached to shake a couple of hands. The man was a wonder. By some strange alchemy he'd even forced some color into his ashen face.

I held his hand, knowing what the effort cost him, never more proud of him than I was at that moment. His harshest critics would have been impressed by Big Duke Wayne's performance that day. He chatted with the reporters, smiled for the cameras that flashed in a blinding barrage of light, assured everyone that he was feeling terrific, and then walked to the waiting car without faltering. Once safely inside, hidden by the limousine's dark windows, he groaned and asked for oxygen.

Duke couldn't wait to see the children when we got home, and he put on such a convincing performance for them that I had a difficult time getting them to treat him with the consideration his condition demanded. Daddy was home, and they wanted him to roughhouse with them as he had just weeks before.

I could hardly meet Duke's eyes as he told the children he was going to bed in the middle of the day. I think he hated that most of all. Deep in his heart he'd been hoping that returning home would miraculously make him well.

He thought the stale hospital air had contributed to his shortness of breath. He'd been so sure he'd feel 100 percent better once he got home. Now Duke had to face the fact that the operation had saved his life, but it hadn't made him whole again. In fact, he confessed in disgust, he'd never felt worse. As far as he was concerned all his suffering had been wasted. He was still a sick man.

Duke walked upstairs slowly, leaning on me for support. Since he couldn't sleep in a prone position I'd put our king size bed in storage, replacing it with two rented hospital beds. They waited for him in our bedroom. He took one look at them and the oxygen tanks standing alongside and muttered something unprintable.

Throughout his recovery shortness of breath and congestion were an ever-present reminder of what he'd been through. I will forever associate the sound of someone trying to clear their throat with those years. His doctor finally told Duke that bringing up phlegm was a habit rather than a necessity.

"But there's a lot of crap down there, Doc," Duke complained.

"Leave it there!" his physician replied in a tone that left no room for argument. "It isn't hurting anything."

Willpower proved to be Duke's biggest asset in his battle for health. He was determined to put the cancer behind him. I'd been very worried about how he'd handle not smoking once he got home, but he never had a cigarette, and he didn't complain about wanting one.

The only reference to his forty-year addiction to tobacco occurred one afternoon when I found him with the strangest expression on his face. "I feel as if something's missing," he said, looking at his empty hand.

Anyone doubting Duke's ability as an actor should watch the films he made from 1965 to 1968. His disability never showed on screen. He moved, rode, fought like a man in the prime of life. In reality he was often in pain and so short of breath that, for the first time in his career, almost all his dialogue had to be dubbed back in the studio.

During those years he made five films, serving as both star and producer-director for one, spending eighteen months on location working twelve- and fourteen-hour days. When he wasn't on location he worked in his office, taking care of Batjac business or preparing for his next film. And this was his recovery period. His determination never flagged.

Six weeks after Duke's operation we realized that the growing rumors about his illness would have a more adverse effect on his career than the truth. Duke, who'd never believed in the cover-up, decided to ignore his advisers and go public with his story. Giving a full-blown press conference was out of the question. Duke was still an invalid who walked with difficulty, coughed heavily, and required constant oxygen. His most strenuous activity consisted of taking the children for a ride on the grounds in a golf cart we'd purchased so he could go outdoors.

Although he intended to tell the truth, it would be his version of the truth. Duke decided to tell the story to an old and trusted friend, the columnist James Bacon, and he planned a flawless performance for Bacon's benefit. Duke was playing the part of a healthy man as they sat in the den having a drink while Duke told a carefully edited version of the last few months: "What the hell," he said, "this whole thing has been crazy. Look, Jim, I'm going to tell you the truth about my operation, and you have permission to quote me. I had lung cancer, the big C, but I've beaten the son of a bitch. Maybe I can give some poor bastard a little hope by being honest. I want people to know cancer can be licked."

The admission proved to be a genuine breakthrough for the medical profession. Before Duke's confession doctors actually debated the wisdom of telling cancer victims that they had the dread disease. Afterward cancer was discussed openly and people were less afraid to get the kind of checkups that would aid in early detection.

Duke looked and sounded very convincing the afternoon of his interview with James Bacon. He managed to suppress his cough, to laugh and joke like a man who's returned from a vacation. The next day Duke's story appeared in the papers, a story of triumph and hope. "John Wayne Beats Cancer," the headlines read. It sounded wonderful, even though it was far from true.

Duke still had a long way to go, five years before the doctors would consider him cured. But John Wayne had to be a winner. Duke's career, his happiness depended on it. He'd vanquished every screen foe, and he had to believe he'd beaten cancer too. He just didn't know any other way to live.

It seemed as if all our friends wanted to see Duke after Jim Bacon broke the cancer story. Duke loved company, and he tried to give all his visitors the impression that he'd made a complete recovery. But there were times when he just couldn't play the part.

I'll never forget the afternoon he had to ask Andy Devine to leave in the middle of their conversation. "I just can't talk anymore," Duke told Andy. It was one of the rare times when Duke's resolve crumbled.

One day during those difficult weeks Duke announced that he planned to sell our home. The decision shocked me. Delighted with the renovations we made after the fire, he always talked about how much he loved the place. Now he argued that the interior was too dark, that he felt isolated by the spacious grounds. He complained that the smog in Encino was making him cough.

"The Valley's had it," he said, staring out the window at a less than blue sky. "We ought to move somewhere down the coast, maybe Newport Beach. I think the sea air would help me, and we'd be closer to the *Goose*.

What Duke said made sense. The sea air might help him breathe easier and, in Encino, we did have a long drive to where we moored the *Goose*. But, despite the logic of his words, I felt certain that emotion motivated the abrupt decision to move. The house in Encino had come to represent a lot of things Duke preferred to put behind him forever.

He'd loved and then grown to hate Chata within those walls. The house echoed with the lost laughter of all the friends he'd buried. The grounds even served as our beloved Blackie's final resting place. Duke had buried the dog himself, wrapped in a vicuna blanket that Blackie loved. Our bedroom, with the hospital beds against one wall, was a constant reminder of the cancer that came so close to killing him.

Always an active man, he wasn't given to introspection. Now he had a great deal of time on his hands, time to look back, to try to see ahead. Occasionally I'd find him standing in an open door, staring into a room as if he saw ghosts inside. The expression in his eyes was so sad. He'd draw in a ragged breath and turn away without saying a word.

One afternoon a few days before Christmas Duke told me that Walt Disney's daughter had just purchased our home. "She made an offer I couldn't refuse," he said, avoiding my eyes.

Tears stung my eyes. I hadn't even known he'd put the house up for sale. There'd never been a sign out front or a bunch of real estate agents showing it. Obviously Duke felt guilty about what he'd done and the way he'd done it, but he'd owned the property prior to our marriage and, legally, he didn't need my signature on a sales agreement.

The series of events, from the cancer diagnosis to the sudden sale of our home, had occurred in less than three months. In that short time my world had turned upside down, and I could only imagine how Duke was feeling. He refused to share his thoughts with me.

We Waynes had a very subdued Christmas that year. The children tiptoed around their father, trying not to upset him or make him angry. Two and a half months after the operations Duke was still a very sick man who used a hospital bed and depended on bottled oxygen.

He was in no condition to go back to work. We had a major battle when he announced that he planned to keep his commitment to film *The Sons of Katie Elder* right after the New Year. "Duke Wayne," I said, "you must be out of your mind. You can hardly walk, let alone ride a horse. You've got two small kids who need their father. You ought to be thinking about retiring instead of planning to go on location!"

Duke didn't even bother to reply. He'd signed his name to a contract, and hundreds of people wouldn't get a paycheck unless he lived up to that contract. Nothing, not even a bout with cancer, would prevent him from keeping his word. Fourteen weeks after two major operations John Wayne was going back to work.

CHAPTER 25

On January 4, 1965, Duke got up from his hospital bed, packed his bags, and left for Durango, Mexico, where his next picture would be filmed. Durango, set high on the eastern edge of the Sierra Madre range, is isolated, primitive, and very cold in the winter. Contrails and other signs of civilization rarely mar the thin mountain air. It's an ideal place for filmmakers who wish to avoid the scars of humankind's occupancy, but it was the worst place in the world for someone convalescing from thoracic surgery.

The Sons of Katie Elder would be the first of Duke's Durango movies—a series of seven formula westerns that firmly cemented his heroic, larger-than-life image in the minds of his fans. The first time I saw Durango I had no idea it would play a pivotal role in our final years together. Although it was the capital of a Mexican state, the modern world had yet to intrude on life there. Comfortable motels or hotels, modern plumbing, television, sophisticated shops, grocery stores—all the things urban men and women take for granted were unheard-of luxuries in that community.

The city seemed to have been caught in a time warp. Pancho Villa or Butch Cassidy would have looked more appropriate on those dusty streets than a twentieth-century movie company. Duke loved it on sight. The surrounding mountains had a timeless quality. Up there, away from his everyday worries, Duke could believe that life was eternal.

I couldn't share his enthusiasm. Within minutes of flying into its primitive airport, I knew I'd never like Durango. That January of 1965, a cold wind whistled off the Sierras, chilling me to the bone. As Aissa, Ethan, and I made our way to the ramshackle building that served as a passenger terminal, the sky was a peculiar lifeless shade of grey which I have always associated with storms. It seemed an ill omen.

Duke had been in Durango for a week when the children and I, accompanied by Mary St. John, joined him. I'd worried about him every minute of our brief separation. Seeing Durango, feeling the gravelike cold, my worry turned to panic. I knew that Duke was in no condition to be filming an outdoor movie, let alone riding and doing stunts in frigid temperatures and rugged landscapes.

When he left the warmth and comfort of our Encino home he'd been a man with a mission. He'd been warned that the press of the world had gathered in Durango to see if he'd really recovered. They wanted to know if John Wayne could still ride and shoot and fight. If he faltered, word would go out on all the wire services. Duke's entire career, particularly after he abandoned romantic leads, had been built around his ability to be absolutely convincing as the hero of action pictures. More important, he loved making them.

When he left Encino I kissed him goodbye, told him how much I loved him, and begged him to be sensible and to take it as easy as possible. The minute I saw him at the airport I knew he'd ignored my request. His skin was white, his expression haggard, he wheezed and coughed in the thin air. Damn it! I thought, he belonged in bed—not on horseback!

It never occurred to him that he was being foolhardy. Duke had established his priorities back in the days when he filmed 'round the clock, making westerns in just seven days. His work would always come first.

Like all westerns, this one had a great number of action sequences, shots any sensible 58-year-old man with one functioning lung would have turned over to a double. But Duke couldn't be sensible or moderate when it came to his craft. He'd rarely used a double for riding sequences, and he had no intention of starting now.

Duke had a history of being injured while working. He'd done so many horse falls and fight scenes that he didn't even bother mentioning backaches unless he was ready for traction. That had only happened once, early in our marriage, when his back hurt so much that he'd been hospitalized for a few days during the filming of Blood Alley. Physical danger didn't intimidate or frighten him. His integrity demanded that he do as much of his stunt work as he could. Duke wouldn't cheat a camera, an audience, or a director. The only thing that could intimidate him was the thought of never working again.

That viewpoint had been fine when he'd been a young man, learning the tricks of the trade from Yakima Canutt. Duke had rarely exceeded his ability when performing a stunt, and, when he did, he'd had a young man's recuperative powers. I'd never opposed his stunt work before, although he'd continued taking risks on into middle age. Now, in his fifty-eighth year, just a few months after two major surgeries, doing them no longer made sense.

Throughout the filming of Katie Elder people thought Duke looked and sounded like a sick man, but he refused to be treated like one. I'd have spoken to the film's director about my husband's condition, breaking my own rule of not interfering with Duke's career, if it would have done any good. But there was no point in talking to this particular director. Henry Hathaway was the man who'd allowed Duke to do the dangerous fire scenes in Circus World. Although Henry and his wife were dear friends, he couldn't have been less sympathetic to Duke's plight. Henry had more than his share of talent, but his perspective on how Duke should act was skewed. Hathaway had survived colon cancer, and his personal prescription for recovery had been work, work, and more work.

"Don't baby yourself," he warned Duke, "or you'll become a psychological cripple. The way to get over what you've been through is to forget it ever happened and get on with your life."

Those two men were kindred spirits. Duke had been doing everything in his power to ignore what he'd endured, and now a trusted friend, someone who'd lived through a similar trauma, agreed with his attitude.

When shooting began Duke still had terrible difficulty breathing. He attempted to solve that problem by keeping supplies of bottled oxygen wherever he happened to be working. Duke made light of his condition in front of the cast and crew, trying to hide his pain and exhaustion. But no one, other than Duke and Henry, thought Duke's role would help speed his recovery.

The night the children and I arrived, Duke's cough sounded dreadful, his breathing labored. He kept a tank of oxygen in the car and another one close by our bed in the old hotel where we would be staying. The children were in the adjoining room, and Duke did his best to muffle his cough after we tucked them in that night.

As we readied for bed I turned to Duke and said, "This is just crazy. What in the world are we doing here? You belong at home in your own bed, not in some seedy old hotel. Nothing can be worth what you're doing to yourself, to me, to the children."

The constant worry was tearing me apart. I was down to 92 pounds. When producer Hal Wallis arrived on location with his wife, Martha Hyer, they were as upset about my condition as they were about Duke's. Wallis took Mary St. John aside and asked if she would talk to me, get me to go home. St. John said it would be useless—she knew that I'd always followed where Duke led, trusting him to do the right thing. But Duke had something to prove to himself, and Durango was the place where he planned to do it. He had to know if he could be the same man he'd been before cancer struck him down. Could he go on being a father to two lively youngsters, a husband and lover to me? Could he go on being John Wayne? He'd despised the nursing in intensive care, the weeks of dependency after he got home. Now, his career, his confidence, his own masculinity, would be tested in Durango.

A part of me, the selfish part that wanted a husband who would stay at home and lead an ordinary life, hoped Duke would falter. The children were beginning to resent leaving their friends, their comfortable home, their schools, and so was I. Although before Duke's illness I wouldn't have dreamed of suggesting retirement, in Durango it seemed only sensible.

The children and I, accompanied by Mary St. John, spent our days in Durango watching the shooting. As St. John viewed Duke gamely struggling through one take after another, she kept her thoughts to herself. But her tight-lipped, dismayed frowns reflected her feelings, so I asked her to talk to him: "He trusts you, Mary," I said. "I know he won't walk away from the picture, but at least convince him to use a double."

"I've tried," she answered, "but you know how he is when his mind's made up."

In the past, on other locations, I'd deliberately stayed away from each day's filming, knowing Duke needed some separation between his work and his family life. On *Katie Elder* I didn't want to let him out of my sight.

The press kept up a nonstop surveillance too. Papparazzi thronged every shoot, their cameras poised to catch my husband looking or acting like the sick man he really was. Inevitably, the day they'd been waiting for, the day that would justify their expense and inconvenience in hanging around Durango, finally arrived.

Hathaway planned to film a major action sequence involving all four Elder brothers, who were being played by Dean Martin, Earl Holliman, Michael Anderson, Jr., and Duke. Despite a temperature which hovered just above freezing, the four were slated to have a free-for-all in the midst of an icy mountain stream.

"Honey, please use a double just this once," I begged when Duke told me about the upcoming scene. "You're not well enough to do it yourself. You could get pneumonia and die." I'd said it, the one word neither of us had mentioned before.

Duke's eyes were angry as he looked down at me. "Mind your own business, Pilar," he said coldly before he walked away. "You take care of the kids, and I'll make the movies."

The location was thronged with media that day. If Duke wanted to retain his image, he did, indeed, need to do the scene himself. I just didn't agree that his image was as important as his life.

The upcoming sequence wasn't really difficult for Duke's younger, healthier costars. During the action Duke would be pulled from his horse, land in the middle of a mountain stream rimmed with ice, and then, while drenched to the skin, fight in a 4- or 5-minute brawl.

To save the principals from having to go through the ordeal a second time, Hathaway planned to use multiple cameras and film the sequence in its entirety, from beginning to end. As I surveyed the milling horses, wranglers, actors, and crew, Hathaway's thoughtfulness failed to impress me. He knew how fragile Duke really was but seemed determined to ignore the problem.

Duke's tall, still-upright figure towered above his costars as they mounted up, moving toward their marks at a leisurely pace. My husband was talking and laughing, sitting the saddle with his accustomed grace as I turned away. Perhaps he was crazy enough to film the scene, but I wasn't masochistic enough to watch him do it. Clutching my children's hands, I marched resolutely toward a nearby trailer, where I planned to remain until the sequence was finished. At the last minute, Ethan, who at 3 years old wanted to grow up to be just like his daddy, insisted on watching. Mary St. John volunteered to stay outside with him.

My daughter and I huddled in the trailer, trying to warm up and forget what was about to happen outside. I heard the distant sound of Hathaway's voice shouting, "Action."

As the scene proceeded, Duke was yanked off his horse right on schedule. He sailed through the air, landing waist deep in the stream. Later that day he confessed that the water was bitter cold, far colder than he'd expected. The icy chill clutched at his legs, numbing them instantly. He'd landed awkwardly, the wind driven from his one good lung. He gasped and rose from the stream, shaking frozen droplets from his hair. Fists bunched, he waded into the fray, commanding his legs and arms to do his bidding.

Duke said the action seemed to last forever; he could feel his body weaken, but he was determined to finish the scene. One shot—one take, Hathaway had said—and it would be over. Duke knew he couldn't force himself back into that stream again. He had to do the scene this time and do it right. In the distance he heard a scream, but he ignored it, although the sound came from his own son. Ethan, terrified by what was happening to his big, strong father, shrieked twice before Mary St. John could hush him.

Hathaway glared at Ethan, knowing the microphones had picked up the boy's cry. The angry director didn't dare stop the action: All the actors were in the icy water, soaked to the skin, throwing punches despite chattering teeth, all caught up by the insane belief that the show must go on. Hathaway couldn't forget the price Duke had paid when he'd allowed the cameraman to stop filming the fire scene in *Circus World*. This time he kept the cameras rolling until the sequence ended.

When Duke staggered out of the water he was ashen, shivering violently. Struggling for breath, he began to cough and couldn't stop. He had to get some air. It felt as if his good lung was collapsing as he strained for breath. Spasm after spasm racked his body as his lips turned a cyanotic blue. Christ, not now, he thought, seeing the press converge toward him. Leave me alone, you bastards!

They reached his side before anyone could interfere, cameras clicking frantically. This was what they'd come to see, what they'd been waiting for. John Wayne seemed about to oblige them by dying while they filmed it all.

Hathaway finally reached Duke's side, screaming at the press, "Get away, you sons of bitches. Can't you see he needs air."

Someone ran up with Duke's oxygen, clamped the mask on his face, and the crisis passed.

The scene was never refilmed. Even Hathaway had the sense to know Duke wouldn't be able to repeat it. To this day, if you listen carefully, you can hear a little boy's shriek rising above the other sounds of action.

The Sons of Katie Elder was a box office success. Although it lacked the complexity of John Ford's westerns, the absence of plot was offset by an abundance of action. The movie depended on the John Wayne image to carry the threadbare plot, and carry it Duke did.

The fact that he appeared to have beaten what he called "the big C," merely enhanced his status. Good old Duke didn't just destroy villains, he faced down death itself.

No one was surprised when Duke appeared in an advertisement for the American Cancer Society. The text read: "My biggest fight wasn't in pictures. It happened in real life. I just finished my 99th ridin', jumpin', fightin' picture. Never felt better in my life. But my wife nagged me into getting a medical checkup. And it turned out I had lung cancer. If I'd waited a few more weeks, I'd be kicking up daisies now."

After the *Katie Elder* ordeal I became a virtual zombie, just going through the motions. A terrible depression overcame me. I couldn't eat, I couldn't sleep, and I couldn't share my feelings with anyone, certainly not Duke. A part of me, a part of our marriage, died in that icy mountain stream.

CHAPTER 26

In the months following his operations, Duke appeared a changed man, physically and mentally. I loved him as much as I had the day we wed, but, at times, loving him didn't seem to be enough to keep our marriage together. His towering rages often left me in tears, wondering how to get through another day. The doctor had mentioned that Duke's personality might be altered by the operation. I'd never dreamed the change would be so dramatic and hard to live with.

Before the cancer diagnosis Duke had been the strongest, kindest, most loving man I'd ever met, a man whose good disposition was only occasionally marred by moments of unpredictable anger. After the operation he was often unreasonably angry. It was especially hard for the children, who didn't understand what was wrong with their father.

Fortunately, during the filming of *Katie Elder*, Duke had neither the time nor the energy to concern himself with disciplining them. He worked like a man possessed, concentrating on his performance, doing everything in his power to ignore his illness. Duke's need to get as far as he could from reminders of the last few months included buying a new house to replace the one he'd sold. We'd been schedule to move in mid-May. Halfway through the filming of *Katie Elder* I returned to California to begin searching for the kind of seaside, Newport Beach home that Duke had decided he wanted. A few days after my return, Virginia Knott, a friend who lived in Newport, called to tell me her next-door neighbor had put his house on the market. Virginia lived in a community that Duke liked very much—the waters of the Newport Harbor bordered her lawn. With the *Goose* moored nearby, I knew the location would be perfect.

I called Mary St. John, who'd come home with me, and she, her husband, and I made the hour and a half drive from Encino to look at the house. It belonged to a professional hunter, and the first thing we saw as we walked through the front door was his 50-foot trophy room. That afternoon the room held dozens of stuffed animals, including a kodiak, a grizzly, and a polar bear in a group that dominated the center of the room. I knew a little work could transform the space into a screening room large enough to do justice to Duke's professional equipment, so I crossed off the first item on Duke's list of priorities.

Waterfront property is at a premium in Newport. Homes stand shoulder to shoulder on narrow lots, a major problem for a superstar such as Duke who already had difficulty maintaining his privacy. However, this house had a magnificent view of the bay from the back patio. I could imagine Duke sitting outdoors with our children, enjoying the wonderful sea air while we watched the sun set. Unfortunately, I also pictured complete strangers motoring up to the dock to ask for his autograph. The property suited some of our needs, but it was a far cry from our beautiful, secluded home in Encino.

That night I called Duke in Durango and described the house, telling him about the potential screening room and the lovely view before discussing the drawbacks. "It's probably as close to what we want as we'll find in Newport," I concluded lamely.

"If you think it's right," Duke said, "buy it."

I almost dropped the phone. Duke made all our major decisions. I couldn't believe he wanted me to be responsible for this one. "Don't you want to see the house?"

"If you like it, buy it," he repeated. "I'll be happy as long as you are."

I bought the house the next day, my hand shaking as I signed the papers.

When the children and I returned to Durango a few days later, I felt hopeful for the first time in months. Duke and I would have a chance at a new life, far from all the memories that he found so painful. I just hoped that new life might include his retirement.

On location Duke continued to push himself beyond the limits of his strength. He was still irritable and short-tempered. One night when the children were already asleep, I turned on him,

asking, "What's the matter with you? Have you lost your mind
along with your lung?"

Duke just stared at me. He didn't want, couldn't tolerate a wife
who questioned his actions. Throughout our marriage I'd made
a practice of not arguing with him. But I'd been through too much,
learned and experienced too much, to go on being a decorative
puppet. Duke was going to have to accept the changes in me, as
I struggled to accept the changes in him, if we hoped to make
our marriage work.

Two people helped us get through the rest of our stay in Durango with our sanity and our marriage relatively intact. Mary
St. John performed above and beyond the call of duty. Because
Duke thought of her as a member of his inner circle, he lost his
temper with her almost as often as he did with me. She ducked
when she could, cajoled, temporized, and reasoned when she
thought it might help, but she never ran out on him.

Dean Martin was the other person who brightened our lives
during the filming. Martin's "laid back" temperament soothed
Duke; Martin's humor kept the two of us laughing even on our
worst days. That laughter was a precious, healing gift.

Martin's mother, a marvelous cook and a real Italian momma,
kept us well supplied with homemade food, which she shipped
to Durango by air two or three times a week. Many an evening
when Duke complained of being too tired to eat, the delicious
aroma of Momma Martin's pasta fazul or ravioli brought him
to the dinner table. After a good meal Duke would unwind by
playing hearts with Martin, as they'd done when they filmed *Rio
Bravo*. As he had so often in the past, Duke found a measure of
contentment in masculine companionship.

When we headed for Mexico City, where *Katie Elder*'s interior
scenes would be filmed at Churubusco Studios, Duke had the
satisfaction of knowing he'd lived through as rough a location
and as rugged a series of stunts as any he could expect to encounter in the future. He couldn't kid himself that he was still
the man he'd been before the operation, but he was a reasonable
facsimile; his fans would never know how much he'd changed.

Mexico City greeted Duke like a conquering hero. Instead of ending his career as he'd feared, his bout with cancer enhanced his appeal to an adoring public.

In Mexico City life resumed a familiar pattern. The studio had rented a home for us, a palace compared with the two small rooms we had in Durango. We got back in the jet set social whirl when Merle Oberon threw an enormous party to celebrate Duke's recovery. Oberon boasted that even reclusive Dolores Del Rio had accepted an invitation because she wanted to see Duke again.

The night of the party Duke said he was too tired to go out. He finally relented when I reminded him that his hostess and his costars would be very hurt if he didn't show up. I knew Duke was on the road to recovery when he went to the party and stayed later, drank more, and had more fun than anyone else. Two weeks after we arrived in Mexico City he declared that he felt better than he had in months. Although he coughed often and hard, and would continue to do so for the rest of his life, his breathing had eased and some of his stamina was returning.

From 1965 on Duke's voice would have a huskier, more gravelled quality, one that would serve him well in his future roles. It was a voice so uniquely American that Duke's speeches and dialogues had the cadence and richness of folk music. I also saw a change in his eyes: They held a world-weary wisdom, a new understanding of life and death. Duke had discovered his own frailty. He could be tolerant and forgiving of weakness in others, but he would never forgive himself for not being superhuman. This was the root of all his anger and frustration.

I'd changed too. In dealing with Duke's illness during the days in the hospital when I'd been "Mom," facing his anger and irritability, and living through my own quiet breakdown, I'd discovered my own personal strength. I may not have lived through those months with grace under pressure, but I'd lived through them, and that's what counted.

We returned to Encino at the end of March to pack our belongings and make the move to Newport. Duke hadn't seen the home I'd bought, and I was very nervous the day we drove down to Newport Beach to look at it together. Duke remained noncommittal as we walked from room to room. He finally paused on the patio, looking out at the harbor as though he'd never seen it before. My knees were shaking by the time he made his first comment.

"Hell, Pilar," he grinned. "It needs a lot of work."

I smiled back at him, knowing it would be all right. Nothing pleased him more than tackling a major remodeling job. We spent the following weeks huddled with architects and builders. The former trophy room proved to be the only room whose dimensions would remain unchanged.

Duke left for Rome two months later to film *Cast a Giant Shadow*, leaving the children and me behind in a rented home in Newport. We would live there while I supervised the remaining work on the Bayshore house.

Duke had a big emotional stake in the upcoming movie. The press had been characterizing Duke as an ultraconservative, creating the impression that he was also anti-minority, anti-black, and anti-Jew. Nothing could have been further from the truth. Duke judged people as individuals, not as members of a race or religion.

Cast a Giant Shadow gave Duke a chance to put an end to some of the misconceptions about him. The movie told the story of Colonel David Marcus, an American soldier who helped prepare the Palestinian Jews to face attacking Arabs in the dramatic months preceding Israel's statehood. Without Batjac's backing and Duke's appearance in a supporting role as General Mike Randolph, the film might never have been made. For the second time in his career he put his money and his reputation on the line to get a story told, and he loved every minute of it.

This film had a fiercely pro-Israel theme. At one point in the movie, when Colonel Marcus, played by Kirk Douglas, is agonizing over his part in the creation of a Jewish state, Duke, as Randolph, tells him "to stand up and be counted. And a lot of us will stand up with you."

That's just what Duke was doing, sending a message at a time when Arab-Israeli tensions were at their height, prior to the Seven Day War. While the U.S. Congress vacillated about risking Arab oil by supporting a Jewish nation, Duke put the full weight of his international popularity squarely behind Israel.

One day in the middle of the filming he surprised me by flying home for an overnight visit. He looked terrific as he walked through the front door, rested and happy despite his tiring trip. Just before twilight we piled into our stationwagon and drove to Bayshore to examine our builder's progress. Afterward we stood in the backyard, watching the sunset and holding hands.

Later that night, when the children were in bed, Duke and I toasted our future with champagne—a great deal of champagne. The next day Duke headed back to Rome, his stay so brief that both of us were to forget all about it.

When Duke came home two months later I wasn't feeling at all well. He took one look at me and insisted that I schedule a check-up. I made an appointment with Dr. Mitchelson in Encino and drove up to see him a few days later. He examined me briefly and then invited me into his office.

"Congratulations," he said. "You're pregnant!"

I thought he was out of his mind. "I can't be!" I protested. "Duke's been away on location for months and he just got back last week."

I'd wanted a large family, but considering the eight years it took me to have two children, and the three miscarriages between those births, I'd reconciled myself to having one girl, one boy, and no more.

My doctor listened to my protests and agreed to do a standard pregnancy test, even though he was confident his diagnosis had been correct. He telephoned a few days later, and this time I couldn't dispute his findings. I was expecting again.

I paced the house all afternoon, wondering how to tell Duke. He was so jealous, he wouldn't believe I hadn't been with another man. And yet, at first I didn't remember making love to him either. I was on the verge of believing in immaculate conception when I remembered Duke's surprise visit and all that champagne. We'd both gone to bed feeling no pain that night. When I woke up the next day to find him gone, I thought his brief visit had been a vivid dream. Now my pregnancy proved that dream had been very real. Duke was in for the surprise of his life.

"Who the hell's the father?" he roared when I told him about the baby.

"You are, Duke! Don't you remember the night you surprised me by flying home from Rome during the filming?"

Suddenly he began to grin. "I guess I surprised both of us."

We named that beautiful surprise Marisa Carmela Wayne. She was born on February 22, four years to the day after her brother Ethan, and she is a beautiful, female version of her father.

Duke was 59 the year he fathered Marisa. He had a new daughter, a new house, and, I prayed, a new lease on life.

CHAPTER 27

Before we moved to Newport Beach, Duke's career, his interests, and his friends kept us busy. But a subtle change took place after we left Encino. Duke's circle had been decimated by illness, alcoholism, and death and he felt those losses keenly.

We were too far from Beverly Hills and Bel Air for his remaining cronies to drop in for conversation or cards as they had when we lived in the valley. In Encino our house had often reverberated to the sound of deep male voices, arguing politics or discussing the film industry. Before we made our own new friends the Newport house reverberated to the sound of children playing. Aissa and Ethan had been isolated on our 5-acre estate. Bayshore Drive was full of boys and girls, all eager to be their playmates. Our children were inundated with new friends while their father mourned the loss of his old ones.

James Grant died in 1966. He'd been an important part of Duke's career since 1946, when they'd done *The Angel and the Badman*, which Grant wrote and directed. During that film Duke discovered Grant's genius for scripting simple, direct speech, tailored to Duke's slow, distinctive delivery.

In 1949 Grant coauthored *The Sands of Iwo Jima*, the film which gave Duke his first Oscar nomination. They went on to collaborate on eight more pictures, including *Hondo* and *The Alamo*. Duke worked with other good writers, often more than once, but Grant was the only one to become "family."

It took James Grant six months to die—a hideously slow and painful death from cancer. Duke, newly recovered from cancer, visited Grant often, going through silent agony as he watched one of his few remaining close friends lose ground each day.

When Duke celebrated his sixtieth birthday, most of his best friends, men he'd worked with all his life, Ward Bond, Grant Withers, Bev Barnett, Pedro Armandariz, James Grant, Bo Roos— were gone. Ford alone remained, a shockingly deteriorated ghost of the roustabout who used to stalk the decks of the *Araner* exhorting the young men around him to ever-wilder stunts and crazier parties.

In semiretirement, Ford was seldom sober, using alcohol to drown the memories of his last, failed movies. On our now rare reunions it was impossible to equate this bleary eyed, rumpled old man with the director who'd made so many masterpieces.

After we moved to Newport Beach it became apparent that there would never be another John Ford in Duke's life or another group of men equal to the friends they'd shared. Duke was accustomed to being surrounded by male companions, men in the industry who understood each other. While he remained one of Hollywood's most accessible stars, easy to meet and quick to strike up a conversation, he didn't have close friends, certainly no Fords or Bonds in Orange County when we settled there.

On the surface, he seemed well pleased with our new home, but adjusting to a new lifestyle was harder than he'd anticipated. There were days when he literally didn't know how to fill the empty hours. Duke could be a monster when he was bored, quick to anger and very demanding. Having filled his life with work or friends, he'd never learned to entertain himself. I grew to dread the mornings when he'd wake up and say, "What's on the agenda today, Pilar?"

As the weeks passed, it became obvious that Duke expected me to schedule social activities for the days he spent at home. If I didn't find a way to keep him entertained, Duke would insist on spending the day aboard the *Goose*. The boat was an escape for him. It was the only place in the world that he could spend time without being approached by fans. But with three small children to oversee, the *Goose* felt more like a prison to me. I hated having to tear them away from their activities just because their father was bored and lonely and needed something to do.

When we lived in Encino, Duke had no problem filling his free time. He'd come home at the end of the day and tell me he'd played cards, worked at the office, visited with an old friend, read a script, seen his business manager, spent an hour talking with Ford. His activities had always been dictated by his career. In Newport, Duke depended on me to stave off boredom. Initially, I wasn't up to the challenge.

After Marisa's birth I had begun to study Christian Science and found it gave me a deep feeling of inner peace after the profound upheavals that had resulted from Duke's illness. The last shreds of my Catholicism had crumbled during those dark months. But I still believed in God and needed a way to express that belief. I wanted to share that peace with Duke, but he couldn't imagine, let alone understand or condone, a religion that forbade smoking and drinking. Although I hoped Duke might attend church, if only to meet some of my new friends, he only accompanied me once. He fidgeted throughout the service. When it was over he turned to me, saying, "I hated sitting still that long."

Duke would never seek the comfort of organized religion. He was too strong in mind and spirit to feel the need. Later, in commenting on my conversion, he told a friend, "I suppose it's better than having her turn to drink!"

My next solo venture proved somewhat less controversial and more rewarding for both of us. One day a new friend called and asked me if I could make a fourth for a mixed-doubles tennis game. I'd never even held a racket in my hand, but being the new kid on the block, I didn't feel as if I should turn down any invitation.

I'd always thought of myself as unathletic, so I was shocked to find out how much I enjoyed running about, swinging wildly at a ball that spun by just out of the reach of my racket. One game and I was hooked.

In the beginning Duke didn't approve of my tennis any more than he'd approved of my new religion. The first time I left the house wearing an abbreviated but standard tennis dress, he looked at me, cocked an eyebrow, and rumbled, "Are you actually leaving the house dressed like that?"

I stopped long enough to explain that women no longer wore long skirts for sports. Early in our marriage I'd made the mistake of allowing Duke to censure my clothes. He dressed me like a

Mother Hubbard. Exposed cleavage or legs were something he liked to see on other women—not on me!

Fortunately tennis became a source of new friends for both of us. I soon learned that I wasn't the only woman who was leaving a bored, disgruntled husband. We solved our problem by introducing these tennis widowers to each other, and they began to play cards, leaving us to improve our backhands in peace. By the time we'd been in Newport a year I had an answer when Duke asked me what was on the agenda: tennis for me, cards for him. The arrangement worked so well that Duke enthusiastically backed the building of the John Wayne Tennis Club in which he maintained an interest until his death.

Going to celebrity tennis tournaments was another favorite activity which stemmed from my passion for the game. The first one that Duke and I attended was the Clint Eastwood tournament in Carmel. The day we arrived in Carmel we were met by Don Hamilton, the man who was in charge of the affair.

"What can I do to make you happy during your stay with us?" Don asked, looking at Duke.

"Well," Duke replied, "I don't play tennis—but I love to drink tequila and play chess."

The next day before the tournament began Don escorted Duke to a trailer which had been set up alongside the courts. The sign on the trailer door read, "John Wayne is inside, and he loves to play chess."

Duke grinned with delight when he opened the trailer door to find a beautiful chess set, a comfortable game table, and a bar well supplied with his favorite, Commemorativo tequila. That weekend the line of eager chess players stretched for a city block.

The celebrities at these events are treated like visiting royalty. They are put up in the best hotels, wined and dined, and even supplied with the finest cars. In Carmel, Duke was given a Maserati to drive. He tried it briefly and then sought Don Hamilton out. "I hate to be a problem," Duke said apologetically, "but I can't drive that damn Maserati. Would you mind getting me a real car like a Ford?"

Duke never took up tennis, although he came to enjoy my participation in the game. After his operation, he devoted his spare time to more sedentary pursuits. Card games, particularly bridge and Klaberjass, were favored occupations. I'll never forget one afternoon when Duke was playing bridge at our Bayshore house.

Duke brooked no interruptions or interference once play began. So he wasn't very pleased when our 10 year old walked into the den to say that a Mr. Davis was at the front door asking to see Duke.

Duke barely lifted his eyes from the cards in his hand. "Tell Mr. Davis that we don't receive anyone at the house unless they have an appointment."

Ethan left the room quickly and returned almost as fast.

"Daddy, Mr. Davis insists on seeing you."

Duke frowned. He hated having a hot and heavy game interrupted. "Ethan, go on out there and get rid of him. I don't care what you say. Tell him if he wants to see me he should call my secretary and make an appointment and I'll see him in the office."

Ethan returned several minutes later looking perplexed. "Dad," he said, "that Mr. Junior was sure angry. He said a couple words that weren't very nice and then he left very fast."

Duke catapulted from his seat at the game table. "My God," he groaned, "that must have been Sammy Davis, Jr." Duke reached the front door in time to see the back of Sammy's limousine speeding away.

CHAPTER 28

Duke always said family came first, career second, and his interest in politics a distant third. In fact, although he loved the children and me, there were times when we couldn't compete with his career or his devotion to the Republican Party.

That devotion was particularly evident during the mid-sixties. It was a time of national turmoil as liberals and conservatives fought it out in the government, in the media, and in the streets. The war in Vietnam was dividing the country as no conflict had since the Civil War.

Duke, in his customary incautious way, threw himself into the middle of the fray when his old friend and political ally, Ronald Reagan, made a run for the governorship of California in 1966. Duke saw Reagan's rising political star as a chance for Republicans to make a comeback from Goldwater's disastrous 1964 presidential campaign. He also knew that the campaign, by one of their own, would reawaken the antipathies that divided Hollywood in the days of the House Un-American Activities Committee investigation.

When Hollywood's most outspoken liberals began to make anti-Reagan, anticonservative television commercials, Nancy Reagan called Duke in Durango, where he was on location with *The War Wagon*, to ask for Duke's help. He was only too happy to oblige, to speak his piece, to once again "stand up and be counted" in the Reagan camp. Duke recalled what he'd done in the following letter which he wrote to President Reagan several years later. It read, in part,

> ...Then when you were running for Governor, they were tearing you apart with the Liberal actor television shorts. Nancy

called me in Mexico. I held up a Batjac picture, made one of those liberals, Kirk Douglas, stand by: and at my own expense, made a short concerning Murphy and Irene Dunne, Jimmy Stewart and John Paul Jones, which showed that fellows who paint their faces can also be valuable in another field of endeavor. [Duke referred to Murphy's tenure in Congress, Irene's service at the United Nations, Jimmy Stewart's career in the Air Force where he was a general.]

Duke's letter continued:

I made radio shorts that said you had proven yourself as an administrator by being head of a multi-million dollar organization and running it well.

Before that, before you made your bid to run for Governor, the Orange County group with Walter Knott, came to me for my opinion and I suggested that the important thing was to get you well briefed in the financial aspects of the state's economy, plus a thorough briefing on everything that the liberals might be able to bring up in questioning you.

When they came to me and said you refused to fly, I suggested that they put you in a car in the San Joaquin Valley and have you stop at about every third or fourth ranch and ask for a glass of water and talk to the farmers about their problems and show an interest, and to their wives if the farmers at not at home; establish a feeling of familiarity and interest in their problems. I suggested you could probably do the same thing in a few city blocks to find out what people were thinking, not so much to find out what they were thinking as to impress upon them your interest in being close to the people rather than the politicians.

The ideas Duke generated for Reagan's campaign give a graphic picture of the kind of folksy, barn-storming campaign Duke might have run for public office. Though Duke confessed to a thorough dislike of all things politic, including politicians, his letter to Reagan clearly demonstrates the fact that Duke had more than a passing interest in the subject.

His Reagan letter continued,

While you were having trouble with the Berkeley people and before Hayakawa came on the scene, Bob Hope did a show for the scholarship fund for the University of Southern California. Naturally they asked me, being a member of the Alumni, to take part.

I recall the night of that show with special clarity. Debate over the Vietnam war had led to a series of violent confrontations on campuses across the country, and USC wasn't immune to the turmoil. Riots and sit-ins which demonstrated contempt for the nation's leaders and the university administrators were as much a part of campus life as panty raids had been in the fifties. When Duke took the stage he would be facing a new breed of college student, young men and women who felt alienated from any authority figure.

Their motto was "You can't trust anyone over thirty." Duke was twice that age, and an authority figure if there ever was one. He'd been asked to say a few innocuous words of greeting as part of the evening's entertainment. Instead, he chose to lecture his young audience about their duties and responsibilities as college students.

Just before Bob Hope went on to do his monologue, he asked if he could see Duke's speech. Hope turned white as he read what Duke had written. "You can't give a speech like that here, Duke," Hope objected, "unless you intend to turn those kids out there into a lynch mob howling for your blood."

Duke didn't share Hope's worry. "Bob, it's time someone talked turkey to those kids. But, since you're so worried, I'll make a deal. If the producer says he doesn't want me to give this speech, I won't."

They called the harried producer over, a man with a half-dozen other things on his mind, and the man gave Duke's speech a cursory glance, okaying it without reading it through. A reluctant Bob Hope introduced Duke that night and then Bob walked to a neutral corner of the stage, as far from Duke as he could get.

Duke proceeded to tell those hostile students that, "a University should be a quiet place where you go to learn, not to destroy property." He made them aware that the property they'd been destroying belonged to taxpayers of the state and not to the students. Duke made no effort to tone down his speech to accommodate the mood of his listeners. "Getting an education is a privilege, not a right," he said with steady conviction. "Your professors and administrators should be treated with courtesy and respect. While you're here you ought to be learning a sense of responsibility. We aren't going to sit by and let you destroy our schools and our system. This is a great University. You owe it your best."

There had been a few scattered boos and hisses as Duke began his speech. As he finished 10,000 people rose to their feet cheering.

When Duke came home and explained what he'd done, my knees went weak. It was one thing to speak his mind; it was another to talk tough to a group of angry students.

"Don't look so concerned," Duke told me. "All those kids wanted was some leadership with a different point of view. The only people they ever hear from are the liberal-thinking malcontents."

"Duke," I replied, "you're probably the only person in the world who could have gotten away with what you said tonight."

Duke didn't see it that way. He was convinced that U.S. youths were being led astray by a very verbal minority group of radical liberals who may have even been infiltrated by communists. Duke believed in the inherent goodness of the nation's youth and thought they would willingly listen to someone who could give them the other side of the story. Unfortunately for my peace of mind, he saw himself as the ideal candidate for the job, and he never turned away from an opportunity to face down a crowd of angry demonstrators.

Shortly after Reagan's election, the Republicans held a victory party which Duke attended with other celebrity Reagan supporters, including Dean Martin, Sammy Davis, Jr., and Frank Sinatra. (Duke had been a little surprised when the super liberal Sinatra had campaigned for Reagan. Duke would never change allegiances that way, but he gladly accepted Sinatra into the conservative fold, hoping he would be more loyal to his new political friends than he'd been to his old ones.)

That night about 300 anti-Vietnam protesters waited outside the hotel where the celebrity's cars and Reagan's limousine were parked. When the affair ended, the police warned us not to try and go out that way. Everyone else turned around, prepared to leave by another door rather than precipitate a confrontation with an angry mob. Not Duke.

He was 61 years old and, as he said, "That's too damn old to run away from a bunch of kids!" All alone, he walked out the door to face the mob. Four of the ringleaders saw him and ran up, waving a Vietcong flag in his face.

Duke stared down at the young men from his superior height and, using a tone that carried over the crowd, said, "Please don't do that, fellows. I've seen too many kids your age wounded or dead because of that flag—so I don't take too kindly to it."

To everyone's amazement the crowd began to applaud Duke. I guess they admired his audacity because one or two called out, "You tell them, Duke!"

But the first four, the ones with the Vietcong flag, weren't about to back down. They continued to wave their banner under Duke's nose until he turned on them and actually chased them down an alley. Meanwhile Governor Reagan and the other fainthearted stars, were able to leave by another exit, undetected.

Like many other Americans, I was confused about our role in Vietnam. As the mother of a son, I hated to see young men go off to fight a war. Duke, on the other hand, felt we had every reason to be fighting in Asia. His only regret was that we refused to commit ourselves to the war 100 percent. He thought we owed total commitment to the men of our armed forces, men who were dying while their countrymen debated the rightness of their deaths. Duke wanted action, not debate. He was a firm believer in the Domino theory, convinced that all Southeast Asia would eventually fall under communist domination if Vietnam toppled. "Nobody enjoys the damn war," he said. "But it happens to be necessary. Besides," he added, "we gave our word."

Duke believed the United States had bound itself to Vietnam through a mutual defense pact and had to live up to its word or lose credibility all over the world. I don't know if Duke was right or wrong, but his willingness to defend the things he believed in was a fundamental part of his character.

I can still hear Duke telling our son, as his father had told him, "Don't give your word easily, but don't break it once you have. Don't start a fight, but if you get in one make damn sure you finish it." Duke lived his life by these rules. He thought they worked as well for nations as they did for individuals. As Duke grew older the message his movies conveyed weighed on his mind as heavily as their entertainment value. He insisted on playing characters who were loyal and courageous. He was the first to admit he'd made lots of mistakes in his life, but now that he had the opportunity through his work, setting a good example was usually uppermost in his mind when he chose a script.

Toward the end of his life in 1974, when he was given the Tuss McLaughery Award by the American Coaches Association, he talked about the importance of setting a good example, saying:

> I don't know of a better way to go through life than guiding others—getting the best out of them, pushing them to do better than they ever thought they could—and all in the framework of fair play and mutual trust.
>
> We were coached into leading legal lives by parents who loved us and who knew the rules of the game of life. The secret was coaching. The other secret is one generation setting a better example for the generation that's pulling up fast. In that area, I plead guilty for not doing more on the positive side. I've tried—but in looking back, maybe I could have tried harder.

Looking back over Duke's life and career, it's hard for me to imagine how he "could have tried harder." I can't think of another movie actor who willingly risked his popularity and his own money in defense of a cause.

Despite the press reports to the contrary, Duke was not a bloodthirsty maniac. He suffered every time he read the casualty figures from Southeast Asia, and he wore his POW bracelet with a great sense of pride and obligation to U.S. fighting men.

By 1967 Duke was deeply disturbed about living in a nation which seemed determined to ridicule men for doing their duty while praising those who burned their draft cards. He had to go to Vietnam to show his support for the soldiers who fought and died in the cause of freedom. Duke told the press, "I can't dance and I can't sing—but I can sure as hell shake a lot of hands."

Once in Vietnam Duke visited the troops wherever he found them, from the holds of ships to the front line. He flew into Pleiku in the midst of the fighting to shake hands with the men. Time and time again he'd walk up to an astonished soldier and say, "I'm John Wayne, and I just want you to know a hell of a lot of folks back home are damn grateful for what you're trying to do over here."

One day, while he was signing autographs for a bunch of marines, a Vietcong sniper began taking pot shots in his direction. Duke was furious when the press called him a hero, exaggerating the danger he'd been in. He didn't think of himself as a hero and resented being portrayed as one while the real heroes, young Americans, were being labeled cold-blooded murderers.

When Duke returned from that trip I could see he was a man with a mission. All the signs were there, the same ones I'd noted as he made plans to film *The Alamo* and *Cast a Giant Shadow*. I wasn't surprised when Duke told me he intended to make a movie about Vietnam, one that would pay tribute to the Green Berets.

Hearing him say he planned to produce, direct, and star in the picture gave me a distinct sense of déja vu. We'd been through it all before. But this time there was a difference. No controversy surrounded the Alamo. Vietnam was another story. The press had been treating Duke more kindly in the aftermath of his cancer. We both knew he'd reawaken a lot of their old hostility if he made this movie.

When I cautioned Duke about his plans, he shook his head in disgust. "Honey," he said, "somebody has to stand up for those guys. They're fighting and dying over there—and damn it, they're doing it for us, for you and me and our kids, for our freedom."

I knew it would be useless to argue further. When Duke had something to say, an Act of Congress couldn't stop him. We spent the last five months of 1967 at Fort Benning, Georgia, where Duke filmed *The Green Berets*. Getting there had taken an all-out effort on his part. No one wanted to be associated with the movie, let alone finance it.

Paramount Studios, to whom Duke was under contract, turned him down cold when he talked to them about distributing the film. Universal turned him down too, saying the script was much too controversial. Despite Hollywood's long history of making war movies, a history that began with World War I and continued through World War II and Korea, Duke had to use all his persuasive powers to convince Jack Warner of Warner Brothers to distribute the film.

War movies were surefire box office when the country was in a patriotic fervor, but no one believed *The Green Berets* would enjoy financial success. A full decade would pass before Hollywood's timid moguls worked up the courage to deal with Vietnam, and then their offerings would be antiwar films that did a great disservice to Vietnam veterans. To this date, *The Green Berets* is the only film to support what the United States tried to do in Southeast Asia. Duke assembled a fine cast including Aldo Ray, David Janssen, Jim Hutton, George Takei (later of *Star Trek* fame), Bruce Cabot, and Patrick Wayne. I think they all knew they were risking their popularity, and possibly their careers, by participating in the picture.

After the film premiered, my worst fears were realized. By defending some of his countrymen, Duke made himself a highly visible target for others. The press attacked him as if he were a traitor rather than a patriot. Duke had long felt that "a little clique back in the East has taken great satisfaction in reviewing my politics, not my pictures." But nothing the critics had written in the past prepared us for the virulence of their attacks after *The Green Berets* was released.

Renata Adler, a highly respected film critic, gave the film a very unfavorable review. She wrote, "The Green Berets is a film so unspeakable, so stupid, so rotten and false in every detail that it passes through being fun, through being funny, through being camp, and becomes an invitation to grieve, NOT for our soldiers in Vietnam (the film could not be more false or do a greater disservice to them) but for what has happened to the fantasy-making apparatus in the country. Simplicities of the right, simplicities of the left, but this one is beyond the possible. It is vile and insane. On top of that, it is dull."

And those were some of the nicer things she had to say about Duke's movie. The rest of the critics tried to outdo each other's scathing remarks. But the great silent majority of Americans seemed to understand and support what Duke was trying to do. They made *The Green Berets* one of his highest grossing pictures.

On the Fourth of July, 1968, in Atlanta, Georgia, Duke unveiled one last testimonial to the men he held in such high esteem. Today a $5\frac{1}{2}$-foot white granite stone stands in front of the Special Forces Memorial Chapel. Its inscription reads, "In tribute to the men of the Green Beret, United States Army Special Forces, whose valiant exploits will ever inspire mankind: John Wayne, July 4, 1968."

Duke's patriotism, his belief in the United States' fundamental goodness, never flagged, although the hate mail arriving at Batjac's office became truly frightening. The press labeled him as the "Apostle of War." They called him a knee-jerk conservative, dredged up his past personal problems, questioned his credentials, his intelligence, his motives.

Duke spent time and energy defending his reasons for making the movie. The final blow was delivered by a U.S. congressman who started an inquiry to discover if the Army had charged Batjac enough for military help and expertise.

Although Duke had made a great deal of money, he couldn't laugh his way to the bank this time. Too many lives were at stake in Vietnam, so he continued to speak out in defense of the American fighting man.

Once again I was praying that he'd consider retiring. Duke seemed so wearied by his fight that I thought he might actually consider quitting the movie business. He even talked about getting a second home down in Baja, where he could just kick back and ignore the rest of the world. But whatever power arranges these matters had other things in mind for both of us.

CHAPTER 29

Duke never saved. He was a spender, an investor with a free-wheeling, eclectic interest in almost everyone on the face of the earth. Just as he backed his moral and political convictions with the films he made, he often backed an idea or an invention which piqued his interest with his own funds, putting his money in such unrelated ventures as manufacturing and repairing fishing nets, cattle ranching, perfecting a method of recovering oil from tires, and prospecting for gold.

He had a terrific memory enhanced by forty years of having to learn scripts, an uncanny eye for detail, and an inborn ability to recognize quality. These attributes should have helped him to be a highly successful businessman. In fact, he lost large amounts in a variety of investments. When it came to money, Duke could be his own worst enemy.

Back in the forties after his initial success in movies, he'd given his accumulated earnings to his first family as part of the divorce agreement. His association with Bo Roos wiped out the next fifteen years of income. What remained went into making The Alamo, and Duke barely broke even when he sold his interest in the film to United Artists.

I was always amazed at his ability to bounce back from disaster. He never complained because things didn't work out the way he hoped they would. He never looked back with regret, in part because he was much too busy planning for the future. He believed in learning from the past, not living in it.

By the late sixties the Wayne family seemed to be financially secure again. Duke had made seventeen pictures in the decade that followed the release of The Alamo, and he was now receiving $1 million a picture plus a percentage of the profit.

Toni Wayne LaCava's husband functioned as Duke's financial manager, working out of Batjac's offices. Don LaCava had come to work for Batjac after Duke and I married. He'd been holding down a part-time job and going to law school at night when he married Toni, but, after she became pregnant, it seemed they were unable to make ends meet. They came to Duke for help. Duke supported most of his family by then, one way or another. Duke's brother Bobby was on Batjac's payroll, and his son, Michael worked as an apprentice in the production department. Duke could always make room for one more relative. Don LaCava joined Batjac in 1958. Like Michael, LaCava started as an apprentice, slated to go on working in the production end of Batjac films.

A year and a half later, after the Roos mess, Duke was looking for a new business manager. He wanted someone he could trust implicitly, someone who would really have his best interests at heart. LaCava, with his college education, his training in law, and his close family ties, seemed like the ideal candidate for the job. Although he had neither experience nor schooling as an investment counselor, Duke felt that a bright young man like Don would have no trouble handling and protecting the millions of dollars Duke earned each year.

"Hell," Duke said, "I don't expect him to make a lot. I told him to be conservative and make damn sure he didn't lose any."

After Don took over Roos's duties, Duke felt secure in the knowledge that his son-in-law, husband to his oldest daughter and the father of his grandchildren, would now have his hands firmly on the wheel of the Wayne financial ship.

Duke often discovered interesting investments on his own. In the fifties he bought several ranches in Arizona. The bulk of their acreage was devoted to growing Pima cotton, considered to be the finest in the world outside of the cotton grown in the Nile Valley. Shortly after Duke and his partner, Louis Johnson, purchased the land, the U.S. government began to pay cotton farmers not to plant a crop. The government's decision proved to be a bonanza for the Wayne ranches.

Duke and Louis stopped growing cotton, collected the government subsidy, and put their acreage to work growing cattle feed and quality beef instead. Within a few years they instituted an annual Thanksgiving sale of thoroughbred bulls held outside of

Casa Grande near the Francisco Grande Hotel. Duke envisioned the event as a western hoedown, and it soon rivaled the splendid livestock auctions held in Texas. The world's wealthiest cattlemen flocked to bid on Wayne bulls, and the value of the ranch herds increased yearly. Although LaCava handled Duke's other investments, Duke and his partner retained control of the Arizona ranches. They would prove to be Duke's most successful business venture as well as a hideaway and vacation spot for our family.

Not all Duke's personal investments fared as well. In many ways he was a naïve man and an easy touch. Close friends often lured him into committing large sums of money in ventures they favored, often with disastrous results.

When Duke and I married, he'd enjoyed a long relationship with the Arias family of Panama. He'd met Harmodio Arias, the only Panamanian president to hold office for his entire elected term, back in the thirties. By the fifties Duke was involved in a wide variety of businesses with Arias's sons, Tito, Tony, and Gilberto. They were such close friends that Duke and I asked Tony Arias to be Aissa's godfather.

The Arias family had widespread connections and a blemish-free reputation. Tito followed his father into politics and served his country as its ambassador to the Court of Saint James. While in England he met, wooed, and married Margot Fonteyn, the world's premiere ballerina. Gilberto served as Panama's minister of finance, and Tony ran the family's various business enterprises.

Duke felt a great affection for all three brothers. He also had a sincere interest in the well-being of the Panamanian nation, a country suffering greatly from lack of venture capital. Duke wasted no time plunging into this void, putting several million dollars into various Panamanian ventures with the Arias brothers, including a ship repair yard. Duke and multimillionaire Eugene McGrath, who had married my friend actress Terry Moore, sank another small fortune into a shrimping fleet.

The money should have been safe, the investments profitable. Gilberto Arias was in a perfect position to oversee and care for Duke's various ventures. But Duke hadn't taken the volatility of Latin American politics into account.

Ernesto de La Guardia, the new Panamanian president, relieved the Arias brothers of their positions shortly after taking office. The change in government coincided with Tony Arias's untimely death. Without Tony's management ability and Gilberto's political pull, the shipyard and the fishing fleet lost money until they went out of business.

Duke never shared the details of his financial life with me, either the disasters or the triumphs. He often brought papers home and asked me to sign them without giving me a chance to read them first. I scribbled my signature willingly, knowing that Duke would always take care of me no matter what happened. Don LaCava sometimes accompanied Duke when papers required my signature. I liked LaCava and enjoyed seeing him, even if those business visits were brief. However my faith in him was later badly shaken. Shortly after Duke and I moved into our Newport Beach home, LaCava arrived on our doorstep one day when Duke was away, saying he had a document that required my signature. There was nothing unusual in the request, nothing to alert me to a problem. The top of the paper read, "Quitclaim Deed," but I signed quickly, without reading further.

Don LaCava was so enthusiastic about his position as Duke's financial manager that he and his brother Paul formed their own management company and began soliciting other clients. With the magic of Duke's name behind them, success was inevitable.

For the first time since Duke and I married, the Waynes seemed to be united by ties of mutual affection as well as financial interdependence. We celebrated our newfound togetherness on Father's Day, 1967, with a gathering of the clan. Duke's mother, his four older children and their husbands or wives, our own three offspring, and nine grandchildren posed for a portrait that day. I thought my problems with the family were finally over.

Duke did a great deal of business traveling. One week when we were in Dallas he decided to go shopping, one of his favorite pastimes. That day we were like two children having fun, going from store to store in a rare and happy time alone together. He wasn't one to count pennies and soon spent $20,000 to $30,000, charging most of his purchases.

A few days later, back in California, the bills arrived at Batjac's office. Don LaCava looked them over, turned pale, and walked into Duke's office, saying, "How could you spend so much money? You don't have this kind of money in the bank! How the hell am I supposed to pay these bills?"

Duke had been earning millions. He should have had more than enough cash in the bank to cover the amount we'd spent. He came home that night and described LaCava's behavior, saying he intended to get to the bottom of the situation. Once again he called in experts to discover what had happened to his money. Their reply sounded like a replay of the Roos incident.

Don LaCava's departure from Batjac was immediate and final, and a year or two later, he and Toni separated.

After Don LaCava was out of our lives, Duke asked me if I wanted to take control of his remaining investments and future earnings. I was shocked by his request. No one knew better than Duke how little I understood business. The fact that he asked showed the measure of Duke's desperate need for a business manager he could trust. Afraid I would bungle his affairs even worse than Roos and LaCava, I told Duke his request was out of the question.

"I guess I'll just handle things myself then," Duke replied. He seemed to recover from this latest setback within a few weeks, finding emotional release in loudly expressed righteous anger. Once the explosion passed, he plunged ahead with new ventures, determined to make several more films as quickly as possible to recoup his recent losses.

I couldn't put those losses behind me as easily. Duke had been talking about retiring before they happened. He'd been serious enough about it to discuss running a charter yacht business out of a Baja port. I'd been looking forward to a new way of life, one that included a full-time husband whose work wouldn't take him away from home six to eight months of the year.

But Duke couldn't retire after the LaCava incident. As far as he was concerned, he had to make up those losses, and that meant more movies, more locations. Duke continued to be a driven man, his career ruling all our lives despite the costs to his health and his family's happiness.

While I worried about the future, Duke became heavily involved in yet another business venture, one he thought deserving of his personal attention. He'd come across an invention which seemed to have great potential—a process for separating the oil and water in a ship's bilge.

The press never reported Duke's interest in environmental issues because it didn't fit the ultraconservative John Wayne image which they'd helped to create. In fact Duke had a firm conviction that clean air and pure water should be part of our national heritage. The growing pollution of his beloved Newport Bay, due in part to the discharge of dirty bilge water, was one of his concerns. The new process gave him a way to help solve the problem.

Duke wasted no time investing in the new company, bringing in a friend, Joe DeFranco, to run it. Separation and Recovery Systems, Inc. was to be Duke's last venture into the world of finance, and this time, thanks to Joe DeFranco, business and pleasure went hand in hand as they traveled the world promoting their product. Today 95 percent of all Coast Guard ships use the device that was financed and promoted by John Wayne.

Duke enjoyed this last business endeavor more than any of the others. He loved the risk, the sense of breaking new ground, the feeling that he was part of larger events. But nothing would replace his love of making movies, and the best was still to come.

CHAPTER 30

Duke followed *The Green Berets* with *The Hellfighters*, a fictionalized version of Red Adair's life. It was an uninspired formula film, tailored to suit Duke's aging screen image. Duke had gathered a road company by 1968, a group he felt comfortable working with, and they played a major role in this and many of his upcoming films. They included Claire Huffaker, the screenwriter who scripted *The War Wagon* and *The Comancheros* before *Hellfighters*, director Andrew McLaglen, the son of Duke's old friend Victor McLaglen, and cinematographer William Clothier.

Hellfighters also featured Vera Miles, who had worked with Duke in *The Searchers* and *The Man Who Shot Liberty Valance*. Miles had played Duke's wife in *The Green Berets*, but her scenes wound up on the cutting room floor. Actor Bruce Cabot, yet another old friend, rounded out the cast.

The story contained all the classic ingredients of a Wayne movie: a diamond-in-the-rough hero, life-threatening action sequences, a senior romance, a junior romance, and a happy ending where all problems are resolved. The picture is a reprise of Duke's work in *The Fighting SeaBees*. He could have walked through it in his sleep, and that's just the way audiences and critics saw his contribution to the film.

Clearly, Duke needed fresh material if he were to go on making pictures. His life and career were at a low ebb early in 1968. There were, thank God, no signs of recurring cancer, but that was small comfort to a man who felt he'd left his middle years, his best years, behind. Both *The Green Berets* and *Hellfighters* had been brutalized by the critics. After four decades, Duke's star seemed to be on the wane. Good scripts didn't come across his desk as often as they had in the past.

Duke had a few projects lined up—nothing he was excited about but at least it was work—when Henry Hathaway telephoned with urgent news: "Duke, I just read a book you ought to take a look at," Hathaway said. "It's called *True Grit*, and I think there's a terrific part in it for you."

Within a few days Duke had read the as yet unpublished Charles Portis novel. He agreed with Henry's assessment of the book—it was a marvelous western, just the sort of story he'd been looking for. The part of Rooster Cogburn was made for a man of Duke's age and talent. He hadn't been as excited about a part since John Ford had given him the *Stagecoach* script thirty years before. Since giving up traditional leading roles, Duke had been looking for a part of an older man with heroic virtues and very human faults. Rooster Cogburn was all of that and more.

Duke thought he had an inside track on buying the movie rights for Batjac, but Hathaway was one step ahead of him. Hathaway preferred making films at major studios; he didn't like the minor inconveniences, the lack of luxury imposed by working for an independent production company such as Batjac. Too penny-pinching to hire a secretary and maintain an office, he knew a big studio would be more than happy to supply him with both, so he'd taken *True Grit* over to Paramount and shown it to Hal Wallis, explaining that Duke was interested in playing the lead.

Wallis had produced the successful film *The Sons of Katie Elder*. He enjoyed working with Hathaway and Duke, and he too had been looking for another property for them. *True Grit* had the smell of a winner. Wallis bid a half-million for the property, far more than Batjac could afford. He gave Hathaway a private office, private secretary, and all the other perks the director desired.

Duke had been eager to make the film himself, but he wasted no time in anger or recriminations. He wanted to play Rooster Cogburn no matter who acted as producer, so he contacted Hal Wallis rather than waiting for the producer to call him. They agreed on salary and terms quickly but clashed hard on their conceptions of how the hero should look. Wallis wanted Cogburn to have a thick mustache and wear an eye patch.

Duke disagreed vehemently. "Hell, the fans pay to see me—not some son of a bitch who looks like a pirate in an Errol Flynn movie."

"The eye patch stays," Wallis insisted, "but I'll compromise. You can forget the mustache."

Once Duke signed with Paramount, Henry Hathaway wasted no time telephoning. He knew Duke liked to tailor a script to suit his own ideas and beliefs; wanting to forestall any arguments, he said firmly, "Duke, I want to talk to you about the picture. We're not going to have any of your moralizing or preaching in this one. This Cogburn fellow is a man who wenches when he wants, gets drunk when he wants, and fights when he's in the mood. He's as much sinner as saint—and you, old friend, are going to play him that way."

Duke didn't argue. He felt jubilant about the upcoming project, more excited about making this picture than he'd been since *The Alamo*. Not only was the part challenging, but Hathaway had told him not to worry about dieting for this film.

Dieting was a bad word in our household. Duke had been plagued by weight problems for years, but extra pounds had been especially troublesome since his cancer surgery because he was less active. His closet now held three complete wardrobes. One fit perfectly when he weighed 210 pounds, one for 240 pounds, and one for those awful times when he tipped the scales at over 260.

He was a big man with a big frame, but at 260 pounds or more, Duke had a paunch. He'd grown to dread the strict diet required for making a film. Duke loved food, especially steak, roast beef, and other heavy meals. He also had a passion for Tootsie Rolls. As each picture loomed, he'd give them up, stop drinking, start counting calories, and exercise by the hour. (If there was anything Duke really disliked about being a movie star, it was the preoccupation with his appearance. Makeup, toupees, minor plastic surgery on his eyelids may have been necessary evils, but he hated them all.)

As Duke grew older, he sought medical help to lose weight. One highly recommended physician gave Duke a whole diet regimen which consisted of different pills, all carefully color coded, to take through the day. Uppers, downers, appetite suppressants—we never knew exactly what they were. All Duke cared about was that they worked wonders—as long as he took the right pill at the right time. Unfortunately, Duke, who had no trouble remembering page after page of dialogue, just couldn't recall which pill was which. The first night on the diet he took his morning pill by mistake. After spending a bored and lonely half hour watching me sleep, he shook me awake.

"You've got to help me," he said as soon as I was able to focus my eyes. "I took the wrong goddamn pill, and I'll be up all night. As long as you're awake too, I might as well teach you to play bridge."

I hadn't been awake, but Duke looked so unhappy that I couldn't help laughing. Normally an impatient teacher, he spent the next eight hours instructing me in the intricacies of the game. My passion for bridge, one that Duke shared, began that night.

The next time Duke made a mistake with his medication he was on his way to NBC, where he was scheduled to make an appearance on Dean Martin's television show. We'd been on the *Goose* all day, docked late, and, in his hurry, Duke grabbed the wrong pill again. By the time he walked into Martin's dressing room, Duke's eyes were half closed and he was fighting the desire to go to sleep any place—the floor, the table, a chair would do.

"I can't do our skit," he told Martin. "I'm too doped up." He peered into the mirror over Martin's head, examining himself. "Goddamn, I look half smashed."

Martin laughed. "Hell, Duke, people think I do the show that way all the time."

Duke encountered some minor difficulties during the filming of *True Grit*. The first was the altitude on location. The second involved Kim Darby, the young actress cast as Mattie Ross. Darby arrived on location determined to show the world that she wasn't at all impressed by working with John Wayne. Several people commented on her rudeness. Duke even called her a "spoiled brat." It wasn't until later we learned she was ill during the filming.

Fortunately, getting to know Glen Campbell, who played a sympathetic character called "Le Boeuf," made up for Duke's problems with Darby. Although Campbell was already a huge success in the music world, this was his first film, and he proved to be hardworking and eager to learn.

Overall, the mood on location was upbeat. Duke and Henry Hathaway shared the belief that this film would be the best of their long collaboration. Duke played the cantankerous Cogburn with skills he'd spent a lifetime acquiring. Everyone knew he was giving one of his best performances. He'd come home at the end of the day, elated and happy with the film's progress.

Duke had three favorite scenes in the picture. The first occurred early in the story when Rooster and Mattie are up late one night. Rooster reminisces about his life, the wife who left him, the things he'd missed. It was one of the longest monologues of Duke's entire career, a real challenge. The cast and crew all broke into applause after the scene was finished.

Duke also loved the scene where he confronted Ned Pepper's gang and takes them on single-handedly, shouting at Ned, "Fill your hands, you son of a bitch."

Last of all, Duke liked his farewell with Mattie at the end of the movie, where he mounts his horse, says "Come see a fat old man sometime," and, in a complete denial of age and infirmity, takes the horse over a four-rail fence. Duke did that jump himself, and the triumph the camera records on his face is very real. He was 61 years old, an overweight man with one good lung, and he could still jump horses and make great movies!

When Paramount's executives viewed the film's rough cut they were united in the feeling that they'd just seen something special, the kind of picture that wins awards. They decided to publicize it as Duke's "fortieth anniversary in pictures" film, and they scheduled three special screenings at the Directors Guild Theater for the movie community.

Duke never cared about the critics, but the approval of his peers meant a great deal. Although he appeared calm and affable during those screenings, he was quite apprehensive. If men such as Jimmy Stewart and Steve McQueen thought he'd done a good job, he'd be more than satisfied no matter what the critics wrote.

To his relief each screening ended in thunderous applause. Each time the houselights came on he was enveloped in a wave of congratulations. Stars such as Clint Eastwood, Lawrence Harvey, Jimmy Stewart, Lee Marvin, Michael Caine, Fred MacMurray, and Ernest Borgnine came to see *True Grit* and pronounced it Duke's best performance. Borgnine, too, suggested that the role would win Duke an Oscar.

Duke thanked Ernie for his sentiments, still doubting he would ever win the coveted award. He couldn't imagine critics appreciating or understanding a John Wayne western. It had never happened before, and Duke wasn't about to count on it now.

The early reviews came as a happy surprise. Vincent Canby of the *New York Times* called *True Grit* one of "the years best films, a major accomplishment," and most of the other critics were equally enthusiastic. The *Village Voice* even suggested that Duke should win an Oscar for his work.

Duke kept his equilibrium through it all, handling the praise the same way he had handled all those years of criticism. He simply ignored all of it and went about his work. Another Batjac film was in the offing. We were on location with that film when Duke got word that he'd been nominated for an Oscar. He tried to control the swift rush of excitement with characteristic modesty: "Hell, I'm honored," he told me, "who wouldn't be? But you can't eat awards and," he added with a grin, "you sure as hell can't drink 'em."

Duke had been nominated once before, in 1949, for *The Sands of Iwo Jima*. Twenty years had gone by since he played Sergeant Stryker, twenty years of critics attacking his worst performances and ignoring his best ones. *The Quiet Man* won an Oscar as the best picture of 1952, but Duke's performance in it went virtually unnoticed and unappreciated. He'd been unforgettable playing the aging Captain Nathan Brittles in *She Wore a Yellow Ribbon*, Ethan Edwards in *The Searchers*, and Tom Dunson in *Red River*. Fans still remembered his riveting portrayal of the Ringo Kid. Yet the critics and the Academy of Motion Picture Arts and Sciences had ignored every one of those performances.

Duke considered himself the underdog in the 1969 Oscar race. His competition was good. Dustin Hoffman and Jon Voight had been nominated for *Midnight Cowboy;* Peter O'Toole, for *The*

Lion in Winter; and Richard Burton, for *Anne of a Thousand Days.*

"At least I keep damn fine company," Duke remarked, studying the list of candidates. Burton and O'Toole had eight previous nominations between them. "One of them is bound to win," Duke told anyone who wanted to know what he thought his chances were.

As soon as we got back from location, Duke screened his competition. Sitting by ourselves in the darkened screening room, I studied Duke's face in the projector's flickering light as he absorbed the other performances. He could never watch a movie for pure enjoyment. Everything happening on screen, every innovative camera angle, every beautiful bit of lighting or photography caught his attention.

Duke wouldn't have watched *Midnight Cowboy* under normal circumstances—he didn't care for the new wave of realism that was sweeping the U.S. film industry. But he viewed this picture with rapt attention. When it was over he sat motionless. I got up and flicked on the lights, waiting for him to say something.

He finally looked at me, his eyes filled with a strange mixture of pain and envy. "Damn," he sighed, "Hoffman and Voight were good. Both of them. More than good—great. That," he concluded, "is acting. But if I had to choose between the two of them, I'd pick Hoffman. He had the better role."

"Did you like the movie?" I asked, wondering what the man who called *High Noon* un-American, thought of *Midnight Cowboy.*

"'Like' isn't the right word." Duke shook his head. "Hell, you know it's not my kind of story, but I know a great performance when I see one—and I just saw two."

He was just as impressed by O'Toole's work in *Lion in Winter* and Burton's in *Anne of a Thousand Days.* Duke never considered himself to be more than a competent, journeyman performer. He knew he'd done a good job, perhaps his best work, as Rooster, but an actor such as O'Toole illuminated the screen with his brilliance as did Burton. Duke wasn't convinced that his own work measured up to those high standards.

He was on location on Oscar night and flew in from Tucson. The children and I met him at the Beverly Hills Hotel, where

we'd reserved a bungalow. By then Duke had convinced himself
Burton would receive a long overdue Oscar.

As it turned out the Burtons were in an adjoining bungalow.
Liz Taylor seemed to have an uncanny way of turning up at critical moments in our lives. We hadn't seen much of her since
Mike Todd's death. That day, after we met Burton, Duke and I
agreed that Taylor had finally found a man who could more than
fill Todd's shoes. In fact Burton reminded us of Todd. He had
the same electrifying presence, the ability to dominate a crowded
room. The major difference between the two men seemed to be
that the teetotaling Todd had been replaced by a real drinker in
Burton.

Before Taylor and Duke left to attend rehearsals, the four of us
agreed to have a private celebration after the ceremony, no matter who won or lost. Duke returned late in the afternoon in time
to dress and go right back to the Dorothy Chandler Pavilion. There
was a wonderful roar of approval as we walked past the fans
waiting outside the auditorium. Once inside we were escorted
to front row center seats, and Aissa, Ethan, and the rest of the
Wayne clan were seated farther back.

Duke and I had been through many an Oscar evening, but this
one was very special. Duke, as private as ever when it came to
his deepest feelings, hadn't said much about being nervous. But
he grabbed my hand as the ceremonies began, clutching it so
tightly that his nails pressed into my palm. I ignored the pain,
pasted a smile on my face, and tried to enjoy the show.

When it was Duke's turn to participate, he slipped away quietly. I glanced down at my palm, seeing the red marks of his
nails. He looked so supremely confident and at ease as I watched
him up on stage that I couldn't believe the same man had been
mangling my fingers seconds earlier.

Minutes later he rejoined me and grabbed my hand in the same
painful grip. By the time Barbra Streisand walked to the podium
to present the Oscar for the year's best actor, Duke's smile had
frozen on his face. We watched the usual brief film clips of each
nominated performance, and then Streisand opened the enve-
lope. She withdrew a single folded sheet, glanced at it, and then
her face was wreathed in a glorious smile.

Duke dropped my hand, preparing to clap enthusiastically for the winner. Streisand leaned toward the microphone, her clear, bell-like voice announcing, "And the winner is...John Wayne for *True Grit*."

For a moment Duke sat as still as a rock, shock on his face. Then he jumped up, smiling broadly, a hint of moisture in his eyes as he raced for the stage. He hadn't prepared a speech, hadn't expected to win. He and Streisand embraced, she handed him his Oscar, and then he leaned down to the microphone, unashamed of the tears that sparkled in his eyes.

"Wow!" Duke exclaimed. "If I'd known that, I'd have put on that eye patch thirty-five years ago." He paused, struggling for composure, choking back sobs that would have exposed Hollywood's most macho male as the world's biggest softie. And then he spoke to his peers, words straight from his heart:

> Ladies and gentleman, I'm no stranger to this podium. I've come up here and picked up these beautiful golden men before—but always for a friend. One night I picked up two; one for Admiral John Ford and one for our beloved Gary Cooper. I was very clever and witty that night—the envy of Bob Hope. But tonight I don't feel very clever, very witty. I feel very grateful, very humble, and I owe thanks to many, many people. I want to thank the members of the Academy. To all you people who are watching on television, thank you for taking such a warm interest in our glorious industry.

Then Duke turned on his heel and, clutching his Oscar, left the podium. I joined him backstage, and we hugged and kissed and hugged some more. After the awards and the interviews, we were waiting for our limousine when I suddenly realized that Duke no longer clutched his Oscar in his hand. But 7-year-old Ethan, who would someday pursue an acting career himself gripped the award firmly, holding it like a machine gun while he pretended to be a soldier ambushing the crowd. The rest of the evening blurs happily in memory, a montage of congratulations and good wishes, the kindest words, a great outpouring of love that took Duke by surprise and brought tears to his eyes.

We spent the small hours of the night with the Burtons, and it is to their credit that not for one minute did we think they didn't share our joy. Burton had great generosity of spirit, a trait he shared with his wife. I'll never forget seeing Duke and Burton embrace and swear undying loyalty. They talked boozily of doing a picture together, but unfortunately the right script never came their way.

Burton was a practiced raconteur, and he held us spellbound, telling one hilarious story after another. I could have listened to him forever, and that evening, it seemed as if I would. Finally Taylor turned to him and said, "Richard, darling, would you please shut up."

Burton stopped talking in mid-sentence, and the strangest look, part amusement, part anger, part pride, came over his face. I'd been holding my breath, waiting to see how he would react. Then some private signal seemed to pass from him to Taylor. He just smiled, winked, and continued his story.

Later, when Taylor finally had the floor, she told us that she had hoped to win an Oscar when she'd been nominated for her work in *Who's Afraid of Virginia Wolf* in 1966. She'd costarred with Burton in that film, their first since *Cleopatra*, and regarded the picture as the best she would ever make. The following year she'd been nominated again, this time for *Butterfield 8*, a film she disliked so much that the studio had to force her to make it. Winning an Oscar for that film had been an anticlimax. "You're lucky," she told Duke, "because you won for a film you love."

Duke returned to location in Arizona the next morning, having gone without any sleep. When he arrived at old Tucson, the entire cast and crew of *Rio Lobo* were wearing eye patches, even Duke's horse.

He called me that evening to make sure the children and I had gotten home safely. And then he said, "It really happened, didn't it?"

"Don't worry, Duke. The Oscar is in our den right now, waiting for you to come home. We all are."

PART THREE

★

That's a Wrap

CHAPTER 31

If I were writing a screenplay instead of the story of Duke's life I would have closed with the last scene, leaving the hero and heroine to live happily ever after in everyone's imagination. The credits would have rolled as the camera dollied away from the happy couple and they danced in each other's arms at the Oscar gala. But this is a story of real lives, lived under great stress, and there isn't going to be a fairytale ending. We never got to walk off into the sunset, hand in hand.

After Duke had won his Oscar, a crowning achievement for any actor's career, I tried to talk him into reconsidering his retirement. He turned on me angrily when I broached the subject. "Are you crazy?" he asked. "What the hell do you think we'd live on?"

Though Duke continued to plead poverty, the reality was that we had more than enough money. I wasn't a financial expert, but I knew that we'd come out of the LaCava affair with the Arizona ranches intact. We had our home in Newport, Duke's old Batjac movies were worth a small fortune as television entertainment, and we had various other assets. True, Duke hadn't accumulated an estate like those of Bob Hope or Gene Autry, but he was a millionaire. He didn't need to go on making money, but he was too old and stubborn to change.

Many people envy a film star's life, not realizing how hard moviemaking can be on marriages. Intense boredom is the lot of a star's family on primitive locations, the kind Duke favored. During filming he'd leave home (mud hut, hotel or motel room, rented house, etc.) at five or six in the morning, depending on how far our temporary residence was from the day's shooting. Since most directors didn't welcome our presence while Duke worked, we usually stayed in our quarters awaiting his return. Duke wasn't around to see how his demands affected the children's behavior. He'd get back somewhere between five and seven o'clock in the evening, take a shower, get a rubdown, climb into his pajamas, eat supper with the family, and then retire to his bed to memorize the next day's script. That's the glamorous life of a working actor and his family.

Twenty years of this routine made me dread going on location. The children, who shared my feelings, were even less willing to leave home in the middle of a school year to go to some lonely place so they could see their father for half an hour at night.

When I remained in Newport with the children, visiting Duke on location for only a week or two at a time, he was terribly hurt. "You're my wife," he'd argue. "Your place is with me."

I'd try to explain that the children were getting too old to be turned over to a nurse or a housekeeper. Aissa was already in her teens. She needed a mother to talk to, not a maid. Ethan and Marisa were still children, but they too wanted me at home. I remembered how empty my own home in Peru had felt when my parents traveled, even though I had a brother and sisters. I couldn't continue to put my children through the loneliness I'd experienced as a child. Unfortunately, Duke wasn't interested in why we didn't want to go on location with him. The only thing that counted was that we were disappointing him. He lived in a black-and-white world, a place with no room for compromise or accommodation. A thing was either good or bad.

As our disagreements escalated, I reluctantly came to the conclusion that I couldn't keep chasing after Duke, that trying to do so was detrimental to our children's welfare, and that he had no reason to go on working so hard. More than anything, I was tired of playing second fiddle to his film career.

While our marriage sagged, Duke's fame peaked. By the end of the sixties, to his amazement and amusement, cars were sporting bumper stickers which read, "God loves John Wayne." He'd never been more popular with the fans. He'd reigned as one of the top-ten box office draws for the past twenty years, a feat no performer has duplicated.

The results of a 1968 poll declared him to be television's most popular star even though he'd never made a television series. His popularity was based solely on his old films, which turned up on the tube with predictable regularity. The 1969 Oscars telecast achieved the highest rating in its history, and insiders claimed this was primarily because Duke appeared on the show. The critics who'd panned *The Green Berets* so mercilessly in 1968 were calling Duke an extra star on the U.S. flag by 1970.

Some years after Duke and I married, he'd written a new will that established trust funds for me and for the children we shared. However, the many financial setbacks he'd experienced in the fifties and sixties prevented that fund from reaching the proportions he'd hoped it would. Duke told me he continued to work so hard because he wanted to assure our future.

I was far more concerned with the present. Duke had been spending his energy and health with a careless disregard for both. Approaching his mid-sixties, he had to face the fact that he'd overdrawn his own physical resources. His breathing problem was aggravated by a newly acquired habit of smoking an occasional cigar. His weight fluctuated wildly, his eating habits were erratic, and his health was obviously deteriorating.

I saw retirement as the answer to all our problems. There'd be no more arguments about going on location, Duke could stop the dieting that made him so short tempered. His health would improve as soon as he began to take it a little easier. It seemed so obviously the right thing to do, I couldn't understand why Duke wouldn't consider it.

Duke said he intended to spend the rest of his life building the trusts funds. He regarded it as a sacred obligation, the very least a man could do for his family. There weren't going to be any Waynes or Morrisons on the street looking for handouts after he was gone! And that meant making movies, lots of movies. Never mind that he was growing old and tired, burdened by a limited lung capacity. Nothing could convince him, not accountants or bank statements or all my pleading, that he didn't need to go on doing films as fast as he could.

From 1939 to 1972 he'd made an astonishing eighty-two feature-length motion pictures, averaging over two a year. That meant putting in six to nine months of sixteen-hour work days each year, spending extra hours in Batjac's offices, holding conferences, and reading scripts at home. It was a killer of a schedule.

People rarely remember him starring in anything other than westerns. However, of the sixty pictures he made from 1940 to 1960, a surprising total of thirty-five were on other subjects. During those two decades he was still groping toward the John Wayne persona, an image that would become equated with apple pie, motherhood, and the U.S. flag.

From 1960 to 1972 he made twenty-two more films, and fifteen of them were westerns. By then the John Wayne image had taken on a life and power of its own. Duke had found his place in film history, and as he grew older he was less inclined to tamper with the colossus he'd created.

He'd always fought changes in our private life. From the late sixties on he fought them in his career as well. He could make a John Wayne western by rote, and he returned to Durango again and again from 1969 to 1972, to make *The War Wagon, The Undefeated, Chisum, Big Jake, The Train Robbers,* and *Cahill, United States Marshall.* Each time he announced that he was about to do another Durango film, I shuddered. Looking back, I can barely tell those Durango films from one another. They had a sameness of story, plot, and location which seemed like a disservice to Duke's fans. Different casts are the only thing which made them stand apart.

The Undefeated, filmed in 1969, was Duke's third Durango picture. Duke's costar, and Duke's attitude toward him, made this film more memorable than the others.

Rock Hudson was a successful leading man in 1969, a Hollywood hunk whom women adored. Insiders knew his sexual preference, even way back then, but that didn't stop ladies from drooling when he was on a set. This film was no exception. Duke had hired several members of the Los Angeles Rams football team to play minor roles in the movie. Their wives, eager for a glimpse of moviemaking, had accompanied them on location. They all adored Hudson, who was adept at flirting in a friendly, nonthreatening way that many women find irresistible.

Hudson had his choice of companions at the end of a day's

work. He spent the early evenings with Duke and me and a fourth, playing bridge. For years afterward, Duke and I got notes from Hudson, detailing spectacular hands he'd played.

To the dismay of the ladies on location, Hudson spent the rest of the night with one of the Ram's more famous members. That alliance ended the football player's marriage, and he moved in with Rock. As gossip swirled around the two men, I couldn't resist asking Duke what he thought about the situation. His reply was characteristic: "What Rock Hudson does—in the privacy of his own room—is his own business. He's a professional on the set and a real gentleman—and he plays a hell of a hand of bridge." Duke could forgive a good bridge player almost anything.

Duke's next picture, *Rio Lobo*, mercifully interrupted the string of Durango films. While we were in Tucson for the filming, Duke received word that his brother, Bobby, had died of cancer at just 58 years old. It was a terrible blow to Duke, who loved his brother in spite of Bobby's crazy escapades and his complete lack of ambition. Duke was finally free of the promise he'd made so many years ago. He no longer had to "look after Bobby." As he said tearfully, "God will have to do it for me."

I felt that Bobby's death was a warning, one Duke should take very seriously. But once again, in 1970 we were back in Durango to make a fifth film. The credits for *Big Jake* looked like "old home week." Duke and Maureen O'Hara were reunited in a move carefully calculated to maximize the movie's box office potential. This picture also marked our son Ethan's first important role in one of his father's pictures. In a rather ironic bit of casting, he played Duke's grandson. Michael Wayne produced the film. Patrick Wayne played Duke's son. Bruce Cabot and Harey Carey, Jr., had supporting roles, and William Clothier was the cinematographer. These names, along with those of director Andrew McLaglen, Jr., writers Harry and Julian Fink, and art director Carl Anderson, appear over and over in the Durango movies.

While I understood and sympathized with Duke's desire to work with reliable people, I felt that doing so again and again contributed greatly to the monotony of Batjac's final films, but all of them made money and pleased Duke's loyal fans, and that seemed to satisfy him.

I made my last trip to Durango in 1973, when Duke was filming *The Train Robbers* with Rod Taylor, Ben Johnson, and Ann Margret. Though they'd never worked together before, Taylor and Duke were already good friends. Ten years earlier, when we still lived in Encino, Duke called one afternoon to announce that Taylor would be our guest for dinner that night. The meal was a convivial affair with lots of storytelling. Knowing Duke liked to stay up late when he had an entertaining male visitor, I retired at a reasonable hour, leaving the two men to their drinks and conversation. To my surprise they were still at it when I got up the next morning. Our family's activities swirled around them all day as they continued drinking and talking.

Taylor stayed for supper that night, and once again I retired early. The next morning Duke and Taylor were still at it, drinking and talking, and, again, they kept it up all day. I didn't even need to ask if Taylor would stay for dinner that night—we just set an extra plate. The marathon conversation ended that night while I slept. When I woke up in the morning Duke was in bed beside me in an exhausted sleep.

Those three days were typical of Duke. When he met someone he liked, he just had to know everything about them—immediately. Duke's need to possess the people he cared for was one of his least attractive traits. After twenty-two years of living with him, I felt completely smothered by it. I was struggling for freedom and an identity of my own, while Duke fought just as hard to maintain his control over me.

One final personal tragedy united us. Ford died on August 31, 1972. He'd been in a long decline, virtually bed-ridden at his retirement home in Palm Desert. Duke had been to see him and came away from those visits saddened and depressed, describing Ford as gaunt and unwashed and usually drunk—a horribly sad end for such a giant, talented figure of the film industry.

Duke said that losing Ford was like losing his father again. We held hands tightly at the funeral and clung together for the next few weeks, painfully aware of life's finite nature.

Then all the old problems resurfaced. My beautiful nineteenth-century man couldn't adapt to the seventies. He was sick about his country's ignominious withdrawal from Vietnam, angered by the entire Watergate incident, furious over the rise of feminism. The angrier Duke became about the world situation, the harder he was to live with at home.

By the fall of 1973 the Bayshore house was beginning to feel like an armed camp. Duke was convinced that my refusal to accompany him on location was caused by a growing selfishness on my part, a lack of interest in him and his well-being. I was just as stubborn and just as blind, certain the children needed me more than he did.

Duke wanted his own idea of a wife, not some female who was struggling to develop a life and an identity of her own. He wanted children who jumped when he said jump, just as he'd done in his youth. I wanted to be able to play tennis, to see my friends, to stay home while Duke was on location without feeling guilty. I wanted to give our children a little more freedom, to allow them to learn by their mistakes.

Duke would have given the children and me anything money could buy. What he couldn't grant us was some degree of independence. Once, I refused to accompany him on a fourth cruise to Alaska and Duke even had my mother fly into town from Lima, Peru, to instruct me on a wife's proper role. I could cheerfully have strangled both of them that day.

I sometimes thought that Duke imagined us existing in a state of suspended animation during his absences. One night after he came home from another stint in Durango, we planned to screen a film at home. Duke was amazed when I loaded the projector by myself, not realizing that I'd done it dozens of times when he was away. Any indication of competence on my part either amazed or angered him. The saddest thing at this point in our lives was that, although we still loved each other, we were better at arguing than talking.

It was time to take a break between rounds, to call in a referee. We both needed a breathing space, a chance to reevaluate our feelings for each other. We agreed to a separation a few days before Thanksgiving 1973. Once the decision had been reached, I told Duke I would move into a condominium we owned in Newport.

Duke told our closest friends that he was sick about the way things worked out. He wanted the "old" Pilar back. He believed that I'd fallen prey to "all that damn bullshit about women's lib."

And so we parted. But I didn't think it would be forever, and neither did he.

CHAPTER 32

Mary St. John reported that Duke spent the first three days of our separation alone, fighting tears. I didn't even bother to fight.

Duke was in New York accepting an award the day the children and I packed our clothes, or I don't think any of us could have gone through with the move. I felt so guilty about leaving, knowing how deeply I'd disappointed him, shattering his expectations of a serene and peaceful old age. Yet I couldn't live with the angry, unyielding man he'd become.

I couldn't help but remember how Duke had asked Scotty to keep the house full of flowers when he and Chata parted. The children, who would be free to spend as much time with their father as they wished, were the flowers I left for Duke. Their brightness would keep the Bayshore house warm and alive in my absence. Ethan stayed behind to greet his father when Duke got home. From then on all three of our children divided their time between the Bayshore house and my condominium just a few blocks away.

Knowing Duke hated even the smallest change in lifestyle, I left our home fully furnished, taking just essentials to the condominium. After camping in my new quarters for a few weeks, sorting out my feelings, I was quite certain Duke and I would get back together. I was miserable, he was miserable. We weren't fighting, and that was a relief, but we weren't happy either.

We'd expected to be married forever. That's what we both wanted. It was inconceivable that we wouldn't overcome our present problems. Duke seemed to agree, because he insisted that I rent furniture rather than buying a house full. "You'll only need it until we get things worked out," he said.

Our first six months apart were not very different from our last few years together. Duke was too restless a man to spend much time at home. When he wasn't working he liked to travel, and he was always going someplace to make a speech, accept an award, or look after his widespread business interests. Duke didn't change his routine after we parted. If anything, he seemed to increase the number and length of his many trips.

In 1974, right after the New Year, the *Harvard Lampoon* dared Duke to show himself in person at their university, a stronghold of liberal activism. A coward might have refused their invitation. Duke had everything to lose and very little to gain by going to Boston.

I urged him to ignore the invitation when he told me about it. "You know they'll try to make a fool of you, Duke," I argued. As usual, Duke was too stubborn to listen to reason. He agreed to visit Harvard in the middle of January, since he would be on his way to London to tape a Glen Campbell television special.

Later, Duke told me that after arriving on campus, he was paraded around Harvard Square in an armored personnel carrier. Then he was taken to the Harvard Square theater for a no-holds-barred question-and-answer session. By the end of that session he'd transformed a mob of rude, hostile students into John Wayne fans. He did it with humor. The dialogue went like this:

STUDENT :   "Where did you get that phony toupee?"

DUKE :   "It's not phony; it's real hair. Of course it's not mine—but it's real."

STUDENT :   "What are your views on women's lib?"

DUKE :   "I think they have a right to work anyplace they want to—as long as they have dinner on the table when I get home."

STUDENT :   "Do you look on yourself as the fulfillment of the American dream?"

DUKE :   "I try not to look at myself any more than I have to."

The session went on like that for an hour, a triumph for Duke.

He also kept busy early in the year traveling with Joe De Franco, promoting their Separation and Recovery Systems business. About this time Duke got involved in a company that had developed a method of extracting oil from old tires. He was quite excited about the nonpolluting process, which seemed to offer one way of combating the oil shortage that existed then. With Duke's financing and name, the Duke Engineering Company was off to a flying start.

While he worked and traveled, I set about trying to build a life that would give me the self-esteem I'd never developed in our marriage. Over the years I'd become involved in two important hobbies—interior decorating and cooking—and I decided to turn these avocations into vocations. It took a little schooling and a lot more legwork than I had anticipated, but the day my Decorator Studio opened was a proud and happy one for me. Opening the Fernleaf Cafe followed in short order. In a matter of months I'd been transformed from a member of the idle rich to a participant in the working world, which I loved. Despite despondent moments when I couldn't help thinking about my relationship with Duke, I was beginning to like myself.

To my surprise, Duke responded positively to my new business activities. When we moved into the Bayshore house he supervised all the decorating. Shortly after my studio opened, he called and asked me to help him redo his living room. I was thrilled. In all the years we'd been together, he'd never given me tangible proof that he valued and respected my opinion. He also liked the restaurant and dined there often. As the weeks went by discussions of reconciliation were often on the menu.

I'd been going to a marriage counselor, trying to understand why two people who still loved one another had made such a mess of their lives. Duke didn't believe in psychologists and psychiatrists, didn't like the idea of airing our "dirty linen" in front of a stranger, but he did agree to attend one of my sessions.

He sat through the meeting politely. When asked why he thought our marriage was in trouble he replied, "My wife won't go on location with me anymore. She'd rather stay home, play tennis, and be with the children."

No matter how the counselor probed, Duke would say no more on the subject. That was the size and scope of our problem as far as he was concerned. For me, that joint visit defined the situation clearly. If I wanted to resume our life together, I was going to have to live it by Duke's rules. At 67 he was too old to change.

Either I played the game his way or he'd take all the marbles and leave. He didn't want to argue, to go on fighting; he just wanted things the way they were twenty years before.

That afternoon in the marriage counselor's office, I realized that I was still Duke's "girl," someone to control and manipulate as well as love and care for. If I couldn't accept the situation, a million women would be more than happy to take my place.

After the session ended, Duke asked me to go to the Arches, a Newport Beach restaurant, to have a drink. It was an amazing invitation. Duke and I had never been out alone together for a private meal, a quiet talk, a romantic evening. Our public excursions were always made in the company of other people. Duke's desire to be surrounded by friends was so much a part of his character that I'd almost forgotten that husbands and wives went out by themselves.

As we pulled into the restaurant's parking lot I felt like a girl on her first date. Good heavens, Duke and I would be all by ourselves, we'd actually have a chance to talk. Perhaps our meeting with the marriage counselor had worked a miracle, perhaps Duke was more willing to try and reach a compromise than he appeared to be. A thousand hopeful thoughts raced through my mind as we walked into the restaurant hand in hand. The proprietor greeted Duke and led us to a prominent table, proud to display John Wayne's patronage. A waiter rushed over and took our order, and we were finally alone.

"Well, Duke," I began, "what did you think of the session?"

He grinned sheepishly. "Not much. Hell, Pilar, you know me. I don't believe in all that mumbo jumbo. We're grown people and we ought to be able to settle our problems ourselves."

"We can't do that, Duke, unless we talk about them."

"That's fine with me," he answered. "I've got all afternoon."

That sounded promising. I couldn't believe we were really going to spend a few hours by ourselves, just talking. It would be a first in our twenty-three years. We'd just begun to discuss the events of the last few months when a movie fan appeared at our table.

"I hope you don't mind, Mr. Wayne," the woman said, "but I just love your movies." She produced a scrap of paper and asked, "Would you please give me your autograph?"

Duke looked up at her, smiled, thanked her nicely, and signed his name. He always treated his fans with consideration. Duke was the first movie actor to achieve stardom without the backing of a major studio. He felt that he owed his success to the people who went to see his pictures. He'd never asked a fan to leave him in peace before, and he didn't start that afternoon at the Arches.

Before the first woman left our table another stood behind her. Within a few minutes a line of eager, excited people stretched from our table to the front door. Duke seemed determined to talk to every one of them, grateful that they liked his films, happy to see them.

I watched him for a few minutes, seeing a man in his glory, a man who'd forgotten his reason for being in that restaurant. When I excused myself, Duke barely nodded in my direction. Feeling completely demoralized, I asked the maitre d' to call a cab. While waiting, I kept on glancing toward Duke's table, wondering if he noticed my absence. He was still signing autographs as I walked out the door.

He called me at home a few hours later, angry and upset. "Where the hell did you go this afternoon?" he blustered. "I thought we were going to have a talk."

Duke and I flirted with reconciliation for a few more months, seeing each other several times a week. We were still unhappy, still eager to work out our differences, and not one step closer to finding solutions. He called me in May to say that he'd be leaving for London soon to film *Branigan*.

Apparently my complaints about those endless Durango westerns hadn't gone unheeded. Duke would be playing a detective in his new movie. Michael was the executive producer, and another old friend, Dominic Frontiere, would be writing the film's score. Duke would be gone for three months.

"I want you and the kids to come and stay for a month," he said, after telling me about the film. "The studio has rented a house for us. Look, Pilar, it's London—not Durango. Please say you'll come."

I couldn't turn down an invitation like that.

The children didn't share my enthusiasm for the proposed visit. Although they wouldn't be in school, they weren't eager to

leave friends and activities behind for what was, in their eyes,
just another location movie. Aissa, already a young lady, had
planned her own jaunt to Europe with friends her age, so I flew
into Heathrow in July accompanied by Ethan and Marisa.

Duke was filming the day we arrived, and he'd made arrangements for one of his employees, a secretary named Pat Stacy, to
pick us up at the airport. Pat was being groomed to replace Mary
St. John, who would be retiring in a few months.

Stacy dropped us at Duke's place on Cheyne Walk. The house
was everything I could have wished, a charming antiquated delight that came complete with a butler and a housekeeper. It was
an ideal place to begin our married life again if that was what
Duke had in mind.

I was still uncertain about his intentions when he walked into
the drawing room late that afternoon. The children rushed into
his arms, and he hugged them ferociously. When the three released each other, Duke turned to me, took three quick steps
across the room, and embraced me tightly. I stayed in his arms
for a moment, feeling as if I'd come home after a long journey,
and then all four of us began talking at once.

Duke had presents for everyone, including a beautiful gold
necklace for me. He'd been bringing me gifts ever since we parted, but none were so costly or carefully chosen. As I held the
heavy golden links in my hand, I knew that Duke was saying, in
the only way he knew, that he wanted us to start over.

The days that followed had a surreal quality. Duke was doing
his best to court me with flowers, small gifts, words of appreci-
ation. We were awkward and hesitant with each other. Our separation had changed me irrevocably. I'd finally become my own
person, and it had wounded Duke deeply. We would draw close
and then back off, like partners in a stately dance. He loved me,
I saw it in every look and touch, but he was still angry. There
were times when I saw so much pain in his eyes that I wanted to
weep. Had I really done so much damage to this wonderful man?

While Duke worked, the children and I went sightseeing. The
Cheyne Walk house boasted a small pool, a purely Hollywood
touch in the midst of its antiquated elegance, and we spent the
afternoons splashing about. Evenings were devoted to family,

which for Duke meant that Marisa and Ethan joined our guests at the dinner table. The film company spent Saturdays shooting and Sundays at our house.

Duke and I appeared to have resumed our lives together as though we'd never been apart. We still weren't sharing a bedroom, but I felt certain that would happen when we were more at ease. We had the rest of our lives to enjoy that part of our relationship. Then one evening, after the children were in bed, Duke and I had a quiet talk about our future. With the saddest expression on his face, he took my hand saying, "Pilar, you know I love you very much. But there's something you have to know. I'm old, tired, I don't feel well, and I'm taking a lot of medication. I just can't be a real husband to you any more."

It broke my heart.

By the third week of our stay, other difficulties that had always plagued our marriage resurfaced. Marisa and Ethan wanted to go home. They were bored and lonely. Four years apart and opposite sexes, they weren't much company for each other. Ethan missed his friends, surfing, sailing, waterskiing, all his normal activities, and Marisa was tired of living out of a suitcase. Nothing had really changed for them. The hour they spent with their father in the evening, in the midst of a houseful of people, didn't make up for other things they were missing. As usual they voiced their dissatisfaction to me rather than Duke, so he had no way of knowing how strongly they felt. So it fell to me to tell Duke that we were going home a week early.

After I told him we would be leaving earlier than we planned, I could see that he was terribly disappointed and upset with us. He began to treat me with a distant politeness, as if we were strangers rather than husband and wife.

On one of our last days together we went to lunch at a restaurant owned by David Niven's son, Noel. We were greeted effusively and given the best table in the house. The wine steward came over and asked what we wanted. Duke ordered a very expensive bottle of red wine for the two of us. I never drank red wine, and he knew it.

Suddenly, with crystal clarity, I realized that trying to go on with our reconciliation was pointless at that particular time. Duke wouldn't fight, shout, or argue, but that bottle of red wine told me more about his feelings than all the words in the world.

Even so, later that day we talked about living together after *Branigan* wrapped. Duke assured me that he wanted me to move back into the Bayshore house as soon as he got home. He was due back in mid-August. Surely by then, I thought, he will have worked his way through what was bothering him and we'll have another chance at a life together.

CHAPTER 33

I returned to Newport Beach at the end of July determined to keep busy with the decorator studio and the restaurant, but no matter how hard I worked, the days dragged. I could no longer ignore the knowledge that life without Duke was a dreary substitute for life with him. The weeks spent in London served to remind me of one inescapable fact: I loved him. Duke's behavior during our nine months' separation gave me every reason to believe that he still loved me. Perhaps we would never have a perfect marriage, but I knew we were still capable of having a very caring one.

Duke expected to be home sometime in mid-August if *Branigan* wrapped on schedule, and I began to count the days. He'd promised that we'd resume our lives together as soon as he got home, and I planned to hold him to his word. Despite his restlessness, Duke was a family man. He needed love more than any other man I've ever known. As long as he had the children and me, there was no reason why he should ever have to be alone again. During those long July days I vowed that we'd find a way to resolve all our problems.

By mid-August I'd convinced myself that it was silly to wait for Duke to return before I moved back into the Bayshore house. So many of my things as well as the children's were still there. We'd been camping out in the condominium, and it had never felt like home. My longing for familiar surroundings, for my own bed, for all the things that represented permanence and stability, was so strong that I decided to call Duke in London to see if he objected to my going home before he got there.

The butler answered the phone at Cheyne Walk. I asked for

Duke without identifying myself, and he told me that Duke was in Paris for the weekend. Then I asked to speak to Pat Stacy, thinking she could tell me how to contact my husband.

"I'm sorry, Ma'am," the butler replied, "but Miss Stacy is in Paris too."

For a moment, I was speechless. I finally managed to say goodbye and hang up, but my mind was in a turmoil. What in the world was Duke doing in Paris with Pat Stacy? I asked myself. A business trip, of course—it had to be a business trip. But what kind of business would Duke have in Paris on a weekend?

My next thought was to call Mary St. John. Although she was semiretired, she kept in close touch with Duke and still filled in when Stacy couldn't keep up with the volume of correspondence and bookkeeping.

"Did you know that Duke has taken Pat Stacy to Paris?" I blurted as soon as St. John said hello.

"Who told you?" she asked.

"I called the house and talked to the butler."

Mary St. John sounded very upset when she replied. "I found out the same way. I'm so sorry, Pilar."

"But why?" I blurted. "Why in the world would he do a thing like that when he knows the children and I have been waiting for him to come home? Did he have business in France?"

"No, Pilar."

I hated having to ask my next question. "Is Duke in love with Pat?"

The reply came with blessed swiftness. "Don't be silly! There isn't anything serious going on between them."

That was some comfort. St. John had trained Pat Stacy as her replacement and had spent more time with her and Duke than anyone else. "Then what are they doing in Paris together?" I demanded.

"Pilar," she replied, "I don't think you realize how much Duke has been hurt by your separation. I think this is his way of getting even." She paused, "And it won't hurt his career to have the fans and the studios thinking of him as a virile man with a young girlfriend."

I couldn't believe what St. John was saying. It seemed so pet-

ty, so foreign to Duke's character. Would he really use Pat Stacy
to hurt me? At first it was unthinkable. But then I began to wonder. Had Duke taken Stacy to Paris to prove something to himself?

Mary St. John and I talked a little longer, about the children,
the weather, inconsequential things. I could barely concentrate
on what she was saying. All I could think about was Duke in
Paris with his secretary. It hurt.

We'd done our best to keep our separation out of the columns,
for the children's sake as well as our own. Fortunately we lived
60 miles from Hollywood, far from the glare of publicity. Duke
liked it that way. He always said that Hollywood had two major
products—gossip and movies. He loved his profession but hated
the endless crop of rumors and scandal that grew in the fertile
soil of the movie industry. He'd chosen to live in Encino and
then in Newport in part because they were far enough from Hollywood to give us some privacy. Now, Duke's sudden trip to Paris
made us, our marriage, our private problems, the subject of some
very public speculation.

While I waited to hear from Duke, a series of disturbing questions raced through my mind. Would the man I respected, the
man whose honesty and integrity I'd never questioned, try to
hurt me by pretending to be involved with another woman?
Would he put his career, his image ahead of our hopes for reconciliation? Had he invited me to London as a test of his feelings
for Stacy? I felt sure he'd call the children as soon as he got home,
but would he want to see me? What would he have to say when
he did?

Fortunately, I didn't have to wait long for answers. Duke returned to Newport within a few days and he telephoned immediately, agreeing to meet me at the Fernleaf Cafe the following
afternoon.

That night just before I finally fell asleep, I remembered how
he used to laugh and say he'd find a younger woman if our age
difference ever got to be a problem. I couldn't believe that Pat
Stacy was that younger woman, but then, I reminded myself un-
happily, they say the wife is always the last to know.

Duke came striding into the restaurant the next day looking

rested and relaxed. He led me to a booth and, for the first few minutes he dominated the conversation, questioning me about what the children had been doing since he'd seen them.

I finally cut him off. "Duke, I heard about your trip to Paris, and I want you to know I won't stand in your way if you want a divorce."

His eyes widened in surprise. "No," he said angrily, "I don't want a divorce. What the hell gave you an idea like that?"

How I hated having to ask my next question. "Are you in love with Pat Stacy?"

"Of course not! She's my secretary—that's all!"

"Then why did you take her to Paris?" I persisted.

"Why the hell did you leave London ahead of schedule?" Duke shot back.

"I told you why. The kids were bored, they wanted to go home." Good Lord, I'd explained it all in London. "What other reason could I possibly have?"

Duke looked at me, flushed, and looked away. In the silence that followed I realized that he had jumped to all the wrong conclusions.

"Why don't we forget London and Paris," I suggested, "and concentrate on all the good years we've had together and on our three children. For their sake I'd like to give our marriage another try." The words were no sooner said than I realized I'd made another mistake. Why hadn't I said, for my sake? It would have been true.

Duke looked completely miserable. "Pilar," he muttered, "we both have to face it. Our marriage is over."

My first instinct was to comfort him—his was to run away. Duke didn't want to discuss his condition. From his bleak expression, I suspected that he already regretted the admission. The best chance we'd ever had for open and honest communication evaporated as he fled the restaurant. That night I wrote Duke a long letter. He had to know how much I cared, how much I wanted to deal with this problem as a couple. I spent hours polishing that letter, wishing I could have written it in Spanish, struggling to put all the love I felt on those few pages.

Duke walked into the Fernleaf Cafe a few days later, without any warning. I'd been praying he'd want to see me after he got the letter. If he could put his pride aside I knew we could work things out.

"I'm so glad to see you," I said, feeling as awkward as a girl with a stranger.

Duke looked equally uncomfortable. "I got your letter and I want you to know it meant a lot to me. I know it wasn't easy for you to write all those things."

He looked at me steadily. "You're still a young woman. One of these days, you're going to need more than I can give and then…" His voice trailed off. "I can't do that to you, or to me. Leave it be, Pilar. Please, just leave it be."

I wanted to shake him, to tell him he shouldn't let pride come between us, not when I knew he needed his family more than ever. But I choked back the words.

Duke always said, "You can take everything a man has as long as you leave his dignity." Dignity was terribly important to him that afternoon. I could see it in the straight way he held himself, the steadiness of his gaze. I had to respect his wishes. He walked out of the Fernleaf Cafe with his pride intact, his broad shoulders silhouetted in the door before he disappeared from my sight. Tears spilled down my cheeks as I struggled to accept what had just happened. In the weeks and months to come, Duke and I would probably go on seeing each other, we might even laugh together again, but I knew that our marriage was over.

Hindsight makes geniuses of us all. If I'd been wiser, I might have anticipated Duke's reaction to my letter. I'd tried to write of love but he interpreted my emotion as pity, and pity was the one thing he couldn't accept from me or anyone else. I had no one to blame but myself. The separation was my fault. I'd wanted independence, a chance to take control of my own life. Now I would have all the independence I could handle. Duke would never return to me unless a miracle made him well again. Instead, he was to become a very sick man.

From then on we were to meet as intimate strangers. I even began dating, although my thoughts and my heart were still with Duke. He still stopped by the restaurant, still called to talk about the children, a new script, an upcoming trip. I continued to offer him the freedom of a divorce, and he always rejected the offer firmly. Our relationship floated along in limbo while the gossip columns printed stories of Duke's new love. Today, years after Duke's passing, it is still difficult for me to write about Pat Stacy and the role she played in our lives.

When Duke left to film *Rooster Cogburn* in September 1974, she accompanied him. That alone wasn't newsworthy, because Duke often took his secretary when he traveled. His business affairs didn't stop just because he happened to be making a movie. There was always an avalanche of mail to answer each day, the recording of expenses had to be reported to the studio, a myriad of details to be handled. In the past Mary St. John had gone everywhere with Duke, but was a happily married woman.

Now, for all intents and purposes, Duke seemed to be a single man traveling with a young woman. It made headlines. Rumors of a romance with Pat Stacy persisted. Duke's constant denials of a romantic link with his secretary simply made the columnists more anxious to "get at the truth."

In fact, Duke was in no condition to have a love affair. He was plagued by a variety of ailments which he struggled to conceal from everyone. His oldest and dearest friends, people he'd counted on for support and companionship, were all gone. His children were busy with their own lives. To my everlasting sorrow, I'd failed him too. Duke, who must have been feeling abandoned and alone, began to rely on Pat Stacy for companionship.

In 1974, when Duke worked with Kate Hepburn during the filming of *Rooster Cogburn*, she described him as "a lovely man." He returned her admiration and loved working with her, but he had a difficult time with his other coworkers during the shooting. Duke felt ill on location, and the worse he felt, the shorter his temper became. He argued with the director and assistant director, had an angry confrontation with one of the wardrobe people.

Mary St. John remarked that Duke no longer seemed to care about much of anything. I wanted to tell her the truth, explain why he no longer cared, share the burden of his confession with someone else who loved him. But I couldn't do that to my husband. Not then.

Meanwhile stories about his relationship with Pat Stacy kept appearing in the columns, and our children were affected by them. One afternoon when Mary St. John was visiting Duke at the Hoag Hospital, she heard him accuse Pat Stacy of being responsible for most of the stories that were appearing in the columns. He'd just seen an article in the gossip magazines that purported to tell the truth about "Duke's new love."

"Damn it, Pat," Duke growled. "This kind of story wouldn't be printed if you didn't talk so goddamn much."

According to Mary St. John, Duke was furious. But Stacy denied talking to the *Enquirer* or any other publication, and the incident was smoothed over. By then Mary St. John was virtually retired, and Duke was too tired to go through the whole complex procedure of finding and training a new secretary. More important, he was lonely, and Stacy was there, ready and anxious to fill the giant gap in his private life. And so the dreary situation dragged on until there was no turning back for any of us.

From 1976 on Duke was almost continuously ill. He came down with pneumonia and had barely recovered when he underwent prostate surgery. Duke's breathing had grown increasingly labored, and, for the first time, he had difficulty speaking. When one of Duke's friends told me that Duke feared a recurrence of cancer, I called Duke at once, urging him to see his doctor.

"I will," Duke said, "as soon as I finish my next picture."

He sounded excited about the new film, more enthusiastic than he'd been about a picture since *True Grit*. Jimmy Stewart, Lauren Bacall, and Ron Howard would costar with Duke in *The Shootist*, the story of an aging gunfighter dying of cancer.

Work on *The Shootist* proved to be the most difficult experience of Duke's long career, even worse than those dreadful days on location for *Katie Elder*. He had severe difficulty breathing and used oxygen constantly. His voice was going, and he couldn't imagine a more useless creature than an actor without a voice. Riding, walking, just sitting and talking tired him. His body was failing, and there didn't seem to be a thing he could do about it.

He tried to concentrate on the pleasures life still held. It was a joy to work with Lauren Bacall and Jimmy Stewart again, and Duke pronounced Ron Howard the most talented young actor he'd ever known.

Despite his growing frailty, Duke gave a strong performance in

The Shootist. Once again, the critics ignored his work and, sadly, this time his fans did too. The picture languished at the box office.

When Duke returned from location I didn't see how he could go on working much longer and everyone, our children, his friends and business associates, myself, urged him to see a doctor. Predictably, Duke ignored all of us.

In March Duke appeared on the Oscars telecast to present a special award to 78-year-old Howard Hawks, the man who'd directed him in five pictures, including *Rio Lobo, Hatari,* and *Red River.* It was a deeply emotional night for both of them.

Duke, who'd never cared for television, suddenly began to appear on a variety of shows, including a Lucille Ball special, a Rodgers and Hammerstein special, and NBC's *The Big Event.* Then he did a Variety Club "all-star tribute to John Wayne" to raise funds for a new cancer wing for a children's hospital. Duke used work to help him forget his loneliness and sickness. When no good scripts turned up, he agreed to do a series of commercials for Bristol Myers and Great Western Savings.

In 1976 he received the last of his many invitations to the White House. This time the occasion was Jimmy Carter's inaugural. (I could just hear Duke saying, "I can't go, I'm a Republican.") But this was more than an invitation to a party. He'd been asked to say a few remarks at a pre-inaugural gala which would be shown on television, and he couldn't pass up the opportunity to talk to the president and the nation. On January 19, 1977, Duke strode to the podium on stage at the Kennedy Center to say a few words to his fellow Americans:

Good evening, my name is John Wayne. I'm here tonight to pay my respects to our thirty-ninth president, our new commander-in-chief—to wish you God speed, sir, in the uncharted waters ahead.

Tomorrow at high noon, all our hopes and dreams go into that great house with you. For you have become our transition into the unknown tomorrows, and everyone is with you.

I'm pleased to be present and accounted for in this capital of freedom to witness history as it happens—to watch a common man accept the uncommon responsibility he won "fair and square" by stating his case to the American people—not by bloodshed, beheadings, and riots at the palace gates.

I know I'm considered a member of the loyal opposition—accent on the loyal. I'd have it no other way.

Later that night, when Duke arrived at the reception following the gala, Carter and Mondale were shaking hands with a long line of guests that included Paul Newman, Shirley MacLaine, Chevy Chase, Linda Ronstadt, and Bette Davis—all good Democrats. But the president and vice president excused themselves as soon as they spotted Duke and walked over to him.

"I've always been a fan of yours," Carter said, shaking Duke's hand.

Duke looked down at the smaller, younger man who now held the fate of the world in his grasp. "It's a pleasure to meet you, Mr. President-elect. I guess you know I didn't vote for you—but don't forget, you're the president of all of us now."

Within a few months Duke and Carter were to be the most unlikely of political allies. The president was fighting for a new treaty with Panama, one that would grant that Central American nation a degree of freedom. His efforts were not meeting with much success when Duke joined him in the battle. Duke supported Carter's new treaty although it was considered to be a liberal document even by other liberals. As usual Duke didn't care whether the press labeled him as a liberal or as a conservative. His only interest lay in doing what he felt was right, in standing up to be counted. That included mailing a position paper to every representative and senator. The carefully researched, seven-page document closed with the following words:

I have carefully studied the Treaty, and I support it based on my belief that America looks always to the future, and that our people have demonstrated the qualities of justice and reason for 200 years. That attitude has made our country a great nation. The new Treaty modernizes an outmoded relation with a friendly and hospitable country. It also solves an international question with our other Latin American neighbors, and finally, the Treaty protects and makes legitimate the fundamental interests and desires of our country.

I like to think that Duke played an important part in convincing the members of Congress to pass the treaty. It was Duke's last political battle.

On March 29, 1978, Duke flew to Boston accompanied by Michael, Patrick, Aissa, and Pat Stacy. He was scheduled to enter Massachusetts General Hospital where the doctors intended to replace his heart's failing mitral valve with a valve from a pig's heart.

Aissa called me several times during Duke's hospitalization to keep me informed about his progress. It was slow going at first, but Aissa was soon able to report that her father was sitting up in bed, breathing easier, and speaking without difficulty for the first time in months. He even joked about his operation, claiming he could "oink with the best of them."

Once again, Duke had cheated death. He seemed indestructible.

CHAPTER 34

Duke's endurance amazed everyone. Three weeks after a twelve-hour heart operation he left the hospital in Boston to return home, and three weeks after that he felt well enough to tape a segment for a Bob Hope special. It would have been an incredible recovery for someone half his age; for a 71-year-old man, it was just short of miraculous. Along with everyone else, I began to think of him as unstoppable, indestructible. We hadn't seen much of each other in the months prior to his operation, and afterward there seemed no need to push things. He was getting better. I was so sure we had time.

Duke began to talk about doing another movie, a sure sign of returning health. He bought the rights to *Beau John*, which he hoped to film with his young favorite, Ron Howard. By August Duke felt strong enough to tape an anniversary special for General Electric with Liz Taylor, Hank Fonda, and Lucille Ball.

November of 1978 saw him in Williamsburg, Virginia, doing a Perry Como Christmas special. At the end of the month he returned to Warner Brothers studio to take part in another Variety Club fund-raiser, this time an "all-star tribute to Jimmy Stewart."

He barely made it through the taping. Though Duke didn't want to admit it, not even to himself, he was sick again, suffering terrible stomach pains and unable to eat. For the first time in years he didn't have to worry about dieting. He was losing weight rapidly.

The doctors suggested another exploratory operation, but Christmas was around the corner, and Duke postponed another trip to the hospital. He wanted to spend the holiday with our children, buy their gifts himself, purchase a tree, and supervise the decorating as he had every year since their births. I think deep down he knew it would be his last Christmas, and he wanted to make it special.

This time his strength failed him. No longer able to pretend that he felt fine for the children's sake, as the doctor had predicted, Duke became irritable and short-tempered with all of them. Christmas morning Aissa reported that he didn't feel well enough to get dressed, and he went back to bed before everyone opened their presents. It was ominous news.

It broke my heart to think of Duke too sick to enjoy the holidays, but I still didn't realize just how sick he really was. After the holidays Duke taped a Barbara Walters special, and the fact that he was well enough to do so allayed my fears. I mistakenly discounted what a superb actor he was. When the interview aired three months later, I saw how concerned Duke had been about his health.

Walters had asked him how he defined a very "good" day and Duke replied, "Getting up in the morning. Being still here."

When she talked about his being called a "legend," as though he "wasn't here anymore," Duke commented, "There's a thing to frighten you. They talk like you're part of the past or something. And rightfully so; I am a part of the past. But I also want to be a part of the future too."

A few days after the interview, Duke stopped by the restaurant to talk to me. We hadn't seen each other for a while, and the changes I saw in him stunned me. He was thin, too thin, and new lines of pain had drawn his face into a mask.

We talked about the children for a while and then, to my surprise, Duke reached for my hand. His skin felt thin and dry, but his grip was as strong as ever. I tried to ignore the instant realization that I'd been missing his touch. Obviously, it was much too late for those kinds of thoughts.

"We had a lot of good times, didn't we?" Duke began.

"Yes, sweetheart," I agreed immediately, "and we've got three wonderful children to show for it."

"You know," Duke said, "I've been thinking about my life, and I guess I'd do it all over the same way except for the last few years. I wish there'd been some way to change that."

Duke's grip grew even tighter, and I had the feeling he was hanging on to me for dear life. "I've got to tell somebody," he said. "I'm sick again. The doc is talking like I've got a bad gall-bladder, but I know better. I can't eat anymore. Hell, I can't even drink."

I held his hand as hard as he held mine, trying to will my own strength into his body, but at the same time I understood what he was trying to let me know.

Duke finally let me go. "Promise that you'll take care of the kids. They're going to need you."

"They need both of us," I said, blinking back tears.

We hugged one another again before he left. I hadn't held Duke in my arms for years, and I was astonished by how thin he was, thinner even than the first time I held him in my arms twenty-five years before. Though we spoke on the phone several times in the next few months, I never touched him or saw him again.

Duke checked into UCLA Medical Center on January 10, 1979. Three days later exploratory surgery revealed that he had stomach cancer. The organ was removed and replaced by a section of his colon. He had survived a terrifying nine and a half hours on the operating table.

All of us were encouraged by his resilience, his will to live. Though the doctors removed all the cancer they could see, they couldn't guarantee that this cancer hadn't already metasticized. The biopsies would tell us what Duke's chances were, and it would be several days before they were completed.

When the test results revealed that the cancer had spread throughout Duke's lymph system, I refused to give up hope. Radiation and chemotherapy had worked wonders in cases like his. It was inconceivable that John Wayne was actually going to die.

Duke returned home in February and actually felt well enough to fulfill his promise to appear at the Oscars in March. Although our children had seen their father almost daily, I'd kept my distance, not wanting to make an event of a visit nor to see Pat Stacy acting the hostess in the home Duke and I shared for so many years. I was certain he'd drop by the restaurant when he felt well enough.

Seeing him on television the night of the Oscars put an end to my wishful thinking. The minute he made his entrance onto the stage to thundering applause, I began to weep helplessly. Duke still walked proud and tall, but he was emaciated, his face a death's head under his makeup. Aissa later told me that Duke was wearing a thick wetsuit under his tuxedo to make him look heavier. His courage never flagged, but his body was failing.

Late in April Duke called me at the restaurant to ask for some of our chocolate mousse. He said he'd been unable to eat for days but thought he might get some of that down.

I was frantic. We didn't have any mousse on hand and it would take hours to prepare, but I promised to deliver some as soon as I could. Before I could keep that promise Ethan called to say he'd just driven his father back to the UCLA Medical Center.

By now, each of us realized Duke would never come home again. He was in terrible pain, fighting to live one more day, so concentrated on that effort that he was barely aware of anything else. Our children told me that Michael and Pat Stacy, on the doctor's orders, had guards on Duke's door and were monitoring all his visitors.

One by one, all of Duke's friends were refused entry to that hospital room. Joe DeFranco, Barry Goldwater, James Bacon, the list went one. Hank Fonda showed up one day and was informed that Duke's doctors weren't permitting visitors. Hank was the last of the bunch that trod the *Araner's* decks, and he wasn't about to be denied a farewell.

He simply took a chair and said, "I'll wait here until I can talk to the doctors if that's what it takes." He was finally granted admittance.

Mary St. John, who had been called back to work in the final weeks of Duke's life, simply sneaked into his room one day.

"Where the hell have you been?" he asked. Apparently, he had no idea how many people called, asking to see him, or how many others were being turned away at the door.

"I've been trying to see you," she replied. "But the doctors have left orders that you need your rest."

"Pilar," Duke asked, "has she tried too?"

"Of course," Mary St. John answered.

"Do me a favor," Duke said. "Tell her not to come. I don't want her to see me this way."

She nodded, trying not to cry.

Frank Sinatra and President Carter were on the approved visitor list. When I read about their visits in the papers I couldn't help thinking they were allowed to see Duke because it made good copy, but by then I was growing bitter. As the unhappy weeks passed the children's reports grew increasingly grim. And then one day Aissa came home and told me that her father had commented on what she was wearing and how pretty she looked. It was the first time since he entered the hospital that he'd paid attention to anything other than his grim battle.

"Dad seemed different today," Aissa continued, "kind of at peace." Her beautiful face brightened. "I think he's feeling better."

But he wasn't feeling better. Duke, having fought long and hard—to the limits of his strength—had finally accepted his fate. It was time to determine what his final wishes were, how he wanted his funeral to be conducted.

Gathering all my courage, I called Pat Stacy. "You must ask Duke what he wants done after he's gone," I said.

"Oh, Pilar," she gasped, "I couldn't do that."

"Someone has to," I insisted.

Pat Stacy finally called back to tell me that Michael Wayne wanted to be in sole charge of the services after his father died. Under the circumstances, I couldn't refuse the request. I agreed to let him make all the arrangements.

Duke was to have two more moments of glory. On May 11, the government of Panama accorded him their highest civilian honor, the Order of Vasco Núñez de Balboa, in recognition of his forty years of service to their country. On May 23, Congress held hearings to vote on the minting of a special medal honoring Duke. The bill had been introduced by Duke's old friend and political ally, Barry Goldwater. Maureen O'Hara and Elizabeth Taylor testified before Congress in behalf of its passage. Many of Duke's friends—Kirk Douglas, Jimmy Stewart, Gregory Peck, Jack Lemmon, and Katharine Hepburn sent telegrams urging Congress to adopt the measure and their messages were read into the Congressional Record. The bill passed unanimously. Duke was modest about this new honor, but it lifted his spirits and helped him survive another pain-filled day.

By the beginning of June, I was praying that Duke's suffering would come to an end. I was relieved to hear that he was being given morphine constantly. From then until the day he lapsed into a final coma, Duke was barely conscious. The papers reported Duke's deathbed conversion to the Catholic faith. It surprised me. Duke had not believed in organized religion. I wondered if he had done it to please his older children.

Forty years after his parents' divorce, Michael finally had his father back. By seeing that Duke died a Catholic, Michael revalidated his parents' marriage. As the executor of Duke's will, Michael took possession of Duke's final days on earth.

I was nearby in a hotel room, as close to my children and my husband as I could be under the circumstances, when Duke died on June 11, 1979. Aissa called to break the news.

"Mom," she sobbed, "it's Dad. He's gone."

I clutched the phone, feeling a giant knot well up inside me. "Oh, sweetheart," I said, "it's a blessing. He's finally at peace."

As the late afternoon shadows darkened the room, I allowed myself to weep. Duke was gone.

CHAPTER 35

"Feo, fuerte y formal"—ugly, strong, and with dignity. Duke always said he wanted those words to be his epitaph. I laughed every time he said it, agreeing that strong and dignified described him perfectly but arguing with his use of the adjective "ugly." I would tell him, "Duke, you are the handsomest man in Hollywood, in the entire world for that matter." And he was certainly one of the best loved. When he died he deserved a funeral befitting a king. He had wanted a huge wake, with friends and jokes, but Michael Wayne arranged one more suited to a pauper.

Before the funeral, Michael called to ask if I would have any objection to having Josephine attend the service. Although I'd been married to Duke for twenty-five years, Josephine and I had never met. It seemed fitting somehow that we would mourn Duke together. But even then we did not meet.

I reminded Michael that Duke often mentioned to me, "When I pass away I would like to be cremated. Then I want all my friends to come to the house and have an Irish type of wake. Let everybody have fun and talk about the good times."

Perhaps, in those final days, Duke had changed his mind, for Michael responded gently, "I would rather do it another way. Don't worry. It will be dignified."

Duke was buried early at dawn on June 15, 1979, at Pacific View Memorial Park with his seven children, myself, and a few friends in attendance. Josephine chose to stay at home.

There is no tombstone to indicate the spot where Duke rests, no place where his fans can come to mourn or remember him. The papers would later report that the family feared grave robbers.

After the funeral there was a small reception at my home; a subdued gathering that was quickly over. At the time it was my opinion that Duke would have hated it all; the religious service, the actual burial, the fact that none of his Hollywood friends and coworkers were permitted to attend.

Since Duke and I never formally separated or established a custody agreement, Aissa, Ethan, and Marisa spent the last five years of their father's life moving at will from my condominium to his Bayshore house. Their clothes and personal possessions were divided equally between the two places. I'd also left many of my belongings, such things as my diaries, family albums, home movies, and clothing, with Duke when we separated. At first I'd left them because I felt certain we'd reconcile. Later, I decided not to upset Duke by picking them up. It had never been an issue between us. Duke knew what belonged to me and that's all that seemed necessary.

A few days after the funeral the children decided to go over to the Bayshore house to retrieve some of their belongings. They came home a few hours later and reported being met at the door by a security guard who watched them while they packed. Nothing was to leave the house with them other than their personal possessions. The belongings I'd left behind were lost to me forever. Although Duke had provided for me financially, establishing generous trust funds for all his heirs, the quitclaim deed I'd signed years before made the house and its contents part of the estate.

After Duke's death a series of events honored his contribution to the film industry and the nation. They were a reason for great pride, but, sadly, they caused dissent within the family as well. The first took place at the White House. President Carter had chosen Duke as the recipient of a Medal of Freedom, our country's highest civilian honor, given to citizens who have made distinguished contributions to security, national interest, world peace, or culture.

The invitation to this important affair came directly to my home. I accepted on behalf of myself and my children and then

passed it on to Michael for his consideration. As I packed to fly
to Washington I thought back over the many times we'd been at
the White House. On this occasion, I knew Duke would have
been happy to be honored by a Democratic president. Duke had
come to respect Carter when they fought for the new Canal Treaty. To my surprise, my children and I were the only Waynes to
show up at the White House. From then on, it seemed to me that
Michael pretended I didn't exist. Little by little, I came to feel I
was excluded from every affair honoring my husband's memory.
This hurt me deeply. Duke had never wanted a divorce. I couldn't
believe he wouldn't want me to celebrate his life and his memory. It's one of the saddest things in my life. I later learned that
Michael was furious because Carter's invitation hadn't been
mailed directly to him.

But Michael was now president of Batjac, and he'd formed a
new corporation, John Wayne Enterprises, through which he intended to control any use of his father's name or image. In the
first few years after Duke's death, Michael commissioned a flood
of artwork—prints, sculptures, plates, all portraying Duke. Michael considered them to be a "proper use" of the Wayne image,
but Michael still is opposed to my using "Mrs. John Wayne" as
my own name.

Late in 1981, when the government of Panama wanted to
present the Order of Vasco Núñez de Balboa to members of the
Wayne family, Michael refused to accept. Duke's good friends in
Panama were understandably upset. The Panamanian Embassy
in Washington responded to Michael's refusal with a letter mailed
to Batjac on November 16, 1981. It said, in part:

> The Embassy has followed the instructions of the Government
> of Panama and, on behalf of our citizens, looks forward to rec-
> ognizing the merits of a good friend, without any desire or in-
> tention of publicity or promotion related to the honors, to our
> country, or to any particular person involved.
>
> As you are aware the Government of Panama, like any na-
> tion in the world, has the right to present awards or decora-
> tions based on the merits of the individual.
>
> The decoration that was granted to Mr. Wayne before his
> death will be delivered to his family in a private reception at

the Embassy of Panama where friends and members of the dip-
lomatic community will be attending as a normal procedure of
our protocol.

I knew Duke had been deeply touched by the honor Panama
accorded him. He would have wanted his entire family in attendance at the embassy, but Marisa and I flew to Washington
alone.

The entire Wayne clan, over thirty of us, were present in the
nation's capital when Michael accepted the special Congressional
Medal on Duke's behalf. Duke was the eighty-fifth American to
be remembered by the government in this way. The unique medal
bears his picture on one side and the image of Monument Valley
on the other. Its simple inscription reads, "John Wayne—American."

A luncheon hosted by Liz Taylor and her then husband, Senator John Warner, followed the ceremony. One by one such men
as Barry Goldwater, Bob Dole, Dick Lugar, Orrin Hatch, Charles
Percy, and Dennis DeConcini paid tribute to Duke. John Warner
was the last speaker. He told of the time, shortly after he'd been
elected, when Duke said, "It's nice to be important, John, but it's
more important to be nice."

After the luncheon ended I found myself on an elevator with
Liz Taylor and her husband. It was our first moment alone that
afternoon, and we hugged and kissed, briefly recapturing the
friendship we'd once shared. Then Taylor stepped away from
me and took Warner's arm. The three of us chatted until the elevator reached their floor, making the sort of vague promises
about staying in touch that people make when they're forced into
unexpected intimacy with former friends. Of course, I never saw
her again. New lives waited for both of us.

Since Duke's death not a day goes by without my thinking of
him. Our three children are a constant, joyful reminder of the
life we shared. Aissa is now married, the mother of three children. Ethan and Marisa are pursuing acting careers.

I don't hear from Duke's older children. Michael continues to
protect his father's image. In the last year the media reported
that Michael brought suit against the distinguished late artist

Andy Warhol, shortly before Warhol's death, for doing a painting of Duke. I can only hope that Michael will one day learn what I learned many years ago: Duke will never belong to any one person, no matter how much that person may love him. John Wayne has always belonged to his fans and to the world. That is the way he would have wanted it.

EPILOGUE

Several years were to pass before I could watch Duke's movies without crying. Gradually, the pain of losing him faded, and I was able to think about what he meant to me and the country he loved so much. In that time, amazingly, his popularity continued to grow, and it is still growing.

The message of his life is a simple one. He got up every morning determined to do his best. Though the results varied, the effort never did. He believed that hard work, sweat rather than talent, was what it took to succeed.

He wasn't born with a silver spoon in his mouth. He struggled and sometimes failed—in his career and in his private life, but he never gave up. Duke was, indeed, the embodiment of the American dream. The legacy he left was so much more than the trust he worked so hard to build. His films are a national treasure, a part of everyone's heritage.

While I worked on this book, trying to weave the strands of his life into a cohesive whole, I came across a speech Duke gave in New York in 1973 to the National Football Hall of Fame foundation. Duke began with his customary modesty, down-playing his own football field experiences, calling himself the only man who'd been nominated as an All American—by the Hollywood Women's Publicist Guild.

He joked about his high school football team, saying they were so tough that half of them went on to become the USC Trojans and the other half, the Dillinger gang. Duke was in rare form, larding his speech with gentle, self-deprecating humor, saying he'd changed his name from Marion Morrison so he wouldn't wind up with Doris Day's movie roles.

But more important than humor was Duke's love for the movie

industry and his concern for its future. He said, "I read some-place that I used to make B pictures. Hell, they were a lot farther down the alphabet than that...but not as far down as R and X. I think any man who makes an X-rated picture ought to be made to take his own daughter to see it....

"My generation not only cared about picture-making, we cared about the country. The only message we wanted to get across was pride—pride in yourself, pride in your history." That's the legacy Duke left for us all, a history on film that is the history of America. He loved this land of ours, and his movies reflected that love.

He closed his talk that night with the following words: "We love this country...warts and all. We love what it has been... what it is now...and even more...we love what America can be. We're lucky God chose us to spend our lives here....In return for that, we should pay our dues....Let's plan the rest of our lives in such a way that America will not forget what we chipped in along our ways...

"...My goodnights to each of you are joined by a wish I have always had for myself...when you play the last scene of your life...may you get to kiss the schoolmarm.

"Thank you and good night."

INDEX